JOSEPH SMITH'S
KIRTLAND

JOSEPH SMITH'S
KIRTLAND
Eyewitness Accounts

Karl Ricks Anderson

Deseret Book Company
Salt Lake City, Utah

First printing in hardbound edition 1989
First printing in quality paperbound edition 1996

Visit us at deseretbook.com

Library of Congress Cataloging-in-Publication Data

Anderson, Karl R., 1937–
    Joseph Smith's Kirtland : eyewitness accounts / by Karl R. Anderson.
        p.   cm.
    Includes index.
    ISBN 0-87579-201-4 (hardbound)
    ISBN 1-57345-205-X (quality paperbound)
        1. Church of Jesus Christ of Latter-day Saints—Ohio—Kirtland—History—
19th century.   2. Mormon Church—Ohio—Kirtland—History—19th century.
3. Smith, Joseph, 1805–1844.   4. Kirtland (Ohio)—Church history—19th century.
I. Title.
    BX8615.O3   A53   1989
    289.3'771334—dc19
    [B]   89-30535

Printed in the United States of America   3170-3851
Alexander's Printing, Salt Lake City, UT

CONTENTS

PREFACE

Joseph Smith's Kirtland is the story of Joseph Smith and of the Church of Jesus Christ during the seven years, 1831 to 1838, the Church was headquartered in Kirtland, Ohio. As a leader he lived there longer than at any other place, and it was there that many pivotal events of the latter-day kingdom of God occurred. The story is not a lengthy recital of historical events, but a visit with over one hundred eyewitnesses who lived there. Their observations and testimonies, which are documented and recorded in letters, journals, contemporary publications, and reminiscences, recount their experiences in living and working with Joseph Smith as he fulfilled his mission as the Prophet of the Restoration. Their firsthand accounts help us to know the Prophet in an unusually intimate way, as well as to gain insights into their own lives. These witnesses, similar to witnesses of the Pentecost in Jerusalem, also recorded their testimonies that the gospel of Jesus Christ, as taught by him in the meridian of time, was restored through Joseph Smith by the power of God, and is encompassed today in The Church of Jesus Christ of Latter-day Saints.

Joseph Smith's Kirtland has been written because of the impact that Ezra Taft Benson, a latter-day prophet and thirteenth president of the Church, has had upon Kirtland and upon me. President Benson loves Kirtland, its history, its early leaders, and the posterity of those who lived there in the early days of the Church. His inspiration and leadership have accelerated in our own day the fulfillment of prophecies made in the 1830s; and through his efforts the Church is once again in Kirtland. He has encouraged Latter-day Saints to find and become acquainted with descendants of the early Kirtland Saints. While in his presence, I have felt my soul burn within me as I have received the sure witness of the Spirit that a prophet, once again standing on sacred Kirtland soil, has lifted a scourge and is prophesying and directing the fulfillment of prophecy.

Moreover, living in the shadows of the Kirtland Temple for over twenty years and having frequently walked Kirtland's streets, hills, and places of history, I have sensed the unspoken sacredness of the area. On Sinai the Lord told Moses to remove his shoes, for he stood on holy ground. As I have become aquainted with the Kirtland Saints, the Moseses and Aarons of the 1830s, I have come to understand that they likewise walked on holy ground. The Lord made Kirtland holy the same way as he made Sinai holy. The Saints in Kirtland also consecrated the ground with their sacrifices. In Kirtland one feels a reverence for the places where they lived and worked and where past prophets and Deity visited.

As I have become acquainted with the Kirtland Saints, I have felt indescribable love, awe, and appreciation for them. They made great sacrifices, they had overwhelming spiritual experiences, and they faced almost overpowering temptations and trials. Some were separated from the Church by trials that might have separated many of us today. All of them, however, have become witnesses to the divinity of the Prophet Joseph Smith's calling in Kirtland. Through my experiences in Kirtland and the writing of this book, I have come to realize I feel an additional affinity with them: I too have become a witness to the divine calling of Joseph Smith in Kirtland.

Joseph Smith prophesied in 1836 that these accounts would be "handed down upon the pages of sacred history to all generations." I have felt compelled to assist in that work by writing this book, with the fervent desire that you, too, will experience the the reality of Joseph Smith's Kirtland.

ACKNOWLEDGMENTS

Many persons made significant contributions to the completion of *Joseph Smith's Kirtland*. First I acknowledge key priesthood leaders who, from its inception, provided direction and encouragement that insured its completion.

Mammoth contributions over several years were made by devoted family members. My wife, Joyce, in addition to her unfailing support and encouragement, has provided endless hours, without complaint, processing every word through numerous drafts, proofs, and revisions. Joyce and our children — Carol, Linda, Bonnie, David, Ruth, Joel, and Martha — have been a part of every major endeavor in my life. I thank them for their support and willingness to share my time and assist in mundane tasks of proofreading and reference checking and over the years in making hundreds of trips through Church history sites in Ohio.

My brother Richard L. Anderson, professor of religion at Brigham Young University, provided seemingly endless source documents, information, patient instruction, guidance, and consulting. His life-long example of careful and precise research and his unselfish dedication to family, church, and his career of teaching and writing have always given me an example to emulate. Richard's wife, Carma, selected the artist and supervised the development of the original drawings. Her combined knowledge of art and historic dress insured their accuracy and quality.

Excellent editors were involved at various stages. Maurine Reintjes and Shayne Bell very skillfully guided the development of the manuscript. Special thanks go to Eleanor Knowles of Deseret Book, who transformed the manuscript into the finished product.

Acknowledgment for the original artwork goes to Douglas M. Fryer, an exceptional artist who labored meticulously. His illustrations precisely recreate Kirtland's people, places, and journal accounts. Many of his illustrations accurately capture important scenes for the first time. Richard Erickson, assistant designer at Deseret Book, was responsible for the page and cover designs.

Appreciation is expressed to professors Keith Perkins and Milton Backman of Brigham Young University. Their deep interest in and love of Kirtland and their willingness to unselfishly share their research and insights has been of great assistance.

Others have helped tremendously. Although I would like to acknowledge each and every contribution, appreciation must of necessity be expressed personally.

To the memory of Karl Vernon Ricks (1892-1904), an uncle who died in his youth and whose name I have been privileged to perpetuate, and to his stalwart pioneer grandfather, Joel Ricks (1804-1888), who knew the Prophet Joseph Smith and was an eyewitness of his divine calling.

1

JOSEPH SMITH GOES TO KIRTLAND

"Go to the Ohio; and there I will give unto you my law; and there you shall be endowed with power from on high."
(Doctrine & Covenants 38:32.)

Joseph Smith, the Prophet of the Restoration, cannot be separated from Kirtland, Ohio, the town that became headquarters for The Church of Jesus Christ of Latter-day Saints in the 1830s. The Church in Kirtland really began when he arrived there and ended when he left. Before summoning Joseph, his twenty-five-year-old prophet, to Kirtland, however, the Lord prepared the area for his coming. For nearly three decades stalwart pioneers were inspired to settle in the Kirtland area.

The preparation commenced as early as 1805, when Oliver Snow moved his wife and two infant daughters, Leonora and Eliza R., to Kirtland from Massachusetts. There a son and future leader of the Church, Lorenzo Snow, would be born. Lorenzo would later be a boyhood friend of future apostles Luke and Lyman Johnson, whose family moved to neighboring Hiram, Ohio, in 1818. The preparation continued when Isaac Morley was led to Kirtland in 1812. This future Church leader became critically ill while serving in the war of 1812, and his wife, Lucy, after remaining in Kirtland "alone in the wild woods, never seeing a human face and continually in fear of Indians and wild beasts," nursed him back to health.[1] The preparation continued in 1829 when two men who later became Church leaders, Parley P. Pratt and Sidney Rigdon, met and became fast friends. The

Lord's hand was manifest again when he called four missionaries from New York to go to the western wilderness; and when Sidney Rigdon, who established a Reformed Baptist congregation, introduced the restored gospel to his members and many were converted. It officially began, however, in 1830, just eight months after the Church was established in upstate New York, when the Lord directed Joseph Smith, his Prophet, to "go to the Ohio." (D&C 38:32.)

The Pioneer Settlement of "The Ohio"

Settlement of Northeastern Ohio actually began in 1796, when a group of men from the Connecticut Land Company surveyed the area. The land, owned by the state of Connecticut, was initially called the Western Reserve. Part of the land, the Firelands, was given to about two thousand people who had been made homeless when their villages were pillaged and burned during the Revolutionary War. The bulk of the land was sold to some of the founders of the Connecticut Land Company. These settlers, mainly from Connecticut and other parts of New England, brought their families and their culture to the new area.

Knowledge of this appealing land spread, resulting in other adventuresome pioneers moving there. The first Kirtland settlers arrived in 1811, and by 1818 they had formed a township. One year later, the first mill was established. In 1823 a pioneer entrepreneur, Newel K. Whitney, established the first general store in a small log house. Mail service began in 1825, with Whitney as postmaster; and by 1827 the first hotel, the Peter French Tavern, was constructed.

One early pioneer described Kirtland's beauty: "The country for many miles around had been for centuries the hunting-ground of the Indians, and surely their most vivid imagination could have portrayed nothing more desirable or delightful concerning their celestial hunting-grounds. The forest-trees were of endless variety and of the tallest kinds. A thick growth of underbrush grew beneath, flowers of rare beauty blushed unseen, birds of varied plumage filled the air with their music, the air itself was fragrant and invigorating."[2]

In 1826 Parley P. Pratt moved from New York State to Ohio, where he determined to "spend the remainder of [his] days in the solitude of the great West, among the natives of the forest."[3] He acquired a piece of forest land about thirty miles west of Cleveland, cleared it of timber, and built a house. About a year later he returned to New York, married his sweetheart, and took her back to Ohio with him.

In 1829 Sidney Rigdon, a Campbellite minister, preached in Pratt's neighborhood. The two men soon formed a friendship, and Pratt became affiliated with the Campbellites. The following summer, impressed that he should return to his former home to preach the Campbellite doctrine, he sold his property and, accompanied by his wife, set sail from Cleveland aboard a schooner bound for Buffalo, New York. There they transferred to a canal boat that would take them to Albany. At Rochester, however, Pratt felt impressed to leave the boat, so he left his wife with some friends when the boat docked at Newark, New York, and began walking into the countryside. That first night he heard about a new book of scripture, called the Book of Mormon, and the next day he began reading it. He later wrote in his autobiography: "I read all day; eating was a burden, I had no desire for food; sleep was a burden when the night came, for I preferred reading to sleep. As I read, the Spirit of the Lord was upon me, and I knew and comprehended that the book was true, as plainly and manifestly as a man comprehends and knows that he exists."[4] Obviously redirected, he immediately set out for Palmyra, where he met Hyrum Smith, the Prophet's brother, and was baptized.

Missionaries Called into the "Wilderness"

After his baptism, Parley P. Pratt joined three other missionaries, Oliver Cowdery, Ziba Peterson, and Peter Whitmer, Jr., to go on a mission "into the wilderness among the Lamanites [American Indians]." (D&C 32:2.) Traveling west, they journeyed through the Western Reserve and arrived in the Kirtland area on October 15, 1830. They stopped at nearby Mentor, where Pratt sought out his friend Sidney Rigdon and told him about his newfound religion. Engaged with his own doctrines and congregation, Sidney Rigdon was not enthusiastic, but because of his friendship for Parley he committed to read the Book of Mormon. He said he would "endeavor to ascertain whether it be a revelation from God or not."[5] Sidney's son, John W. Rigdon, said that when he was informed that Joseph Smith was a young man with "hardly a common school education," Sidney replied, "If that is all the education he has got, he never wrote this book."[6]

President A. W. Cowles of Elmira College interviewed Sidney Rigdon in 1868 and recorded that Sidney's beliefs on this point had not changed: "Rigdon expressed the utmost amazement that such a man should write a book which seemed to shed a flood of light on all the old scriptures, open all their profoundest mysteries, and give them perfect consistency and complete system. In his fresh enthusiasm he exclaimed that if God ever gave a revelation, surely this must be divine."[7]

After prayer and much meditation, Sidney decided to be baptized. This decision imposed a dilemma upon him, a dilemma that was described by Joseph Smith in the Prophet's history:

> The honors and applause of the world were showered down upon him, his wants were abundantly supplied, and were anticipated. He was respected by the entire community, and his name was a tower of strength. His [counsel] was sought for, respected and esteemed. — But if he should unite with the Church of Christ, his prospects of wealth and affluence would vanish; his family dependent upon him for support, must necessarily share his humiliation and poverty. He was aware that his character and his reputation must suffer in the estimation of the community.[8]

Realizing that baptism, with the subsequent loss of employment and of the home and property provided by his congregation, would greatly affect his family, Sidney asked his wife, Phebe, "My dear, you have once followed me into poverty, are you again willing to do the same?" Phebe's devotion to the Lord and to her husband were clear in her answer: "I have weighed the matter, I have contemplated on the circumstances in which we may be placed; I have counted the cost, and I am perfectly satisfied to follow you; it is my desire to do the will of God, come life or come death."[9]

After meeting with Sidney Rigdon, the four missionaries requested permission to speak to his Mentor congregation. He agreed. In *History of the Church* we read:

> The appointment was accordingly published, and a large and respectable congregation assembled. Oliver Cowdery and Parley P. Pratt severally addressed the meeting. At the conclusion, elder Rigdon arose and stated to the congregation that the information they had that evening received, was of an extraordinary character, and certainly demanded their most serious consideration: and as the apostle advised his brethren "to prove all things and hold fast that which is good," so he would exhort his brethren to do likewise, and give the matter a careful investigation; and not turn against it, without being fully convinced of its being an imposition, lest they should, possibly, resist the truth.[10]

Other members of Sidney Rigdon's Campbellite congregation also joined The Church of Jesus Christ of Latter-day Saints, and a branch was established in Mentor, one of four branches organized in the Kirtland area early in 1831.

After introducing the gospel to Sidney Rigdon and preaching to his congregation, the four Mormon missionaries stopped at the Isaac Morley farm in Kirtland. One of the first persons they approached was Lyman Wight, who had just been put in charge of a group of five families who were preparing to join a communal organization in Mayfield, about seven miles from Kirtland. He was loading his wagon when the missionaries from New York approached him. He recorded in his journal:

> When I had my goods about half loaded, there came along four men (namely P. Pratt, O. Cowdery, P. Whitmer, and Ziba Peterson) and brought with them the Book of

Mormon, which they wished to introduce to us. I desired they would hold on till I got away, as my business was of vital importance, and I did not wish to be troubled with romances nor idle speculations. But nothing daunted, they were not to be put off, but were as good-natured as you please. Curiosity got uppermost, and I concluded to stop for a short time. We called meeting, and one testified that he had seen angels, and another that he had seen plates, and that the gifts were back in the church again, etc. The meeting became so interesting withal that I did not get away till the sun was about an hour high at night, and it was dark before I arrived at my new home.[11]

Wight concluded, "I shall therefore content myself by saying that they brought the Book of Mormon to bear upon us, and the whole of the common stock family was baptized."[12]

One of the earliest baptisms as a result of the missionaries' proselyting efforts was of John Murdock, who was baptized in the Chagrin River on November 5, 1830, by Parley P. Pratt. He wrote of his conversion and baptism:

I . . . was soon introduced to those four men from New York, and presented with The Book of Mormon. . . . I stayed alone, and read the Book of Mormon. . . . I read till it was late. . . . The Spirit of the Lord rested on me, witnessing to me of the TRUTH of the work. . . . I told the servants of the Lord that I was ready to walk with them into the waters of baptism. Accordingly, Elder Parley P. Pratt baptised me in the Chagrin River and the Spirit of the Lord sensibly attended the ministration, and I came out of the water rejoicing and singing praises to God, and the Lamb! An impression sensibly rested on my mind that cannot, by me, be forgotten. . . . This was the third time that I had been immersed, but I never before felt the authority of the Ordinance, but I felt it this time and felt as though my sins were forgiven! . . .

On Sunday evening they confirmed about thirty; I was one of the number. Elder Oliver Cowdery was administrator. I was also Ordained an Elder and it was truly a time of the outpouring of the Spirit! I know the Spirit rested on me as it never did before and others said they saw the Lord, and had visions.[13]

Another convert, Philo Dibble, described a similar feeling of elation:

> When I came out of the water, I knew that I had been born of water and of the spirit, for my mind was illuminated with the Holy Ghost. I spent that evening at Dr. F. G. Williams'. While in bed that night I felt what appeared to be a hand upon my left shoulder and a sensation like fibers of fire immediately enveloped my body. . . . I was enveloped in a heavenly influence, and could not sleep for joy. The next morning I started home a happy man.[14]

After the missionaries preached in Painesville, the local newspaper noted:

> About two weeks since some persons came along here with the book [of Mormon], one of whom pretends to have seen angels and assisted in translating the plates. He proclaims that the ordinances of the gospel have not been regularly administered since the days of the apostles till the said Smith and himself commenced the work. . . . In the neighboring township of Kirtland, we understand that twenty or thirty have been immersed into the new order of things, many of whom had been previously baptized.[15]

One of those who was taught by the missionaries was Edward Partridge, who owned a hatter's shop on Painesville's town square. His wife, Lydia, wrote concerning the missionaries' visit, "[Edward] told them he did not believe what they said, but believed them to be imposters. Oliver Cowdery said he was thankful there was a God in heaven who knew the hearts of all men. After the men were gone my husband sent a man to follow them and get one of their books."[16] Partridge was subsequently baptized during a visit to Palmyra, New York, where he had gone to investigate the Prophet Joseph Smith. This trusted businessman represented himself and others who esteemed him as "a man who would not lie for his right arm!"[17] He later became the first bishop of the Church.

The message of the restored gospel was received and took root in Ohio. The four missionaries baptized about one hundred people in less than two months.

The Command to "Go to the Ohio"

As the missionaries were completing their work in Kirtland, the Lord revealed to Joseph Smith in New York that members of the Church should "assemble together at the Ohio." (D&C 37:3.) "There I will give unto you my law; and there you shall be endowed with power from on high." (D&C 38:32.) "Inasmuch as my people shall assemble themselves at the Ohio, I have kept in store a blessing such as is not known among the children of men, and it shall be poured forth upon their heads. And from thence men shall go forth into all nations."(D&C 39:15.)

At about that time, Newel K. Whitney, who owned the Gilbert and Whitney store in Kirtland, and his wife, Elizabeth Ann, had an unusual experience. Elizabeth Ann related:

> One night—it was midnight—as my husband and I, in our house at Kirtland, were praying to the father to be shown the way, the spirit rested upon us and a *cloud* overshadowed the house. It was as though we were out of doors. The house passed away from our vision. We were not conscious of anything but the presence of the spirit and the cloud that was over us. We were wrapped in the cloud. A solemn awe pervaded us. We saw the cloud and felt the spirit of the Lord. Then we heard a voice out of the cloud saying: "Prepare to receive the word of the Lord, for it is coming!" At first we marveled greatly, but from that moment we knew that the word of the Lord was coming to Kirtland.[18]

On about February 1, 1831, a sleigh stopped in front of the Gilbert and Whitney store. A man jumped out and went into the store, where he approached Newel Whitney, extended his hand, and called him by name. Newel, bewildered, responded,

"I could not call you by name as you have me." "I am Joseph the Prophet," the stranger said. "You have prayed me here, now what do you want of me?"[19]

Newel's grandson, Orson F. Whitney, later wrote: "By what power did this remarkable man, Joseph Smith, recognize one whom he had never before seen in the flesh? It was because Joseph Smith was a seer, a choice seer; he had actually seen Newel K. Whitney upon his knees, hundreds of miles away, praying for his coming to Kirtland."[20]

Elizabeth Whitney described the Prophet's arrival as "the fulfillment of the vision we had seen of a cloud as of glory resting upon our house."[21] Joseph wrote that he and his wife "lived in the family of Brother Whitney several weeks, and received every kindness and attention which could be expected, and especially from Sister Whitney."[22]

A glorious new era had begun in Kirtland.

2

FAITHFUL SAINTS GATHER TO KIRTLAND

"They came, men, women, and children, in every conceivable manner, some with horses, oxen, and vehicles rough and crude, while others had walked all or part of the distance." (History of Geauga County.)

Most of the faithful Saints who followed the Lord's command to "go to the Ohio" acted out of pure faith. Like the children of Israel who had faith that God would sustain them in their journey to the promised land, many came on foot, leaving behind them their worldly goods as well as family and friends. What few possessions these faithful converts were able to carry could not sustain them for long. But the Saints already in Kirtland welcomed these pilgrims and shared their meager substance willingly. These stalwart individuals formed the foundation for the Church's amazing growth and progress.

One of the thousands who converged on Kirtland, Oliver B. Huntington, described his journey with a group of the Saints: "We left Sackets Harbor . . . but [were] driven back, the wind blowing a perfect gale; we landed in Rochester the next morning before sunrise. . . . From Rochester we took the canal to Buffalo and from Buffalo to Fairport, 12 miles from Kirtland we sailed on a steamboat, and in four days from the time we left Sackets we were in Kirtland. We all walked the 12 miles with joy, rejoicing at the privilege of getting there no matter how."[1]

Nearly all who gathered to Kirtland needed assistance of some kind. Even Brigham Young, who, because of his industry and good business sense, was generally able to provide very well for himself and his family, had virtually nothing when he arrived in Kirtland. He described how he responded with faith to the Prophet's call to gather:

> When we arrived in Kirtland [in September [1833], if any man that ever did gather with the Saints was any poorer than I was — it was because he had nothing. . . . I had two children to take care of — that was all. I was a widower. "Brother Brigham, had you any shoes?" No; not a shoe to my foot, except a pair of borrowed boots. I had no winter clothing, except a homemade coat that I had had three or four years. "Any pantaloons?" No. "What did you do? Did you go without?" No; I borrowed a pair to wear till I could get another pair. I had travelled and preached and given away every dollar of my property. I was worth a little property when I started to preach. . . . I had traveled and preached until I had nothing left to gather with; but Joseph said: "come up;" and I went up the best I could.[2]

Amasa Lyman was another immigrant to Ohio. A note in *History of the Church* describes his experience:

> Elders Orson Pratt and Lyman E. Johnson passed through the section of New Hampshire where young Lyman lived, on a preaching tour. He believed the message proclaimed by these new evangels and was baptized on the 27th of April 1832. . . . In consequence of the ill feelings which arose in his uncle's family [where he was living], owing to his joining the Church, Amasa departed from the home of his kindred, and set out on foot for the gathering place of the Saints in Ohio. After a journey of some seven hundred miles, in which he endured many hardships — for much of the journey was made on foot and with but scant means of subsistence — he arrived at Hiram in Portage county. . . . About the first of July [1832] . . . Amasa had the joy of meeting the Prophet of the new dispensation. Of that meeting and the impressions it produced, he says: "Of the impressions produced I will here say, although there was nothing strange or different from other men in his personal

appearance, yet when he grasped my hand in that cordial way (known to those who have met him in the honest simplicity of truth), I felt as one of old in the presence of the Lord."[3]

Phoebe Carter told of leaving her family behind and traveling alone to Kirtland in 1835:

My friends marveled at my course, as did I, but something within impelled me on. My mother's grief at my leaving home was almost more than I could bear; and had it not been for the spirit within I should have faltered at the last. My mother told me she would rather see me buried than going thus alone out into the heartless world. "Phoebe," she said, impressively, "will you come back to me if you find Mormonism false?" I answered, "yes, mother; I will, thrice." These were my words, and she knew I would keep my promise. My answer relieved her trouble; but it cost us all much sorrow to part. When the time came for my departure I dared not trust myself to say farewell; so I wrote my good-byes to each, and leaving them on my table, ran downstairs and jumped into the carriage. Thus I left the beloved home of my childhood to link my life with the saints of God.[4]

Housing those who gathered to Kirtland became a constant challenge. Caroline Crosby described this problem: "Several families came in at that time [1836] from [New York State] and as houses were very hard to be rented, every place being filled, Mr. C[rosby] rented the cellar kitchen to a man, and his wife, with two small children. His name was Lewis, a blacksmith by occupation, and very poor people. But they found it rather uncomfortable, and staid only a short time."[5]

New arrivals often appeared at the doorstep of friends, acquaintances, and strangers with no notice. Brotherly love dictated that members move over and offer hospitality, however meager—at times even sleeping on the floor and giving up their own beds. Caroline Crosby wrote in her journal:

About the middle of July a co[mpany] came from Boston

Mass. . . . And no house could be found for their accomodation. John [Boynton] was building, but could not get it ready in season. He therefore came to us and offered to give us four times the amount of rent we paid, if we would go in with sister Sabre Granger, a maiden lady near by us, who was living alone, and let him have our house for his friends. My husband left it with me to say, to which I hesitated some time, but at length consented, rather reluctantly. The remuneration I considered no object; [but] to leave my pleasant little house, and go in with another, after living by ourselves so short a time; but the idea of accomodating friends, stimulated me to make the sacrifice.

Sister Granger's house was small, only one room, besides cellar, pantry, a small closet, and chamber. She had however a stove room, outside where she cooked her food. She had many peculiarities, which in some respects were not as agreeable to us, as we could wish. Notwithstanding being kindhearted, and friendly, atoned in my estimation, for many imperfections.[6]

Many years later, the memory of thousands arriving with nowhere to live was still vivid enough that this description appeared in a short six-paragraph history of the Latter-day Saints in Kirtland: "The future 'City of the Saints' appeared like one besieged. Every available house, shop, hut, or barn was filled to its utmost capacity. Even boxes were roughly extemporized and used for shelter until something more permanent could be secured."[7]

Until 1832, most of the Saints gathering to Kirtland settled on the Isaac Morley farm. Later they settled on the Frederick G. Williams farm and other land purchased by the Church. Home building was a constant activity. In January 1836, William W. Phelps, in a letter to his wife, Sally, described the construction work: "I must relate the marvelous works here. There have been built during the past year nearly 20 houses, mostly very small—only one of note called the 'Boston House.' It is 53 feet by 32 feet—three stories high. It is not yet enclosed. It is almost a miracle how such a large number of people live—but the Lord is merciful."[8]

14

By the end of 1836, houses and land were fully occupied. Minutes of a conference on December 22, 1836, reflect the problem:

> Whereas the Church in this place being poor from the beginning, having had to pay an extraordinate price for their lands, provisions, etc; and having a serious burthen imposed upon them by comers and goers, from most parts of the world, and in assisting traveling Elders and [their] families, while they themselves have been laboring in the vineyard of the Lord, to preach the Gospel; and also having suffered great loss in endeavoring to benefit Zion, it has . . . become a serious matter. . . .
>
> A stop [must be] put to churches or families gathering or moving to this place, without their first coming or sending their wise men to prepare a place for them, as our houses are all full, and our lands mostly occupied, except those houses that do not belong to the Church, which cannot be obtained without great sacrifice, especially when brethren with their families are crowding in upon us, and are compelled to purchase at any rate, and consequently are thrown into the hands of speculators, and extortioners, with which course the Lord is not well pleased.[9]

Kirtland history is filled with examples of Saints who willingly sacrificed their worldly possessions to gather to Kirtland. Three families, the Millets, the Tanners, and the Huntingtons, exemplify how sacrifice and spiritual commitment overshadowed worldly concerns.

The Millet Family

Artemus Millet was a wealthy builder in Canada at the time he and his wife learned of the restored gospel in late 1832. A family history tells the story:

> Brigham Young was given a special mission [by the Prophet Joseph Smith] to go to Canada and baptize Bro. Artemus Millet, . . . which call resulted from a consultation held at Kirtland respecting the building of the Temple there,

and as to who they could get that was capable of taking charge of the work. When Elder Lorenzo Young exclaimed to the Prophet "I know the very man who is capable of doing this work," "Who is he?" asked the Prophet. Lorenzo replied ["It] is Artemus Millet." The Prophet turned to Brigham and said "I give you a mission to go to Canada and baptise Brother Artemus Millet, and bring him here. Tell him to bring a thousand dollars with him." Artemus was much surprised when Brigham announced his mission to him and [he] asked "What kind of a church is that?" Then Brigham explained the principles of the Gospel to him and he accepted and was baptized.[10]

Artemus, obedient to the Prophet's call, left his family and went immediately to Kirtland, where he selected stone for the temple foundation. He later returned to Canada, disposed of his property on credit (which became difficult to collect), and took his family to Kirtland to supervise the masonry work on the temple. He deposited money in the Kirtland Safety Society Bank and loaned money to the Church that he never collected. Despite his financial sacrifices, however, Artemus Millet maintained his testimony. He later immigrated with his family to Utah, where his large posterity now enjoy the blessings of the gospel.

The Tanner Family

John Tanner sold several flourishing businesses, including land in New York, a hotel, and other properties, in order to gather to Kirtland. The proceeds of these sales went mainly to the Church. John's move to Kirtland is described in a biographical account:

About the middle of December [John] received an impression by dream or vision of the night, that he was needed and must go immediately to the Church in the West. He told his family of the instruction he had received and forthwith made preparations for the start, while his neighbors, with deep regret at what they considered an insane

16

purpose, tried their utmost to dissuade him; but he knew the will of God in the present crisis and nothing could deter him from doing it.

On Christmas day he commenced his journey with all his earthly effects, and in the dead of Winter traveled the distance of five hundred miles, to Kirtland where he arrived about the 20th of January, 1835, on the Sabbath.

On his arrival in Kirtland, he learned that at the time he received the impression that he must move immediately to the Church, the Prophet Joseph and some of the brethren had met in prayer-meeting and asked the Lord to send them a brother or some brethren with means to assist them to lift the mortgage on the farm upon which the temple was being built.

The day after his arrival in Kirtland, by invitation from the prophet, he and his son, Sidney, met with the High Council, and were informed that the mortgage of the before mentioned farm was about to be foreclosed. Whereupon he loaned the prophet two thousand dollars and took his note on interest, with which amount the farm was redeemed.[11]

It is estimated that at various times John gave or loaned over fifty thousand dollars to Joseph Smith and the Church. By the time he was forced to leave Ohio with the Saints, he had lost a virtual fortune:

In April, 1838, [John] fitted up with a turnpike-cart, a borrowed wagon, one horse of his own and three borrowed ones, twenty dollars in cash and a keg of powder to pay expenses, and started for Missouri with his family—eleven persons in all. When the money and powder were spent, they were under the necessity of appealing to the benevolence of the inhabitants on the road for buttermilk and sometimes for other food to sustain life. He had two children. . . . One of these, a lovely girl, died on this tedious journey.[12]

Later John forgave the remaining debts incurred in Kirtland, as the following incident illustrates:

17

At the April Conference in 1844, [John] was called on a mission to the Eastern States. Before starting, he went to Nauvoo, where he saw the Prophet Joseph, and, meeting him on the street, gave him his note of hand for the two thousand dollars loaned in Kirtland, January 1835, to redeem the temple land. The Prophet asked him what he wanted done with the note. Elder Tanner replied, "Brother Joseph, you are welcome to it." The Prophet then laid his right hand heavily on Elder Tanner's shoulder, saying, "God bless you, Father Tanner; your children shall never beg bread."[13]

Historian Leonard Arrington researched the fulfillment of this prophecy. He writes:

When the family moved west after the martyrdom of the Prophet, John Tanner . . . had time to see his family settled and thriving . . . before his death in 1850. His ten children who came west fulfilled the Prophet's prediction, as they participated in the colonization, not only of South Cottonwood, [Utah], but of San Bernardino, California; of such Utah communities as Beaver, Fillmore, Payson, and North Ogden; and of Arizona. . . . Consistently devoted and hard-working, they gave their families economic and spiritual security and left an honorable legacy of commitment that has not decreased with time.[14]

The Huntington Family

Joseph Smith Sr., while visiting in upstate New York in 1835, asked Oliver Huntington's father to sell his farm and move to Kirtland at "the first opportunity." The new convert "sold his farm, after much anxiety and concern, by sacrificing about fifteen hundred dollars, in selling it for that much less than it was really worth for the sake of living with the church and obeying the word of God as given to Joseph Smith."[15]

Upon arriving in Kirtland, Huntington was counseled to buy Jacob Bump's house and thirty acres of land. Oliver related how they trusted Jacob Bump with a mortgage on the property, commenting, "We thought all the brethren were honest then."

Within one year, Bump "denied the faith and refused to lift the mortgage."[16] Oliver wrote:

> My poor old father who but six months ago was in affluent circumstances, and surrounded with everything to make him comfortable, and render life desirable; [with] a farm of upwards of 230 acres; a good stone house and two frame barns . . . from all these earthly comforts and conveniences, in six months he was brought to live by day work, and that but very poorly, still my mother was the same mother and the same wife.
>
> It was a torment to each, to see the other in want and still more see their children cry for bread and have none to give them nor know where the next was coming from, and after all their trials and sufferings not only there but elsewhere, never did I hear either of them utter a murmuring, or complaining word against any of the authorities of the church, or express a doubt of the truth of the work. . . . John and I, though small, felt for them as much as our age would and could be expected; we often would kneel beside each other in the woods, and in the barn, daily, and pray to God to have mercy and bless father and mother, that they should not want nor see us want for bread.[17]

The Huntington family left Kirtland in the spring of 1838. They had to borrow money and a yoke of oxen, and they sent their "best goods, and everything but just what we really needed" by riverboat to Missouri. All of their goods, however, were lost, which caused Oliver to reflect on their poor circumstances and rapid loss of material wealth: "We never saw anything more of our goods, which left us as bare as a sheered sheep; we had the hide left, but not whole; and all that change wrought in two years."[18]

3

HARDSHIP AND CONFLICT IN KIRTLAND

"The Saints in the city of Kirtland have been called to endure great affliction for the truth's sake and to bear a heavy burden." (Newel K. Whitney.)

Though life in Kirtland was difficult for the early Saints, journal accounts do not indicate that they viewed their lives as such. Rather, they apparently had a sense of gratitude and challenge associated with the opportunity to live as they believed. An example of this feeling was expressed by Mary Fielding Smith after a spiritual experience in the temple, when she wrote, "What I felt that day seemed to [outweigh] all the afliction and destress of mind I have sufferd since I came here."[1] John Tanner reflected on this experience and said, "Well, if others have come up easier, they have not learned so much."[2]

Even considering the rigorous missionary journeys, the Saints adjusted to circumstances beyond their control, such as sickness, death, inclement weather, and difficult travel conditions. More difficult for them, however, were external conflicts thrust upon them — economic boycotts, extreme poverty, lawsuits, persecution, and violence. Many persons sold all they had just to get to Kirtland. Others, who had financial reserves, sacrificed greatly to build up the city and the Church.

Since northeastern Ohio in the 1830s was essentially an agrarian area, the Saints' livelihood revolved around agriculture. Most men spent plodding hours planting, plowing, and harvesting crops and cutting wood. The women tended to domestic matters, including cooking over primitive stoves, sewing and mending, housecleaning, and laundering clothes and bedding. Families had to make their own household materials and equipment, such as soap, candles, clothes, leather and wood items, bowls, pitchforks, and brooms.

Wilford Woodruff tells of his first encounter with Joseph Smith:

> My first introduction to him was rather singular. I saw him out in the field with his brother Hyrum: he had on a very old hat, and was engaged shooting at a mark. I was introduced to him, and he invited me home with him.
>
> I accepted the invitation, and I watched him pretty closely, to see what I could learn. He remarked, while passing to his house, that this was the first hour he had spent in recreation for a long time.
>
> Shortly after we arrived at his house, he went into an adjoining room, and brought out a wolf-skin, and said, "Brother Woodruff, I want you to help me to tan this;" so I pulled off my coat, went to work and helped him, and felt honoured in so doing. He was about going up with the brethren to redeem Zion, and he wanted this wolf-skin to put upon his waggon seat, as he had no buffalo robe. . . .
>
> I have felt to rejoice exceedingly in what I saw of brother Joseph, for in his public and private career he carried with him the Spirit of the Almighty, and he manifested a greatness of soul which I had never seen in any other man.[3]

During Kirtland's cold winters, men usually stayed at home, devoting time to their families. Home life centered around the family, and families spent long evenings together. Church meetings were frequently held in the evenings at "early candlelight." Schools were generally conducted during the winter months, when people could not go outdoors.

Some of Joseph Smith's everyday activities provide insight into typical Kirtland life in the 1830s:[4]

> I went to a place near Lake Erie, and spent the day in fishing, and visiting the brethren. [April 12, 1834]
> Hauled a load of hay; and on Wednesday plowed and

sowed oats for Brother Frederick G. Williams. [April 15, 1834]

Labored in Father's orchard, gathering apples. [October 15, 1835]

Went to Chardon to attend the County Court. [October 26, 1835]

Attended school during school hours, returned and spent the evening at home. [November 6, 1835]

In the forenoon, at home, studying the Greek language. [December 23, 1835]

At early candle-light I preached at the school house to a crowded congregation, who listened with attention for about three hours. [December 29, 1835]

After attending to the duties of my family, retired to the council room to pursue my studies. [December 31, 1835]

Attended at the schoolroom, as usual, . . . and did not feel like studying, but commenced conversing upon heavenly things. [January 23, 1836]

At school in the forenoon. In the afternoon met in the printing office. Received and waited upon those who called to see me, and attended to my domestic concerns. In the evening met in the printing office and listened to a lecture on grammar. [March 15, 1836]

Opposition and Persecution

Unable to appreciate that the Lord's purposes were being fulfilled, settlers who had lived in Kirtland before the Mormons arrived suddenly found themselves outnumbered. Before 1830, the population was 1,018. The Mormons began arriving in 1830, and by 1838 their numbers had increased to over two thousand. Within the same period the non-Mormon population grew only to about twelve hundred. With the growth of the Church in the area, the Mormons were able to control much of the development and direction of the community, and there was growing fear that they would gain control of county offices as well. Undoubtedly, this contributed to an increase in violence and persecution against them.

The fact that the Church was not politically aligned with the community also caused conflict. A majority of the Mormons supported the Democratic party, led by President Andrew Jackson, while most non-Mormons supported candidates of the Whig party. Joseph Smith later called the period in Kirtland a "long seven years of servitude, persecution, and affliction in the midst of our enemies."[5]

The persecution began barely a year after the Saints arrived, starting with the tarring and feathering of the Prophet and Sidney Rigdon, one of his chief supporters, in Hiram, a farm community about thirty miles from Kirtland. On the morning following the tarring and feathering, Joseph went to see Elder Rigdon and "found him crazy, and his head highly inflamed, for they had dragged him by his heels, and those, too, so high from the ground that he could not raise his head from the rough, frozen surface, which lacerated it exceedingly; . . . and he continued delirious some days."[6]

In 1833 George A. Smith, the Prophet's cousin, expressed grave concern about the situation: "In consequence of the persecution which raged against the Prophet Joseph and constant threat to do him violence it was necessary to keep continual guard to prevent his being murdered by his enemies. . . . During the fall and winter I took a part of this service going two and a half miles to guard at President Rigdon's."[7]

Joseph Smith wrote that "all of the Church in Kirtland had to lie every night for a long time upon our arms to keep off mobs, of forties, of eighties, & of hundreds to save our lives and the press, and that we might not be scattered & driven to the four winds!"[8]

Benjamin F. Johnson, who as a youth had moved to Kirland with his family, later recalled how the Saints were forced to guard and protect their homes: "Much of my time in boyhood was spent in assisting to prepare arms for the protection of the Saints. The lower story of my mother's house in Kirtland was at that time used by Brother M. C. Davis as a gunsmith shop, for the manufacture of defensive weapons for the use of the people."[9]

Finally it became necessary for Joseph Smith and other leaders to have bodyguards. Ira Ames wrote: "Ever since my arrival in Kirtland, I had stood guard at night in consequence of the mob and persecutions we endured. Especially this winter of 1835, I [was] frequently taking my blanket and sleeping in Joseph's house and guarding my portion of the time and continued as one of Joseph's body guards until I left Kirtland."[10]

On January 21, 1834, Oliver Cowdery wrote in a letter to Missouri: "Our enemies have threatened us, but thank the Lord we are yet on earth. They came out on the 8th. about 12 oclock at night, a little west & fired cannon. we suppose to alarm us, but no one was frightened. but all prepared to defend ourselves if they made a sally upon our houses."[11]

In 1835, some merchants mounted an economic boycott of the Saints. George A. Smith later recalled:

A majority of the inhabitants of Kirtland combined together and warned all the saints to leave the town. This was done to prevent any of our people becoming a town charge in case of poverty. They then bought up all the grain that was for sale in the country around, and refused to sell a particle of it to our people. Mr. Lyman, a Presbyterian owning the Kirtland Mills, was at the head of the movement. He accumulated several thousand bushels of grain in his mill and refused to sell the least portion of it to any of the saints. This arrangement was brought a combination of all the religious sects in the vicinity. Mr. Chase, a Presbyterian neighbor of ours, who had a quantity of grain on hand and had refused to sell a particle at any price, came to my father one morning and asked him if he could board the school mistress his portion, assigning as a reason that he had not got provisions to feed her on. My father, although he had eaten the last [morsel] of bread stuff we had, told him he could board her as well as not. This was done to ascertain our [straitened] condition, but Joseph in learning the plan of our enemies, got the brethren to put their mites together, and sent to Portage County and bought a supply of wheat at a reasonable price and carried to a mill owned by one of the brethren several miles from town. By so doing, our Christian friends not only had the mortification of not starving out the saints, but when the harvest came round had a large quantity of grain on hand and no market for it, as our people had raised a supply for themselves.[12]

An Impoverished People

Building the kingdom consumed what little money and resources the Saints had brought to Kirtland with them. It was important that buildings such as the temple and the schoolhouse/printing office be constructed. Money was also needed to buy land, print books, support missionaries and their families, and finance various Church operations. Building up financial resources and finding jobs were difficult as a result of the boycott by the non-Mormons. Jonathan Crosby described the poverty:

> Shortly after we got to Kirtland, Brother B. Young, H. C. Kimball, [and] P. P. Pratt came to me to borrow money. I had nearly 100 dol[lar]s . . . they were very poor. Pres. Young said he had nothing in the house to eat, and he knew not where to get it. . . . He stood in the door of the printing office thinking of his condition and he felt so bad the sweat [rolled off] him. Soon P. P. Pratt came along, and he said to him, "What shall we do?" I have nothing to eat and I don't know where to get it. Broth. Pratt said there was a brother and his wife just come to my house he got some money and I think he will lend us some (I had let Brother Pratt have 7 doll[ar]s. before). So they all came and gave me their joint note and I let them have 75 doll[ar]s—25 each, this was Jan. of [18]35.[13]

W. W. Phelps described the destitute conditions to his wife, Sally, in a letter in May 1835: "It is hard living here, flour costs from six to seven dollars per barrel and cows from twenty to thirty dollars a head. . . . It is a happy thing that I did not move [you and the family] back for everything here is so dear. Our brethren are so poor and hard run for money that it would have been more than I could have done to maintain my family."[14]

Oliver Huntington wrote: "There was nothing to be had

either for love or money, for Mormons, when they had anything to buy with. Many a time did my mother go without her meal of victuals to leave enough for the children, when there was nothing but beach leaves, after string beans and sometimes a very scanty allowance of corn bread, to leave. Once in a while when we were most starved out we would kill a starved to death hen we had wintered over on nothing, and eat as necessity called hardest."[15]

An urgent letter dated September 18, 1837, from Bishop Newel K. Whitney and his counselors to all members of the Church, asked for financial support:

> It is a fact well known that the Saints in the city of Kirtland have been called to endure great affliction for the truth's sake, and to bear a heavy burden in order that the foundation of the kingdom of God might be laid on a sure and certain basis. . . . The exertions of the enemy . . . have given to the Saints great trouble, and caused them much expense. In addition to this, they have had to publish the word of the Lord, which has been attended with great expense. These things, together with building the House of the Lord, have embarrassed them very much; for when subscriptions failed they went on and accomplished the work of building the house themselves, plighting all that they had, property, credit, and reputation, and by these means accomplished this great work which is the wonder and admiration of the world. This they have done in faith. . . . And besides all this there have been a large number of poor who have had to receive assistance from the donations of the Church, which have tended to increase its embarrassment.[16]

"Poor laws" were enacted in Ohio, allowing communities to expel destitute persons, those who could possibly become wards of the community. Townships elected officers, called Overseers of the Poor, to report such people to the constable; he, in turn, had the authority to force them to leave the city. George A. Smith wrote that "if a person, who had been warned out of town, applied for assistance, he was to be carried to the next town and so on till he was taken out of the state or to the town from which he formerly came."[17] The Mormons were harassed as a result of the laws, but generally they just ignored the notices. In an address to the Saints in Salt Lake City in 1860, Brigham Young described his experience in Kirtland:

> You have frequently heard me refer to my poverty when I moved to Kirtland in the fall of 1833. Not a man ever gathered with the Saints, so far as I have known, but had more property than I had. When I came into the Church I distributed my substance and went to preaching, and when I gathered with the Saints I had nothing. . . . I went to work for Brother Cahoon, one of the Kirtland Temple Committee. He had little or no means, and only a shell of a house. I helped him, and the Lord threw things in his path, and he paid me for my labor.
>
> When I went to Kirtland, I had not a coat in the world, for previous to this I had given away everything I possessed . . . neither had I a shoe to my feet, and I had to borrow a pair of pants and a pair of boots.[18]

Changes in the Economy

Kirtland went through a short-lived surge of rising prosperity during 1836-37, as did the rest of Ohio and the Western Reserve, and many businesses sprang up. Latter-day Saints founded six mercantile firms, and the Church itself operated a brickyard, printing office, bank, ashery, tannery, shoe shop, forge, pottery, steam sawmill, and lumber kiln. In addition, non-Mormons operated two mercantile firms, a blacksmith shop, a sawmill, a grist mill, a carding mill, and a clothing factory.

Jacob Butterfield described the improving economy in a letter to his mother:

> Provisions are high but not so high as they are in Maine — flour is 8 dollars a barrel, wheat $1.25 to $1.50 per bushel, corn 75 cts. per bushel, potatoes 25 cts. per bushel, oxen and cows and sheep are high. This is partly on account of so many moving into the place. There is no lack of work

here but it is a better place to work than it is in Maine. Wages are from 12 dollars to 30 or 40 dollars per month. I have 12 or 13 dollars per month to work on a farm or build road or drive a horse team. There is plenty of work of most kinds for men, women or horses.[19]

When Wilford Woodruff returned from a mission in November 1836, he found Kirtland changed:

Two & a half years since I left Kirtland with my Brethren in their Poverty to go forth . . . our Brethren in Kirtland were poor, despised, & even looked upon . . . with disdain & disgrace. . . . But how changed the scene[. N]ow I behold a cheerfulness beaming upon every countenance that indicates Prosperity & the noise of the ax & the hammer & the sight of their walls & dwellings newly erected & their Bank & market & especially house of God speaks in language loud as thunder that the saints will have a City in prosperity.[20]

Warren Cowdery wrote in January 1837: "Our streets are continually thronged with teams loaded with wood, materials for building the ensuing season, provisions for the market, people to trade. . . . The number of new buildings erected the last season, those now in contemplation and under contract . . . are evincive of more united exertion, more industry and more enterprise than we ever witnessed in so sparse a population."[21]

By July, Cowdery wrote, "The starting up, as if by magic, of buildings in every direction around us, were evincive to us of buoyant hope, lively anticipation, and a firm confidence that our days of pinching adversity had passed by.[22]

It could be argued that the rising prosperity of 1836 came too fast, probably due to population growth. Land prices spiraled. An editorial in the *Messenger and Advocate* in June 1837 indicated that land prices had increased eight hundred percent in one year "and in many cases more."[23] Many of the Latter-day Saints became wealthy on paper because of the value of their properties; however, this wealth never materialized.

4

STAGGERING TRIALS FOR JOSEPH AND EMMA

"Thou hast seen much sorrow because the Lord has taken from thee three of thy children." (Blessing given to Emma Smith.)

Just as the official activities and contributions of Joseph Smith cannot be separated from Kirtland, so the personal lives of Joseph and his twenty-six-year-old wife of four years, Emma Hale Smith, cannot be separated from the Church in Kirtland. Everything that happened — the trials, the persecution, financial problems, the gathering and the subsequent growth of the community, and massive spiritual outpourings — deeply affected their home life.

For Joseph and Emma, life in Kirtland was not easy. They lived with other families for almost half of the time they were there; they lost three children; they suffered financial reverses; Church responsibilities placed inordinate demands on their time; visitors and curiosity seekers frequently visited their home; they were often separated because of Joseph's frequent travels for the Church; their living quarters were, in essence, the Church's headquarters; and persecution aimed at the Church invaded their home and personal lives.

In the seven Ohio years, Joseph and Emma lived in five locations. For at least the first three years they shared quarters as guests of other families. The shortest stay was a few weeks, when they lived with Newel K. Whitney and his wife and five children. When they were finally able to build a larger home, intense persecution and financial problems apparently prevented their occupying it before they had to leave Kirtland.[1]

Joy and Sorrow

When Joseph and Emma arrived in Kirtland in February 1831, Emma was in her seventh month of pregnancy with twins. Their first child, a boy named Alvin, had died immediately after birth on June 15, 1828, at Harmony, Pennsylvania. On April 30, 1831, while living on the Isaac Morley farm, Emma gave birth to twins, a girl and a boy. They lived for only three hours. Emma's father-in-law, Joseph Smith, Sr., who later became the Patriarch to the Church, told Emma in a special blessing, "Thou hast seen much sorrow because the Lord has taken from thee three of thy children."[2]

Joseph and Emma's sorrow was somewhat softened when one of the new converts, John Murdock, approached Joseph and Emma with an unusual request. On April 30, 1831, the same day the Smith twins were born and died, Murdock's wife had died while giving birth to twins, a boy and a girl. After he buried her, he realized he could not care for the twins alone, so he asked Joseph and Emma to raise them. In his biographical sketch, he said the adoption was motivated by a desire to "place them where they can be taught in the faith and principles of Salvation."[3] The Smiths accepted the twins and gave them the names of Joseph and Julia Smith.

Further tragedy came to Joseph Smith's family in March 1832 while they were living at the John Johnson farm. The Prophet described what happened:

> On the 24th of March [1832], the twins before mentioned, which had been sick of the measles for some time, caused us to be broken of our rest in taking care of them, especially my wife. In the evening I told her she had better retire to rest with one of the children, and I would watch with the sicker child. In the night she told me I had better lie down on the trundle bed, and I did so, and was soon after awakened by her screaming murder, when I found myself going out of the door, in the hands of about a dozen men; some

of whose hands were in my hair, and some had hold of my shirt, drawers, and limbs. . . . I made a desperate struggle, as I was forced out, to extricate myself, but only cleared one leg, with which I made a pass at one man, and he fell on the door steps. I was immediately overpowered again, and they swore . . . they would kill me if I did not be still, which quieted me. As they passed around the house with me, the fellow that I kicked came to me and thrust his hand, all covered with blood, into my face and with an exulting hoarse laugh, muttered: " . . . I'll fix ye."

They then seized me by the throat and held on till I lost my breath. After I came to, as they passed along with me, about thirty rods from the house, I saw Elder Rigdon stretched out on the ground, whither they had dragged him by his heels. I supposed he was dead. I began to plead with them, saying, "You will have mercy and spare my life, I hope." To which they replied, ". . . call on yer God for help, we'll show ye no mercy;" and the people began to show themselves in every direction; one coming from the orchard had a plank; and I expected they would kill me, and carry me off on the plank. They then turned to the right, and went on about thirty rods further; about sixty rods from the house, and thirty from where I saw Elder Rigdon, into the meadow, where they stopped, and one said, ". . . pull up his drawers, pull up his drawers, he will take cold." Another replied: *"Ain't ye going to kill 'im? Ain't ye going to kill 'im?"* . . . They held a council, and as I could occasionally overhear a word, I supposed it was to know whether or not it was best to kill me. They returned after a while, when I learned that they had concluded not to kill me, but to beat and scratch me well, tear off my shirt and drawers, and leave me naked. One cried, "Simonds, Simonds, *where's the tar bucket?"* "I don't know," answered one, *"where 'tis, Eli's left it."* They ran back and fetched the bucket of tar, when one exclaimed, . . . *"Let us tar up his mouth;"* and they tried to force the tar-paddle into my mouth; I twisted my head around, so that they could not; and they cried out, *". . . hold up yer head and let us giv ye some tar."* They then tried to force a vial into my mouth,

33

and broke it in my teeth. All my clothes were torn off me except my shirt collar; and one man fell on me and scratched my body with his nails like a mad cat, and then muttered out: ". . . *that's the way the Holy Ghost falls on folks!*"

They then left me, and I attempted to rise, but fell again; I pulled the tar away from my lips, so that I could breathe more freely, and after a while I began to recover, and raised myself up, whereupon I saw two lights. I made my way towards one of them, and found it was Father Johnson's. When I came to the door I was naked, and the tar made me look as if I were covered with blood, and when my wife saw me she thought I was all crushed to pieces, and fainted. During the affray abroad, the sisters of the neighborhood had collected at my room. I called for a blanket, they threw me one and shut the door; I wrapped it around me and went in. . . .

My friends spent the night in scraping and removing the tar, and washing and cleansing my body; so that by morning I was ready to be clothed again. This being the Sabbath morning, the people assembled for meeting at the usual hour of worship, and among them came also the mobbers . . . With my flesh all scarified and defaced, I preached to the congregation as usual, and in the afternoon of the same day baptized three individuals.[4]

A contemporary newspaper called the tar and feathering "a base transaction, an unlawful act, a work of darkness, a diabolical trick."[5] As a tragic consequence of the mob action, Joseph and Emma lost their adopted son, Joseph, on that night. The twins were sick with the measles, and the eleven-month-old boy caught a severe cold and died four days later.[6]

The Trials Continue

On April 1, 1832, Joseph Smith had to leave for Missouri on Church business. Fearing for his family's safety because of the recent mob action in Hiram, he suggested to Emma that she go to Kirtland and stay with the family of Newel K. Whitney. He later wrote:

She went to Kirtland, to Brother Whitney's, and Sister Whitney's aunt, Sarah Smith, (who was then living with her,) inquired of her niece if my wife was going to stay there; and, and on being answered in the affirmative, said she should go away, for there was not room enough for the both of them; accordingly sister Whitney invited my wife to leave, which she did immediately; having enjoyed about two hours visit. She then went to Brother Reynolds Cahoon's, and father Smith's, and Doctor Williams, where I found her, very disconsolate on my return.[7]

At the time, Emma had no home of her own and was trying to manage without the help of her husband. After two ill-fated pregnancies, she was in the fourth month of another one, and was mourning for her lost son and caring for Julia, the surviving adopted twin. During the two and a half months that Joseph was in Missouri, she lived with three different families. Joseph also struggled with his trials during this trip. He was poisoned, and except for a healing blessing from Elder Whitney, he probably would have died. On June 6, the Prophet expressed his own loneliness in a letter to her:

Dear Wife:
I would inform you that Brother Martin has arrived here and brought the pleasing news that our family were well when he left there which greatly cheered our hearts and revived our spirits. We thank our Heavenly Father for his goodness unto us and [all of you]. . . . My situation is a very unpleasant one although I will endeavor to be contented, the Lord assisting me. I have visited a grove . . . almost every day . . . and there give vent to all the feelings of my heart. . . . I was grieved to hear that Hyrum had [lost] his little child. I think we can in some degree sympathize with him but we all must be reconciled to our lots and say the will [of the Lord] be done. Sister Whitney wrote a letter to [her husband] which was very cheering and being unwell at that time and filled with much anxiety it would have been very consoling to me to have received a few lines from you. . . . I hope you will excuse . . . my inability in

conveying my ideas in writing. . . . I should like [to] see little Julia and once more take her on my knee and converse with you on all the subjects which concerns us. . . . I subscribe myself your husband. The Lord bless you, peace be with [you]. So farewell until I return.[8]

Not long after Joseph Smith returned from Missouri, he and his family moved into rooms above the Whitney store in Kirtland. That fall he left again, this time on a trip to Boston, Albany, and New York City. During his absence he communicated with Emma through letters that expressed his feelings of tenderness, love, and support. In a letter dated October 13, 1832, he wrote:

My Dear Wife:
    This day I have been walking through . . . the City of New York. . . . [A]fter beholding all that I had any desire to behold . . . the thoughts of home of Emma and Julia rushe[d] upon my mind like a flood and I could wish for [a] moment to be with them. My breast is filled with all the feelings and tenderness of a parent and a Husband and could I be with you I would tell you many things. . . . I hope you will excuse me for writing this letter so soon after writing for I feel as if I wanted to say something to you to comfort you in your peculiar trial and present affliction. I hope God will give you strength that you may not faint. I pray God to soften the hearts of those around you to be kind to you and take [the] burden off your shoulders as much as possible and not afflict you. I feel for you for I know your state and that others do not but you must comfort yourself knowing that God is your friend in heaven and that you have one true and living friend on Earth your Husband.[9]

On November 6, just hours before Joseph returned from this trip, Emma gave birth to a son, whom they named Joseph Smith III. Another son, their second surviving child, was born June 20, 1836. Because of their love for Frederick G. Williams, who served as scribe and counselor to the Prophet, they named their new son Frederick G. W. Smith. This time the Prophet was able to remain in Kirtland with Emma during the full length of her pregnancy.

"Malicious and Vexatious Lawsuits"

The end of Joseph and Emma's stay in Kirtland was foreshadowed by numerous lawsuits against the Prophet and the Church. Seventeen lawsuits have been identified as being filed between 1837 and 1839 in Chardon, the county seat of the county in which Kirtland was situated,[10] and many others were filed in Painesville.

One example of such harassment occurred on July 27, 1837, when the Prophet, accompanied by Sidney Rigdon and Thomas B. Marsh, set out to visit members in Canada. At Painesville, the Prophet recorded, "We were detained all day by malicious and vexatious lawsuits. About sunset I got into my carriage to return home to Kirtland; at this moment the sheriff sprang into the carriage, seized my lines, and served another writ on me." The writ had been sworn out by a traveling salesman who contrived to have the Prophet test "a new fashioned cooking stove . . . in [Joseph's] kitchen, saying it would give credit to his stove, wishing to have it tested by our people." This, of course, turned out to be a ploy for a lawsuit. The Prophet concluded, "I gave my watch to the officer for security and we all returned home."[11]

One historian, in researching the lawsuits, has found that on that same day six writs were served on the Mormon leader in Painesville. "On the first two writs he was tried and released with no action taken against him. He was then arrested a third time and on being examined was held over for the trial. A release was available, however, on a five hundred dollar bond if an acceptable signor could be found. The court would not allow any in his party to sign for him."[12] Anson Call, a recent convert to the Church, knew the sheriff, and so his signature was accepted. However, after Joseph was released, the sheriff pursued him again with another writ and immediately took him back to Painesville, where he stood trial and was acquitted. He was then arrested a fifth time, and this case also was dropped.

Intense mob action and additional evidence of harassment brought on by lawsuits is evident in an account by Apostle Heber C. Kimball: "Joseph was sued before a magistrate's court in Painesville on a vexatious suit. I carried him from Kirtland to Painesville, with four or five others, in my wagon every morning for five days, and brought them back in the evening. We were often waylaid, but managed to elude our enemies by rapid driving and taking different roads. . . . Mobs were organized around Kirtland, who were enraged against us, ready to destroy us."[13]

E. D. Howe, publisher of the Painesville *Telegraph,* indicated that the suits were devised to hinder the Church's progress in Ohio: "All their [the Mormons'] vain babblings and pretensions were pretty strongly set forth and noticed. . . . [T]he surrounding country was becoming somewhat sensitive, *and many of our citizens thought it advisable to take all the legal means within their reach to counteract the progress of so dangerous an enemy in their midst, and many law suits ensued."*[14]

Grandison Newell, who owned a chair factory in Kirtland, was a particularly bothersome adversary of Joseph Smith and the Church. It has been estimated that he filed as many as thirty civil suits against the Prophet. In one lawsuit, he claimed that the Prophet was plotting to assassinate him, and a warrant was issued for Joseph's arrest. Several individuals from Painesville, evidently a self-appointed committee to make a citizen's arrest, went to Kirtland to apprehend Joseph and take him back to Painesville. Joseph, who was away at the time, was arrested when he returned and taken to Painesville. At the trial, held on Saturday, June 3, 1837, at the Methodist church, Joseph was charged with attempting "to take the life of said complainant, by inducing two individuals to lay in wait for said Newell, near his dwelling in order to shoot him." Joseph was bound over to the Geauga County Court in Chardon and fined five hundred dollars bond, while Sidney Rigdon, Orson Hyde, and Solomon Denton, who had appeared as his witnesses, were fined fifty dollars bond each. The editor of the Painesville *Republican* wrote: "I attended the trial and took down the evidence, but was much surprised to find that no testimony appeared, on which, any reliance could be placed, that went in the least degree to criminate the respondent, but rather to raise him in the estimation of men of candor."[17]

Whether Joseph and Emma's trials stemmed from lawsuits, persecutions, personal tribulation, or separation while Joseph was away, those trials no doubt posed enormous challenges for Emma. She could usually only support Joseph from afar. Through all these trials, though she was often in delicate health and forced to manage without her husband, she remained steadfast and supportive. Her mother-in-law, Lucy Mack Smith, wrote of her:

> She did not favor herself on this account, but whatever her hands found to do, she did with her might. . . . I have never seen a woman in my life, who would endure every species of fatigue and hardship, from month to month, and from year to year, with that unflinching courage, zeal, and patience, which she has ever done. . . . [S]he has been tossed upon the ocean of uncertainty — she has breasted the storms of persecution, and buffeted the rage of men and devils, which would have borne down almost any other woman.[16]

Both Joseph and Emma set obedience to the Lord and devotion to Joseph's calling over personal desires.

5

THE PROPHET JOSEPH
AT HOME

*"I spent the evening around my fireside,
teaching my family grammar." (Joseph
Smith.)*

When persecution and outside pressures crowded upon
Joseph Smith, he generally found solace and peace in
his home, even during periods when guards were
posted. As one examines his diary, it is obvious that he enjoyed
his home and truly found peace there, whether teaching his
family around the fireplace, spending Christmas with them, or
entertaining guests and strangers.

The first house Joseph and his wife, Emma, could really call
home was built in 1834 in Kirtland, after they had been married
seven years. This home, built on a hill near the site of the Kirtland
Temple, provided some measure of privacy and family life.
Nevertheless, because Joseph Smith was President of the
Church, much religious activity centered around his home. Journal entries and records give glimpses into his home life:[1]

> Remained at home and had great joy with my family.
> [March 27, 1834]
> Spent the evening around my fireside, teaching my fam-
> ily grammar. It commenced snowing this afternoon; wind
> very heavy. [November 10, 1835]
> Enjoyed myself at home with my family, all day, it being
> Christmas, the only time I have had this privilege so sat-
> isfactorily for a long period. [December 25, 1835]

Some notations mention illnesses of the Prophet:

> Much afflicted with my cold, yet I am determined to overcome. . . . Brother Parrish, my scribe, being afflicted with a cold, asked me to lay my hands on him in the name of the Lord. I did so, and in return I asked him to lay his hands on me. We were both relieved. [November 27, 1835]
>
> I am laboring under some indisposition of health. Slept awhile, and arose feeling tolerably well, through the mercy of God. [December 5, 1835]
>
> I was taken sick, and kept [in] my room. [June 12, 1837]
>
> My afflictions continued to increase, and were very severe, insomuch that I was unable to raise my head from my pillow when the brethren called to bid me farewell. [June 13, 1837]
>
> Dr. Levi Richards, at my request, administered to me herbs and mild food, and nursed me with all tenderness and attention; and my heavenly Father blessed his administrations to the easing and comforting of my system, for I began to amend in a short time, and in a few days I was able to resume my usual labors. [June 14, 1837]

When apostates reported, and the doubtful believed, that his afflictions resulted from transgression, Joseph wrote, "But of this the Lord judge between me and them."[2]

Chores and duties had to be done, and Joseph Smith did his share of mundane household and family tasks. On November 7, 1835, he wrote in his journal that he spent the day at home "attending to my domestic concerns." In December 1835, he mentioned that he was "at home attending to the duties of my family." He also recorded that he was chopping wood. On December 24, he spent the afternoon assisting the commissioner in "surveying a road across my farm."

In his teachings, the Prophet emphasized the importance of learning. Here are some entries from his journal:

> I returned home, being much fatigued from riding in the rain. Spent the remainder of the day in reading and meditation. [October 5, 1835]

Spent the day at home, in examining my books, and studying the Hebrew alphabet. [November 21, 1835]

Spent this day at home, endeavoring to treasure up knowledge for the benefit of my calling. [December 21, 1835]

Continued my studies. O may God give me learning, even language; and endue me with qualifications to magnify His name while I live. [December 22, 1835]

At home, studying the Greek language. [December 23, 1835]

Wherever he lived, Joseph Smith had an office in his home for official Church business, which included working on translations, receiving revelations, instructing the members, entertaining visitors, and holding council meetings. From 1835 through 1837, he also had an office outside of his home, first in the schoolhouse/printing office and then in the temple.

Many visitors, often insensitive and inquisitive individuals, stopped in Kirtland to visit the Prophet. In his journal he tells of some of the visits:

I was this morning introduced to a man from the east. After hearing my name, he remarked that I was nothing but a man, indicating by this expression, that he had supposed that a person to whom the Lord should see fit to reveal His will, must be something more than a man. [November 6, 1835]

This afternoon, Erastus Holmes, of Newbury, Ohio, called on me to inquire about the establishment of the Church, and to be instructed. . . . I gave him a brief relation of my experience . . . my first vision . . . also the revelations that I received afterwards concerning the Book of Mormon. . . . He listened very attentively, and seemed highly gratified, and intends to unite with the Church. [November 14, 1835]

Elder Josiah Clark, from the state of Kentucky, called on me. . . . Elder Clark . . . was bitten by a mad dog some three or four years since; has doctored much. . . . He came here that he might be benefitted by the prayers of the

Church. Accordingly we prayed for him and laid hands on him . . . and anointed him with oil, and rebuked his afflictions. [November 28, 1835]

A number of brethren from New York called to visit me and see the Egyptian records. [December 14, 1835]

The Smiths often entertained overnight guests in their home. The Prophet was generous in his hospitality to the point that he was criticized for being too generous. Some of the guests were sincere in seeking for truth and some were not. For example, one person, John Hollister of Portage County, Ohio, wanted to discuss religion with the Prophet. Joseph wrote, "He tarried overnight with me, and acknowledged in the morning that, although he had thought he knew something about religion, he was now sensible that he knew but little." The Prophet, showing his wit, added, " . . . which was the greatest trait of wisdom I could discover in him."[3] Another guest, Samuel Barnum, "came to my house, much afflicted with a swollen arm." The Prophet commented that "he had not sufficient faith to be healed, my wife applied a poultice of herbs, and he tarried overnight."[4]

Joseph and Emma had their share of obnoxious guests. Luke Johnson, a Kirtland constable, observed an overnight guest taking advantage of their hospitality: "A Baptist Clergyman from the State of New York, who had been acquainted with the Prophet Joseph in his early life, called upon him and staid all night. Joseph made the minister welcome, and treated him hospitably and respectfully; but, when breakfast was over next morning, he called Joseph a hypocrite, a liar, an imposter and a false Prophet, and called upon him to repent."[5]

One of the strangest visitors was "Joshua, the Jewish Minister," who arrived in mid-morning on Monday, November 9, 1835. The Prophet described him as "having a beard about three inches in length, quite grey; also his hair was long and considerably silvered with age; I thought him about fifty or fifty-five years old; tall, straight, slender built, of thin visage, blue eyes, and fair complexion; wore a sea-green frock coat and pantaloons, black fur hat with narrow brim; and, while speaking, frequently shut his eyes, with a scowl on his countenance."[6] Joseph invited him to stay for dinner and overnight. After a lengthy doctrinal discussion and questioning, it turned out that "Joshua" was really a notorious lawbreaker from New York who had been tried in court for murder, manslaughter, contempt of court, and whipping his daughter. Despite this, and knowing that the man had been convicted and imprisoned for contempt and the whipping, the Prophet fed him and put him up in his home for two more nights.

Joseph Smith was constantly faced with financial problems. Because his duties required that he be available at all times, he had to ask members of the Church for financial assistance. In his history, he listed the names of those who contributed and the amounts given. In one entry he commented, "My heart swells with gratitude inexpressible when I realize the great condescension of my heavenly Father, in opening the hearts of these my beloved brethren to administer so liberally to my wants. . . . Whether my days are many or few, . . . let me enjoy the society of such brethren."[7]

One notation stated that an Elder Tanner "brought me half of a fatted hog for the benefit of my family." Another noted, "Elder Shadrach Roundy brought me a quarter of beef." The Prophet then expressed a wish that "blessings . . . be poured upon their heads, for their kindness towards me."[8]

Postage was expensive in the 1830s; mailing a letter cost twenty-five cents, which was a half-day's wage. Joseph frequently received letters that had been sent C.O.D. To make matters worse, some of the mail contained insults. The Prophet wrote: "It is a common occurrence [to receive C.O.D. letters], and I am subjected to a great deal of expense by those whom I know nothing about, only that they are destitute of good manners; for if people wish to be benefitted with information from me, common respect and good breeding would dictate them to pay the postage on their letters."[9]

This problem continued until the Prophet finally put a notice in the Church newspaper, *Messenger and Advocate*: "I wish to inform my friends and all others, abroad, that whenever they wish to address me thro' the Post Office, they will be kind enough to pay the postage on the same. My friends will excuse me in this matter, as I am willing to pay postage on letters to hear from *them;* but am unwilling to pay for insults and menaces, — consequently, must refuse *all,* unpaid."[10]

In his family relationships, Joseph Smith manifest a strong and tender love. Journal notes indicate he longed to be with them when he was separated from them. When he was at home, he frequently made note of his joy to be with them.

His love for others outside his family circle was also frequently manifest. Perhaps this love was tested most when friends turned against him and the Church. As difficult as it must have been for him to undergo persecution from enemies, his hardest trials came as friends and associates deserted him. But he was always quick to forgive and to welcome back the transgressor. His feelings are revealed in a letter to one such individual: "I have received your letter of the 28th of September, 1835, and I have read it twice, and it gave me sensations that are better imagined than described, let it suffice that I say that the very flood gates of my heart were broken up — I could not refrain from weeping. I thank God that it has entered into your heart to try to return to the Lord, and to this people."[11]

Joseph was particularly fond of children. Louisa Littlefield, who was baptized in 1834 at age fourteen, recalled: "In Kirtland, when wagon loads of grown people and children came in from the country to meeting, Joseph would make his way to as many of the wagons as he well could and cordially shake the hand of each person. Every child and young babe in the company were especially noticed by him and tenderly taken by the hand, with his kind words and blessings. He loved innocence and purity, and he seemed to find it in the greatest perfection with the prattling child."[12]

Lorenzo Snow, who later would become President of the Church, was impressed by the Prophet's deep feelings of kindness toward animals: "There was a steep hill in Kirtland which was being leveled, and quite a number of workmen were engaged. President Smith was there and I met him with his first counselor, Sidney Rigdon. The Prophet was overseeing the work. One of the brethren came up to the Prophet, carrying a nest full of young mice. He showed them to Joseph, who after looking at them, seemingly with great interest, said to the workman: 'Pretty little innocent things, take them back and put them where their mother can find them.' "[13]

The Prophet Develops and Matures

In Kirtland, the Prophet Joseph Smith developed and matured as a leader through facing and overcoming many challenges and difficulties. Lorenzo Snow made two observations of the Prophet's development. The first was in 1832 at the home of John Johnson:

> I made a critical examination as to his appearance, his dress, and his manner as I heard him speak. He was only twenty-five years of age and was not, at that time, what would be called a fluent speaker. His remarks were confined principally to his own experiences, especially the visitation of the angel, giving a strong and powerful testimony in regard to these marvelous manifestations. He simply bore his testimony to what the Lord had manifested to him, to the dispensation of the Gospel which had been committed to him, and to the authority that he possessed. At first he seemed a little diffident and spoke in rather a low voice, but as he proceeded he became very strong and powerful, and seemed to affect the whole audience with the feeling that he was honest and sincere. It certainly influenced me in this way and made impressions upon me that remain until the present day.[14]

Five years later, Lorenzo again met the Prophet, this time at Joseph's home on the hill, and noted:

> He seemed to have changed considerably in his appearance since I first saw him at Hiram, four and a half years before. He was very ready in conversation, and had apparently lost that reserve and diffident feeling that he seemed to have before. He was free and easy in his con-

versation with me, making me feel perfectly at home in his presence. In fact, I felt as free with him as if we had been special friends for years. He was very familiar.[15]

Christopher G. Crary, a longtime Kirtland resident and non-Mormon, recognized that experiences with people and a "native ability" polished Joseph Smith in spite of his lack of formal education. He observed that "contact with mankind and native ability had given him [Joseph] polished manners, and his language, so far as I was qualified to judge, was correct, forcible, right to the point, and convincing. From my acquaintance and dealings with him, I considered him far superior to the educated Rigdon in intellectual ability."[16]

Joseph as a Businessman

In an attempt to provide for his family and to meet his financial obligations, Joseph Smith opened a store in the latter part of 1836. He apparently operated the store for less than one year. Accounts written about the store indicate that his compassion for the Saints took precedence over profit. He apparently found it difficult to refuse many of the Saints who came into the store asking to purchase goods on credit. Brigham Young wrote a scenario of possible transactions in the store:

> Joseph goes to New York and buys 20,000 dollars' worth of goods, comes into Kirtland and commences to trade. In comes one of the brethren, "Brother Joseph, let me have a frock pattern for my wife." What if Joseph says, "No, I cannot without the money." The consequence would be, "He is no Prophet," says James. Pretty soon Thomas walks in. "Brother Joseph, will you trust me for a pair of boots?" "No, I cannot let them go without the money." "Well," says Thomas, "Brother Joseph is no Prophet; I have found *that* out, and I am glad of it." After awhile, in comes Bill and sister Susan. Says Bill, "Brother Joseph, I want a shawl, I have not got the money, but I wish you to trust me a week or a fortnight." Well, brother Joseph thinks the others have gone and apostatized, and he don't know but these

goods will make the whole Church do the same, so he lets Bill have a shawl. Bill walks off with it and meets a brother. "Well," says he, "what do you think of brother Joseph?" "O he is a first-rate man, and I fully believe he is a Prophet. See here, he has trusted me this shawl." Richard says, "I think I will go down and see if he won't trust me some." In walks Richard. "Brother Joseph, I want to trade about 20 dollars." "Well," says Joseph, "these goods will make the people apostatize; so over they go, they are of less value than the people." Richard gets his goods. Another comes in the same way to make a trade of 25 dollars, and so it goes. Joseph was a first-rate fellow with them all the time, provided he never would ask them to pay him. In this way it is easy for us to trade away a first-rate store of goods, and be in debt for them.[17]

Brigham Young noted the negative consequences of Joseph's charity in the store:

I have known persons that would have cursed brother Joseph to the lowest hell hundreds of times, because he would not trust out everything he had on the face of the earth, and let the people squander it to the four winds. When he had let many of the brethren and sisters have goods on trust, he could not meet his liabilities, and then they would turn round and say, "What is the matter brother Joseph, why don't you pay your debts?" "It is quite a curiosity that you don't pay your debts; you must be a bad financier; you don't know how to handle the things of this world." At the same time the coats, pants, dresses, boots and shoes that they and their families were wearing came out of Joseph's store, and were not paid for when they were cursing him for not paying his debts.[18]

Financial problems connected with the store no doubt created further pressures on Joseph and Emma. After they left Kirtland, he was still settling debts connected with this business venture.

6

FAMILY HERITAGE AND SUPPORT

"I saw Mother on her knees under an apple tree praying for us. . . . From that moment we were healed." (Hyrum Smith.)

Joseph Smith's family heritage was crucial to the success of his life and mission. From noble parents and grandparents, he was blessed with character traits and faith that prepared him to meet opposition and persecution in his life.

Joseph and Emma were greatly blessed by the association and support of Joseph's family, who followed them to Kirtland. The family included the Prophet's parents, Joseph Smith Sr. and Lucy Mack Smith; his brothers, Hyrum, Samuel, William, and Don Carlos; several sisters, uncles and aunts, and cousins. Many of them served in Church callings, gave moral support when it was badly needed, assisted in blessings and prayers, and helped to build up the Church in Kirtland.

Joseph Smith Sr.

While living in Kirtland Joseph Smith Sr. served missions, preached, baptized, underwent persecution, helped build the temple, frequently gave blessings to the Saints, and conducted meetings. He was a member of the first high council, served as Patriarch to the Church, was president of the high priesthood, and served in the First Presidency. Joseph Smith Sr. was described as "six feet, two inches high, was very straight, and remarkably well proportioned. His ordinary weight was about two hundred pounds, and he was very strong and active. In his younger days he was famed as a wrestler, and, Jacob like, he never wrestled with but one man whom he could not throw."[1]

Lorenzo Snow made the following observation: "Anyone seeing Father Smith as he then appeared and having read of old Father Abraham in the scriptures, would be apt to think that Father Smith looked a good deal like Abraham must have looked; at least, that is what I thought. I do not know that any man among the Saints was more loved than Father Smith; and when any one was seriously sick Father Smith would be called for, whether it was night or day. He was as noble and generous a man as I have ever known."[2]

Lorenzo first met Joseph Smith Sr. following a meeting in the Kirtland Temple. The Patriarch boldly predicted that Lorenzo "would soon be convinced of the truth of the Latter-day work, and be baptized." Lorenzo recorded this impression: "The old gentleman's prediction, that I should ere long be baptized, was strange to me, for I had not cherished a thought of becoming a member of the 'Mormon' Church. . . . I looked at Father Smith, and silently asked myself the question: Can that man be a deceiver? His every appearance answered in the negative. At first sight, his presence impressed me with feelings of love and reverence. I had never seen age so prepossessing. Father Joseph Smith, the Patriarch, was indeed a noble specimen of aged manhood."[3] His lack of worldly possessions is evident from his comment during a conference on October 25, 1831, when many priesthood brethren had expressed willingness to consecrate all that they possessed to the Lord. Father Smith responded that he "had nothing to consecrate to the Lord of the things of the Earth, yet he felt to consecrate himself and family."[4]

Lucy Mack Smith

Throughout the Kirtland period, Lucy Mack Smith was supportive and involved with the Church. Her leadership ability surfaced when she led a group of twenty adults and thirty children from Fayette, New York, traveling part of the way by flat boat on the Erie Canal. When a blockage of the canal delayed the barge for more than a day and there was a great deal of murmuring by the Saints because of a food shortage, Lucy stood up and declared, "You will not starve. . . . I have no doubt but the hand of the Lord is over us."[5] In Buffalo, she was not afraid to let people know that she and her group were members of the Church, though another group of Saints there told her that such an admission might prevent them from getting lodging. She succeeded in finding a place for the women and children to stay. When scoffers said that the ship on which the group were to cross Lake Erie could not sail because of ice, she led the Saints aboard ship and told them:

> "If you will all of you raise your desires to heaven, that the ice may be broken up, and we be set at liberty, as sure as the Lord lives, it will be done." At that instant a noise was heard, like bursting thunder. The captain cried, "Every man to his post." The ice parted, leaving barely a passage for the boat, and so narrow that as the boat passed through[,] the buckets of the waterwheel were torn off with a crash, which, joined to the word of command from the captain, the hoarse answering of the sailors, the noise of the ice, and the cries and confusion of the spectators, presented a scene truly terrible. We had barely passed through the avenue when the ice closed together again, and the Colesville brethren were left in Buffalo, unable to follow us.
>
> As we were leaving the harbor, one of the bystanders exclaimed, "There goes the 'Mormon' company! That boat is sunk in the water nine inches deeper than ever it was before, and, mark it, she will sink — there is nothing surer." In fact, they were so sure of it that they went straight to the office and had it published that we were sunk, so that when we arrived at Fairport we read in the papers the news of our own death.[6]

In Kirtland, Lucy took in visitors, supported those working on the temple, and assisted in building the schoolhouse/printing office. She was noted for her missionary zeal. While traveling with her son Hyrum on a visit to Detroit to visit her brother's family, she spoke rather plainly, with her customary missionary zeal. When someone expressed concern about her outspokenness, Hyrum proposed that "Mother Smith should say just what she pleased, and if she got into difficulty, the Elders should help her out of it."[7]

Her zeal led many people to convert to the Church. During the trip to Michigan, she was introduced to a Mr. Ruggles, her niece's Presbyterian pastor. In her history, she wrote:

"And you," said Mr. Ruggles, upon shaking hands with me, "are the mother of that poor, foolish, silly boy, Joe Smith, who pretended to translate the Book of Mormon."

I looked him steadily in the face, and replied, "I am, sir, the mother of Joseph Smith; but why do you apply to him such epithets as those?"

"Because," said his reverence, "that he should imagine he was going to break down all other churches with that simple 'Mormon' book."

"Did you ever read that book?" I inquired.

"No," said he, "it is beneath my notice."

"But," rejoined I, "the Scriptures say, 'prove all things'; and, now, sir, let me tell you boldly, that that book contains the everlasting gospel, and it was written for the salvation of your soul, by the gift and power of the Holy Ghost."

"Pooh," said the minister, "nonsense—I am not afraid of any member of my church being led astray by such stuff; they have too much intelligence."

"Now, Mr. Ruggles," said I, and I spoke with emphasis, for the Spirit of God was upon me, "mark my words—as true as God lives, before three years we will have more than one-third of your church; and, sir, whether you believe it or not, we will take the very deacon, too."

This produced a hearty laugh at the expense of the minister.

Not to be tedious, I will say that I remained in this section of country about four weeks, during which time I labored incessantly for the truth's sake, and succeeded in gaining the hearts of many, among whom were David Dort and his wife. Many desired me to use my influence to have an elder sent into that region of country, which I agreed to do. As I was about starting home, Mr. Cooper observed that our ministers would have more influence if they dressed in broadcloth.

When I returned, I made known to Joseph the situation of things where I had been, so he despatched Brother Jared Carter to that country. And in order that he might not lack influence, he was dressed in a suit of superfine broadcloth. He went immediately into the midst of Mr. Ruggles' church, and, in a short time, brought away seventy of his best members, among whom was the deacon, just as I told the minister. This deacon was Brother Samuel Bent, who now presides over the High Council.[8]

Records indicate Lucy Mack Smith's prayers sustained her family. Her son Joseph wrote an account of her prayerful entreaties during the time when he and other brethren had gone with "Zion's Camp," a company of men who went to Missouri to help members of the Church who were being harassed there by mobs. An epidemic of cholera broke out in the camp, and Joseph and Hyrum were both in danger of losing their lives. Joseph wrote:

The disease instantly fastened itself upon us and in a few minutes we were in awful distress. . . . [W]e were scarcely able to stand upon our feet . . . and we were greatly alarmed fearing that we should die in this western wilderness. . . . [T]he cramp siezed the calves of my legs . . . gathering the cords into bunches and then the [operation] extended in like manner all over my system[.] I cried heartily unto God but the Heavens seemed sealed against us and every power that could render us any assistance shut within its gates. . . . [I]n a short time afterwards Hyrum sprung to his feet and exclaimed Joseph we shall return for I have seen an open vision in which I saw Mother on her knees under an apple tree praying for us and she is even now in tears asking God to spare our lives that she may behold us again in the flesh and the spirit testifies to me that her prayers and ours shall be heard—

and from that Moment we were healed and went on our way rejoicing.[9]

After relating the experience to his mother, Joseph told her, "Oh My Mother . . . how often have your prayers been a means of assisting us when the shadows of death encompassed us."[10]

Lucy Mack Smith and her husband were generous to those who needed help, in their concern for the Saints and desire to see the Church prosper. Members gathering to Kirtland frequently sought them out. Later in life Lucy vividly recalled sacrifices that she and Emma had both made for visitors and guests: "How often I have parted every bed in the house for the accommodation of the brethren, and then laid a single blanket on the floor for my husband and myself, while Joseph and Emma slept upon the same floor, with nothing but their cloaks for both bed and bedding."[11]

The Prophet, realizing the hardships his parents' generosity created for them, made it a matter of prayer. The Lord responded through a revelation on March 8, 1833: "Let your families be small, especially mine aged servant Joseph Smith's, Sen., as pertaining to those who do not belong to your families; . . . that those things that are provided for you, to bring to pass my work, be not taken from you and given to those that are not worthy — and thereby you be hindered in accomplishing those things which I have commanded you." (Doctrine and Covenants 90:25-27.)

Despite the revelation, the Smiths could not refuse hospitality to those in need. Lucy wrote: "In 1835, we were still living on the farm, and laboring with our might to make the company which was constantly coming in, as comfortable as possible. Joseph [the Prophet] saw how we were situated, and that it would not answer for us to keep a public house, at free cost, any longer; and, by his request, we moved into an upper room of his own house, where we lived very comfortably for a season."[12]

After his father's death in 1840, Joseph noted that "he was one of the most benevolent of men; opening his house to all who were destitute."[13]

Hyrum, Joseph's Beloved Brother

Throughout his life, Joseph Smith was very close to his older brother Hyrum. Their lives were intertwined in family as well as Church affairs, and they were seldom separated for more than a few months. Hyrum was one of the Eight Witnesses to the Book of Mormon and one of the six original members of the Church. He served as chairman of the building committee for the Kirtland Temple. In 1837 he was appointed a counselor in the First Presidency.

Indicative of the closeness of the brothers, Joseph wrote, "I could pray in my heart that all my brethren were like unto my beloved brother Hyrum, who possesses the mildness of a lamb, and the integrity of a Job, and in short, the meekness and humility of Christ; and I love him with that love that is stronger than death, for I never had occasion to rebuke him, nor he me, which he declared when he left me to-day."[14]

Hyrum assisted Joseph in family matters and responsibilities. He was a peacemaker between Joseph and their brother William, who was very headstrong. And when the Prophet was away on Church assignments, Hyrum would look after Emma and other family members.

Hyrum spent a great deal of his time in missionary service and other Church assignments. On one of his missions, he met the Tyler family near Erie, Pennsylvania. Daniel Tyler later reminisced:

> About December, 1832, Elder Hyrum Smith, brother to the prophet, came to our neighborhood. My father told him that his daughter, who was present, was bent on being baptized into his church, stating at the same time, that the Elder who baptized her would do so at his peril. The Elder quite mildly remarked in substance as follows: "Mr. Tyler, we shall not baptize your daughter against your wishes. If our doctrine be true, which we testify it is, if you prevent your daughter from embracing it, the sin will be on your head, not on ours or your daughter's."
>
> This remark pricked him to the heart. He began to think that possibly the "Mormons" were right and he was wrong.

He therefore decided to counsel his daughter in the matter and then permit her to exercise her free agency. He would thus relieve himself of any responsibility.

His remarks to my sister were to the effect that if this new religion was true, it was the best religion in the world, but, if false, it was the worst. "These men," said he, "know whether it is true or false, but I do not." He wished her to reflect upon all these things before making a move in the matter. She replied that she had weighed them long ago and believed it to be her duty to be baptized. He took her on an ox-sled to Lake Erie, a distance of two miles, where, after a hole was cut through three feet of solid ice, she was baptized and confirmed into the Church by Elder Hyrum Smith.[15]

In January 1836, Joseph sent for Hyrum to administer to and heal Lorenzo Young, who had become ill while working on the temple. Lorenzo described his miraculous healing and a prophecy that Hyrum uttered:

My disease was pronoun[c]ed to be the quick consumption. . . . Dr. Williams, one of the brethren, came to see me, and, considering my case a bad one, came the next day and brought with him Dr. Seely, an old practicing physician. . . . [H]e said to my father, as he left the house:

"Mr. Young, unless the Lord makes your son a new pair of lungs, there is no hope for him!" . . .

The next morning after the visit of the doctors, my father came to the door of the room to see how I was. I recollect his gazing earnestly at me with tears in his eyes. As I afterwards learned, he went from there to the Prophet Joseph, and said to him: "My son Lorenzo is dying; can there not be something done for him?"

The Prophet studied a little while, and replied, "Yes! Of necessity, I must go away to fill an appointment, which I cannot put off. But you go and get my brother Hyrum." . . .

Brother Hyrum Smith led. The Spirit rested mightily upon him. He was full of blessing and prophecy. Among other things, he said that I should live to go with the Saints into the bosom of the Rocky Mountains, to build up a place there, and that my cellar should overflow with wine and fatness.

At that time, I had not heard about the Saints going to the Rocky Mountains; possibly Brother Smith had. After he had finished he seemed surprised at some things he had said, and wondered at the manifestations of the Spirit. I coughed no more after that administration, and rapidly recovered.

I had been pronounced by the best physicians in the country past all human aid, and I am a living witness of the power of God manifested in my behalf through the administration of the Elders.[16]

During the Kirtland years, Hyrum supported Joseph even while wrestling with his own personal tragedies. In 1832 Hyrum and Jerusha, his wife, lost their three-year-old daughter, Mary. He wrote in his journal, "I was called to view a scene which brought sorrow and mourning. Mary was called from time to eternity on the 29th day of May. She expired in my arms—such a day I never before experienced, and oh may God grant that we may meet her again on the great day of redemption to part no more."[17]

One of Hyrum's greatest trials came in 1837, while he was fulfilling a mission in Missouri. Jerusha was expecting their sixth child, and on October 2, she gave birth to the baby girl, whom she named Sarah. Less than two weeks later, Jerusha died. Joseph Smith wrote: "My brother Hyrum's wife, Jerusha Bardon Smith, died on the 13th of October while I was in Terre Haute, and her husband at Far West. She left five small children and numerous relatives to mourn her loss; her demise was severely felt by all. She said to one of her tender offspring when on her dying bed, 'Tell your father when he comes that the Lord has taken your mother home and left you for him to take care of.' She died in full assurance of a part in the first resurrection."[18]

Lucy Mack Smith, Hyrum's mother, wrote of the death of her daughter-in-law, "A calamity happened to our family that wrung our hearts with more than common grief. Jerusha, Hyrum's wife, was taken sick, and after an illness of perhaps two weeks, died while her husband was absent on a mission to Missouri. She was a woman whom everybody loved that was acquainted with her, for she was every way worthy. The family were so warmly attached to her, that, had she been our own sister, they could not have been more afflicted by her death."[19]

As soon as news of Jerusha's death reached him, Hyrum returned home. Within weeks he proposed marriage to Mary Fielding, a convert to the Church from Canada who taught school in Kirtland, and they were married on December 24. Hyrum later remarked, "It was not because I had less love or regard for Jerusha, that I married so soon, but it was for the sake of my children."[20]

Hyrum's name is strongly associated with Kirtland, not only for his contributions toward the building of the temple, his Church service, and his devotion to his family, but also for a prophecy concerning the eventual rebuilding of Kirtland. It was through him that the Lord said, referring to a future time, "Thus saith the Lord . . . I will send forth and build up Kirtland."[21]

Mary Duty Smith

Death touched the Smiths again when the Prophet's grandmother, Mary Duty Smith, passed away while visiting the family on May 27, 1836, at the age of ninety-three. Of her visit, the Prophet wrote:

> She had come five hundred miles to see her children, and knew all of us she had ever seen. She was much pleased at being introduced to her great-grandchildren, and expressed much pleasure and gratification on seeing me.
>
> My grandfather, Asael Smith, long ago predicted that there would be a prophet raised up in his family, and my grandmother was fully satisfied that it was fulfilled in me. My grandfather Asael died in East Stockholm, St. Lawrence county, New York, after having received the Book of Mormon, and read it nearly through; and he declared that I

was the very Prophet that he had long known would come in his family.

On the 18th, my uncle Silas Smith and family arrived from the east. My father, three of his brothers, and their mother, met the first time for many years. It was a happy day, for we had long prayed to see our grandmother and uncles in the Church. [Mary Duty Smith, however, had not been baptized because of the opposition of her eldest son, Jesse Smith.]

On May 27, after a few days visit with her children, which she enjoyed extremely well, my grandmother fell asleep without sickness, pain or regret. She breathed her last about sunset, and was buried in the burial ground near the Temple, after a funeral address had been delivered by Sidney Rigdon.[22]

7

THE MISSIONARY PROPHET
LEADS BY EXAMPLE

*"I made this my rule: when the Lord
commands, do it." (Joseph Smith.)*

During the seven years the Church headquarters were in
Kirtland, the membership grew rapidly under Joseph
Smith's inspired leadership and example. He continually
taught the principles of the gospel, groomed new leaders, and
comforted those in need. During those years, the Lord directed
the young prophet to go throughout the eastern and central
United States as well as Canada to conduct church business and
spread the gospel. As a result of his efforts, honest seekers of
truth flocked to the restored church. The response of Mary Noble
typified reactions to his message: "Never did I hear preaching
sound so glorious to me as that did. I realized it was the truth
of heaven."[1]

Between 1831 and 1838, the Prophet took twelve major missionary and business trips, which consumed a total of almost
twenty months. Though such extensive travels and obligations
to the Kingdom of God were taxing, he had resolved always to
follow the will of the Lord. During one particularly busy time,
he declared a rule of obedience that governed his life: "No month
ever found me more busily engaged than November; but as my
life consisted of activity and unyielding exertions, I made this
my rule: when the Lord commands, do it."[2]

The twelve journeys and their purposes were as follows:

1. June to August 1831, Missouri; designate Jackson
County as the center place of Zion and dedicate a temple site.

2. April to June 1832, Missouri; establish printing facilities and oversee the implementation of the united order.

3. October and November 1832, New York City, Albany, and Boston; purchase goods for Newel K. Whitney store.

4. October and November 1833, Canada; preach and baptize.

5. February and March 1834, Pennsylvania and New York; preach and recruit members for Zion's Camp.

6. May to August 1834, Missouri; Zion's Camp march.

7. October 1834, Michigan; visit members and preach.

8. August 1835, Michigan; visit members and preach.

9. July to September 1836, New York, bank business; Boston, preach.

10. February 1837, Michigan; bank business.

11. July and August 1837, Canada; preach, baptize, and bless the Saints and strengthen the branches.

12. September to December 1837, Far West, Missouri; organize stakes, purchase land, and survey the town.

Accounts from some of these trips indicate how Joseph created lasting impressions and touched lives. They also tell of some of his encounters and give insight into his feelings for his wife and family.

Missouri Mission, 1832

After completing their business in Missouri, Joseph Smith and Newel K. Whitney, who had accompanied him, were returning to Kirtland by stagecoach. Near Greenville, Indiana, the horses pulling the coach became frightened and started to bolt. As the two men leaped from the stagecoach, Bishop Whitney caught his foot in the wheel, breaking his leg and foot in several places. The Prophet nursed him for four weeks at a "public house," or inn, in Greenville. At dinner one evening, poison was placed in the Prophet's food. A violent attack of vomiting followed, and he began to hemorrhage. Great "muscular contortions" caused his jaw to become dislocated, and he replaced it himself. He made his way to Bishop Whitney's bedside and asked for a blessing. Bishop Whitney, he said, "laid his hands on me and administered to me in the name of the Lord, and I was healed in an instant."[3] The poison's effect was so powerful, however, that much of the Prophet's hair fell out.

At the time of this experience he wrote to his wife, Emma, in Kirtland: "I will try to be contented with my lot. . . . God is my friend. In him I shall find comfort. I have given my life into His hands. I am prepared to go at his call. I desire to be with Christ. I count not my life dear to me, only to do his will."[4]

Mission to Canada, 1833

The Prophet and Sidney Rigdon preached to many congregations as they traveled through upper New York State to Canada. Lydia Knight wrote of their visit to the home of Freeman Nickerson in Mount Pleasant, Ontario, Canada:

> As evening drew near, Mr. Nickerson became anxious to hear something of the newcomer's faith. "Oh," said he, "just let him talk; I'll silence him if he undertakes to talk about the Bible. I guess I know as much about the scriptures as he does." This was to his wife whom he directed to place the family Bible on the table in the parlor.
>
> As soon as supper was over, he invited his visitors and family to go up stairs to the parlor, where he said they would have some talk. All, accordingly, repaired to the large well-furnished room, and then Mr. N. said to the Prophet: "Now, Mr. Smith, I wish you and Mr. Rigdon to speak freely. Say what you wish and tell us what you believe. We will listen." Turning to his wife, he whispered, "Now you'll see how I shall shut him up."
>
> The Prophet commenced by relating the scenes of his early life. He told how the angel visited him, of his finding the plates, the translation of them, and gave a short account of the matter contained in the Book of Mormon.
>
> As the speaker continued his wonderful narrative, Lydia, who was listening and watching him intently, saw his face become white and a shining glow seemed to beam from every feature. As his story progressed he would often allude to passages of scripture. Then Mr. N. would speak

up and endeavor to confound him. But the attempt was soon acknowledged even by himself to be futile.

The Prophet bore a faithful testimony that the Priesthood was again restored to the earth, and that God and His Son had conferred upon him the keys of the Aaronic and Melchisedek Priesthoods. He stated that the last dispensation had come, and the words of Jesus were now in force — "Go ye into all the world and preach the gospel to every creature. He that believeth and is baptized shall be saved; but he that believeth not shall be damned." . . .

You may be sure that by this time Mr. N. was quite willing to sit and listen, saying but little to interrupt or confound. After both men were through speaking, many questions were asked by all present for information. The listeners were honest-hearted people, and when truth is told to such, they are constrained to accept and believe.

"And is this then," said Mr. N., "the curious religion the newspapers tell so much about? Why if what you have just said is not good sound sense, then I don't know what sense is."[5]

The Prophet baptized the Nickersons and at least fourteen others in Mount Pleasant.

Mission to Recruit for Zion's Camp

In February and March 1834, Joseph Smith and other Church leaders were on simultaneous trips in the East to recruit men for an army to march to Missouri, where the Saints were facing expulsion from Jackson County as a result of confrontations with angry mobs.

In upstate New York the Prophet rendezvoused with some of the others. Mary Noble describes the group's visit to her parents' home:

> The spring of 1834, Brother Joseph Smith came from Kirtland, Ohio, to my father's New York estate, Avon, Livingston County. This was the first time I ever beheld a prophet of the Lord, and I can truly say at the first sight that I had a testimony within my bosom that he was a man

chosen of God to bring forth a great work in the last days. His society I prized, his conversation was meat and drink to me. The principles that he brought forth and the testimony that he bore of the truth of the Book of Mormon made a lasting impression upon my mind.

While he was there, Sidney Rigdon and Joseph and Brigham Young, Luke and Lyman Johnson, and 12 or 14 of the travelling elders had a council to my father's. I, in company with my sisters, had the pleasure of cooking, and serving the table, and waiting on the[m], which I considered a privilege and a blessing.

Brother Joseph and Elder Rigdon held a meeting in Geneva, which is called the Orton neighborhood, in a barn. Elder Rigdon preached, Brother Joseph bore testimony of the truth of the Book of Mormon, and of the work that had come forth in these last days. Never did I hear preaching sound so glorious to me as that did. I realized it was the truth of heaven, for I had testimony of it myself.[6]

Zion's Camp March, 1834

From May to October 1834, Joseph Smith led an army of about two hundred men to Missouri to aid the beleaguered Saints there. The group called itself Zion's Camp. Soon after starting out on this journey of over one thousand miles, while camped in Indiana, the Prophet wrote to his wife, Emma, the following letter, which gives insight into his feelings for her:

My Dear Wife
Meeting being over I sit down in my tent to write a few lines to you to let you know that you are on my mind and that I am sensible of the duties of a Husband and Father and that I am well and I pray God to let his blessings rest upon you and the children and all that are around you until I return to your society. The few lines you wrote and sent by the hand of Brother Lyman gave me satisfaction and comfort and I hope you will continue to communicate to me by your own hand, for this is a consolation to me to converse with you in this way in my lonely moments which is not easily described. I will endeavor to write every Sun-

day if I can and let you know how I am. . . . O may the blessings of God rest upon you is the prayer of your husband until death.

Joseph Smith Jr.[7]

Visit to Michigan, 1834

Accompanied by his brother Hyrum, David Whitmer, Frederick G. Williams, Oliver Cowdery, and Roger Orton, Joseph Smith went to Pontiac, Michigan, in October 1834 to visit some Saints there. One of those whom he visited, Edward Stevenson, recalled:

> I first saw him in 1834 at Pontiac and the impression made upon my mind by him at that time causes me now much pleasure. . . . The love for him, as a true Prophet of God, was indelibly impressed upon my mind, and has always been with me from that time. . . .
>
> In that same year, 1834, in the midst of many large congregations, the Prophet testified with great power concerning the visit of the Father and the Son, and the conversation he had with them. Never before did I feel such power as was manifested on these occasions, and, although only a small percentage of those who saw and heard him accepted the restored Gospel, there was not one who dared to dispute it. Many of our neighbors were heard to say: "Well, if Mormonism is true, it will stand; if not true, it will fall." Many of them lived to see it stand and increase, and while they themselves passed away in death's embrace, the work continued to flourish and prosper. . . .
>
> Joseph said, "If you will obey the Gospel with honest hearts, I promise you in the name of the Lord, that the gifts as promised by our Saviour will follow you, and by this you may prove me to be a true servant of God."
>
> I am, with others, a witness that these gifts did follow many in the branch of the Church which was raised up in Pontiac.[8]

While the group was traveling on Lake Erie aboard the steamer *Monroe*, Oliver Cowdery met a man by the name of

Ellmer, who said he was "personally acquainted with Joe Smith, had heard him preach his lies, and now, since he was dead, he was glad!" This man claimed to have heard Joseph preach in New York and described him as a "dark-complexioned man." The Prophet responded, "God have mercy on such, if they will quit their lying. I need not state my complexion to those that have seen me."[9]

Mission to Canada, 1837

On his mission to Canada in 1837, Joseph Smith traveled with Sidney Rigdon and Thomas B. Marsh. In Toronto they stayed on the farm of Mary Horn and her husband. Mary wrote:

> In the latter part of the summer of 1837, I had the great pleasure of being introduced to, and entertaining, the beloved prophet, Joseph Smith, with Sidney Rigdon and T. B. Marsh. I said to myself, "O Lord, I thank thee for granting the desire of my girlish heart, in permitting me to associate with prophets and apostles." On shaking hands with Joseph Smith, I received the holy spirit in such great abundance that I felt it thrill my whole system, from the crown of my head to the soles of my feet. I thought I had never beheld so lovely a countenance. Nobility and goodness were in every feature.[10]

Mission to the West, 1837

Joseph Smith and Sidney Rigdon traveled to Far West, Missouri, in 1837 according to the Prophet, "to fulfill the mission appointed to us on the 18th of September by a conference of Elders, in establishing places of gathering for the Saints." David Osborn tells about a meeting that the Prophet conducted there from a wagon box:

> The first time I saw Joseph Smith was at Far West, in 1837. There were but three houses in town at that time. On the south side of the elder Peter Whitmer's house was a wagon with a box on. Here were seated Joseph, Sidney Rigdon and others. There was quite a congregation in-

cluding old residents (Gentiles) of Caldwell County. I remember many of his sayings. A few things he said on this occasion I will relate. Said he, "You have heard many reports about me. Some perhaps are true and others not true. I know what I have done and I know what I have not done. . . . You may hug up to yourselves the Bible, but except through faith in it you can get revelation for yourself, the Bible will profit you but little. . . . The Book of Mormon is true, just what it purports to be, and for this testimony I expect to give an account in the day of judgment. . . . If I obtain the glory which I have in view I expect to wade through much tribulation."

In closing his remarks he said, "The Savior declared the time was coming when secret or hidden things should be revealed on the house tops. Well," says he, "I have revealed to you a few things, if not on the house top, on the wagon top."[11]

Future Church Presidents

It was in Kirtland that Joseph Smith groomed four future presidents of the Church for responsibilities to come. Brigham Young, John Taylor, Wilford Woodruff, and Lorenzo Snow were baptized during the Kirtland years and led the Church, in succession, until 1901. In addition, the next three presidents — Joseph F. Smith, Heber J. Grant, and George Albert Smith, whose administrations lasted until 1951 — were direct descendants of stalwart Kirtland pioneers.

Seven months after his baptism, Brigham Young met the Prophet. He described the experience:

In September, 1832, Brother Heber C. Kimball took his horse and wagon, Brother Joseph Young and myself accompanying him, and started for Kirtland to see the Prophet Joseph. We visited many friends on the way, and some branches of the Church. . . . We proceeded to Kirtland and stopped at John P. Greene's, who had just arrived there with his family. We rested a few minutes, took some refreshments and started to see the Prophet. We went to his father's house and learned that he was in the woods chopping. We immediately repaired to the woods, where we found the Prophet, and two or three of his brothers, chopping and hauling wood. Here my joy was full at the privilege of shaking the hand of the Prophet of God, and receiving the sure testimony, by the spirit of prophecy, that he was all that any man could believe him to be as a true prophet.[12]

John Taylor, who had been a Methodist preacher in Canada, first came to Kirtland in March 1837, almost one year after he was converted by Parley P. Pratt. Although hesitant at first to listen to Elder Pratt, John gradually warmed up to the message brought from Kirtland. He boldly told a group of friends, "I desire to investigate his doctrines and claims to authority, and shall be very glad if some of my friends will unite with me in this investigation. But if no one will unite with me, be assured I shall make the investigation alone. If I find his religion true, I shall accept it, no matter what the consequences may be; and if false, then I shall expose it."[13]

Following his baptism, John Taylor traveled to Kirtland, which was staggering under the pressures of apostasy. He boldly proclaimed to apostates critical of the Joseph Smith, "It is not man that I am following, but the Lord."[14]

Wilford Woodruff, a convert of barely four months, first went to Kirtland in April 1834. Though friends and neighbors in New York State warned him of the dangers involved in joining the Mormons, he responded: "Parley P. Pratt told me it was my duty to lay aside all my temporal matters, go to Kirtland, and join Zion's Camp. I obeyed his counsel."[15] He described his first meeting with the Prophet:

> I was introduced to Brother Joseph, and he shook hands with me most heartily. He invited me to make his habitation my home while I tarried in Kirtland. This invitation I most eagerly accepted, and was greatly edified and blest during my stay with him. . . .
>
> That night we had a most enjoyable and profitable time in his home. . . . He said in relation to Zion's Camp,

"Brethren, don't be discouraged about our not having means. The Lord will provide, and He will put it into the heart of somebody to send me some money." The very next day he received a letter from Sister Vose, containing one hundred and fifty dollars. When he opened the letter and took out the money, he held it up and exclaimed: "See here, did I not tell you the Lord would send me some money to help us on our journey? Here it is." I felt satisfied that Joseph was a Prophet of God in very deed.[16]

Lorenzo Snow, who lived near Kirtland, experienced a spiritual conversion similar to that of the other future prophets. He first met Joseph Smith at the John Johnson home in Hiram, Ohio:

As I looked upon him and listened, I thought to myself that a man bearing such a wonderful testimony as he did, and having such a countenance as he possessed, could hardly be a false prophet. He certainly could not have been deceived, it seemed to me, and if he was a deceiver he was deceiving the people knowingly; for when he testified that he had had a conversation with Jesus, the Son of God, and had talked with Him personally, as Moses talked with God upon Mount Sinai, and that he had also heard the voice of the Father, he was telling something that he either knew to be false or to be positively true. There for the first time I heard his voice. When I heard his testimony in regard to what the Lord had revealed to him, it seemed to me that he must be an honest man. He talked and looked like an honest man. He was an honest man.[17]

After his conversion and baptism in Kirtland, Lorenzo made a commitment that was to characterize his leadership: "I made up my mind that I would do my duty and that this principle would be my guide through life. I made up my mind solidly that whatever I was asked to do in the Church and Kingdom of God, I would try to do it."[18]

In Kirtland, Joseph Smith not only set a missionary example but also labored to instill a missionary spirit and vision in his followers. At a meeting at the schoolhouse on the hill above the Morley Farm, Wilford Woodruff heard the Prophet make an astounding prophecy:

> On Sunday night the Prophet called on all who held the Priesthood to gather into the little log school house they had there. It was a small house, perhaps 14 feet square. But it held the whole of the Priesthood of the Church of Jesus Christ of Latter-day Saints who were then in the town of Kirtland. . . . When we got together the Prophet called upon the Elders of Israel with him to bear testimony of this work. . . . When they got through the Prophet said, "Brethren, I have been very much edified and instructed in your testimonies here tonight. But I want to say to you before the Lord, that you know no more concerning the destinies of this Church and kingdom than a babe upon its mother's lap. You don't comprehend it." I was rather surprised. He said[,] "[I]t is only a little handfull of Priesthood you see here tonight, but this Church will fill North and South America — it will fill the world. . . . This people will go into the Rocky mountains; they will there build temples to the Most High. They will raise up a posterity there."[19]

Though Wilford recorded the instruction and prophecy, he did not understand it at the time. Sixty-four years later, however, standing in the Tabernacle in Salt Lake City, he declared: "I want to bear testimony before God, angels and men that mine eyes behold the day, and have beheld for the last fifty years of my life, the fulfillment of that prophecy. I never expected to see the Rocky Mountains when I listened to that man's voice, but I have, and do today."[20]

As the Church fulfills its destiny, one can see the literal fulfillment of that prophecy that the gospel message would fill the Americas and then the world.

8

MISSIONARIES GO FORTH FROM KIRTLAND

*"I left with the twelve. . . . for Fair-
port . . . and went immediately on
board of a steamboat which. . . . the
Lord in his mercy provided . . . at the
very moment we arrived which was according to our prayers." (Orson Pratt.)*

S ending the message of Christ's restored church to the world
was perhaps the greatest work done by the early Latter-
day Saints. Joseph Smith taught the priesthood holders in
Kirtland that "the greatest and most important duty is to preach
the Gospel."[1] Based on revelations from the Lord that stated
that the gospel would go to all nations from "the Ohio"(D&C
39:15-16), faithful brethren journeyed to other parts of the United
States, to Canada, and to England on missions. The Twelve
Apostles, men ordained to be special witnesses, set the example.
Shortly after their call to the apostleship, on May 4, 1835, they
left as a body for various missions.

The missionaries were often armed with little more than
faith, the Spirit of the Lord, and all the copies of the Book of
Mormon they could carry. Hardship, rejection, persecution, and
exhausting travel characterized their labors as they delivered
their divine message to the world. Nevertheless, with the Lord's
help, they converted great numbers of people, many of whom
converged upon Kirtland, the first gathering place of the Church.

The missionaries' mode of travel to and from Kirtland in the
1830s was mostly by foot, horseback, wagon, stagecoach, and
steamboat. Though railroads were emerging in New York and

a few other areas, there were none near Kirtland. On one mission, Joseph Smith and his companions used the railroad to travel from Schenectady to Albany, New York.

Some missionaries could afford to travel by stagecoach. This was convenient because the main road connecting Cleveland to western Pennsylvania and New York was close to Kirtland. But though stagecoach travelers could cover as much as six to eight miles an hour on good roads, it was usually an uncomfortable way to travel. Many journals refer to rough roads with ruts. It could also be expensive, since the travelers had to pay for food and lodging at stagecoach stops along the way.

A rider on horseback could probably cover only forty to fifty miles a day because of the need to feed, water, and rest the animal. Traveling by wagon was even slower: a loaded wagon averaged only about two miles an hour.

Steamships, which averaged about twenty miles an hour, were a favorite mode of travel. Missionaries often boarded a steamship at Fairport Harbor on Lake Erie to go to Buffalo, Detroit, and other cities. Sometimes they would travel by boat on the Ohio River to visit the southern states and Missouri. The Prophet mentioned that his spring 1832 trip to Missouri included travel on the Ohio River through Cincinnati and Louisville.

For most missionaries, travel was by foot, carrying cloth knapsacks or leather valises. Walking for thirteen or fourteen hours, they could go about forty miles a day if the weather was favorable and the roads were good. George A. Smith described his experience:

> My shoes, which Brother Brigham Young gave me, were worn out, and Brother Sherman Brown gave me another pair. There had just been a flood which had destroyed many bridges in the county; this subjected us to great annoyance in traveling and increased the distances we had to walk. . . . From Freedom we walked 35 miles to Lodi; the road was very muddy and my feet sore. We walked 10 miles the next morning and stopped for breakfast accidentally at the house of a Latter-day Saint who recognized us as Traveling Elders and made us welcome. My feet were

very sore. I had blisters on all my toes and one on the ball of each foot and one of my heels was one complete blister. Brother William Tinney and Brother Murdock collected a congregation and we preached in the evening. In the morning I proposed to Lyman Smith to rest till my feet got well.[2]

As George prepared for his mission, his cousin, Joseph, gave him a copy of the Book of Mormon, some cloth to make a coat, and some advice: "Preach short sermons, make short prayers, and deliver your sermons with a prayerful heart."[3]

Missionary Hardships and Trials

There are numerous examples in Church history of hardships endured by missionaries and their families, as well as stories of incredible faith. Families left behind usually had to sustain themselves or be taken care of by other Church members. In 1831 Joseph Smith declared that "the Lord held the Church bound to provide for the families of the absent Elders while proclaiming the Gospel."[4]

Many men would serve on their missions for as long as possible, return to Kirtland to accomplish necessary tasks at home and receive further inspiration and instruction from the brethren, and then leave on another mission. Lorenzo Barnes, who was baptized on June 16, 1833, followed such a pattern. Within one month after his baptism, he was ordained an elder and left for Pennsylvania on a mission that lasted for two months, August and September. In October, he returned to Kirtland, where he worked on the temple for three or four weeks. He then returned to his home in Norton to teach school during the winter. In the spring of 1834, he went with Zion's Camp to Missouri. The group disbanded in the summer and he remained in Missouri until October, when he started another missionary journey, which lasted more than six months. He returned home for less than a month before leaving on another mission, which lasted for five and a half months. Upon his return, he was called to study English grammar and Hebrew at the School of the Elders in Kirtland.[5]

Despite the primitive modes of transportation, some missionaries traveled thousands of miles to preach the gospel. Wilford Woodruff summarized his 1835 experience: "During the last year, I travelled 3,248 miles, held 170 meetings, baptized 43 persons; procured 22 subscribers for the Messenger and Advocate; also 73 on the petition to the Governor of Missouri; wrote 18 letters, and ordained two Teachers and one Deacon. Held three debates &c."[6]

Many of the missionaries tried to convert their nonmember families. Orson Hyde, the converted Kirtland Campbellite preacher, traveled to Great Falls, New Hampshire, to teach his sister and brother-in-law. Although their greeting was warm, they rejected his message. He wrote: "We saw that they objected to our testimony, and, must I tell? — we took our things and left them, and tears from all eyes freely ran, and we shook the dust of our feet against them, but it was like piercing my heart; and all I can say is 'The Will of the Lord Be Done.' "[7]

An experience common to numerous missionaries was harassment. Parley P. Pratt, while preaching in Mentor, attempted to hold a meeting on the steps of a meetinghouse owned by the Campbellites because they "refused to open the house" to him. He described what happened:

> Some came to hear, and some to disturb the meeting; and one Mr. Newel soon appeared at the head of a mob of some fifty men and a band of music. These formed in order of battle and marched round several times near where I stood, drowning my voice with the noise of their drums and other instruments. I suspended my discourse several times as they passed, and then resumed. At length, finding that no disturbance of this kind would prevent the attempt to discharge my duty, they rushed upon me with one accord at a given signal, every man throwing an egg at my person. My forehead, bosom, and most of my body was completely covered with broken eggs. At this I departed, and walked slowly away, being insulted and followed by this rabble for some distance. I soon arrived in Kirtland, and was assisted by my kind friends in cleansing myself and clothes from the effects of this Christian benevolence.[8]

In Ohio, Pennsylvania, New York, and Massachusetts in 1832, Orson Hyde narrowly missed harm when he and his companion held a meeting in a private home. A mob of several hundred men surrounded the house to tar and feather the elders. Orson noted that "a little boy came into the house to see if we were there and he did not see us, and went out and told them that we were not there, and they then disappeared swearing and scolding, and thus the Lord delivered us."[9]

While George A. Smith was delivering a sermon at a meeting near Syracuse, New York, in 1835, a Baptist deacon "furnished a pop gun and ammunition, which he passed in through the windows to a man who fired pop-gun wads of tow at me all the time I was preaching. He was an excellent shot with the pop-gun, the most of the wads hit me in the face. I caught several of them in my hands. Many of them tickled, but some of them paid good attention. I finished my discourse without noticing the insult."[10]

Some missionaries were arrested on frivolous charges. While Parley P. Pratt was teaching the gospel to Simeon Carter in Amherst, Ohio, he was arrested and convicted after being subjected to a mock trial at which he was forced to sing and preach. After spending a night locked in "a public house," he was taken to an inn for breakfast. He recounts what happened:

> After sitting awhile by the fire in charge of the officer, I requested to step out. I walked out into the public square accompanied by him. Said I, "Mr. Peabody, are you good at a race?" "No," said he, "but my big bull dog is, and he has been trained to assist me in my office these several years; he will take any man down at my bidding." "Well, Mr. Peabody, you compelled me to go a mile, I have gone with you two miles. You have given me an opportunity to preach, sing, and have also entertained me with lodging and breakfast. I must now go on my journey; if you are good at a race you can accompany me. I thank you for all your kindness — good day, sir."
>
> I then started on my journey, while he stood amazed and not able to step one foot before the other. Seeing this,

I halted, turned to him and again invited him to a race. He still stood amazed. I then renewed my exertions, and soon increased my speed to something like that of a deer. He did not awake from his astonishment sufficiently to start in pursuit till I had gained, perhaps, two hundred yards. I had already leaped a fence, and was making my way through a field to the forest on the right of the road. He now came hallooing after me, and shouting to his dog to seize me. The dog, being one of the largest I ever saw, came close on my footsteps with all his fury; the officer behind still in pursuit, clapping his hands and hallooing, "stu-boy, stu-boy—take him—watch—lay hold of him, I say—down with him," and pointing his finger in the direction I was running. The dog was fast overtaking me, and in the act of leaping upon me, when, quick as lightning, the thought struck me, to assist the officer, in sending the dog with all fury to the forest a little distance before me. I pointed my finger in that direction, clapped my hands, and shouted in imitation of the officer. The dog hastened past me with redoubled speed towards the forest; being urged by the officer and myself, and both of us running in the same direction.

Gaining the forest, I soon lost sight of the officer and dog, and have not seen them since.[11]

Three of the Twelve Apostles—Orson Hyde, Brigham Young, and Wilford Woodruff—give a flavor of missionary hardships in 1833. Orson Hyde summarized his experiences:

To travel two thousand miles on foot, teaching from house to house, and from city to city, without purse or scrip, often sleeping in school houses after preaching—in barns, in sheds, by the way side, under trees, &c., was something of a task. When one would be teaching in private families, the other would frequently be nodding in his chair, weary with toil, fatigue and want of sleep. We were often rejected in the afterpart of the day, compelling us to travel in the evening, and sometimes till people were gone to bed, leaving us to lodge where we could. We would sometimes travel until midnight or until nearly daylight before we could find a barn or shed in which we dare to lie down; must be away before discovered least suspicion rest upon us. Would often lie down under trees and sleep in daytime to make up loss.[12]

Brigham Young described his travels:

I used to travel without purse or scrip, and many times I have walked till my feet were sore and the blood would run in my shoes and out of them, and fill my appointments — go into houses, ask for something to eat, sing and talk to them. . . . Converse with them until they have given you what you want, bless them, and, if they wish, pray with them, and then leave, unless they wish you to stay longer. . . .

The second time I went to Canada, which was after I was baptized, myself and my brother Joseph traveled two hundred and fifty miles in snow a foot and half deep, with a foot of mud under it. We travelled, preached, and baptized forty-five in the dead of winter. When we left there, the Saints gave us five York shillings with which to bear our expenses two hundred and fifty miles on foot, and one sister gave me a pair of woollen mittens, two-thirds worn out. I worked with my own hands and supported myself.[13]

Wilford Woodruff described persecution and other trials he experienced while serving on a mission to the Fox Islands off the coast of Maine:

Success did not come without many obstacles. . . .

Notices were posted up, warning me to leave town, but I thought it was better to obey God than man, and, therefore, did not go. . . . I baptized three . . . [and] subsequently a couple of others.

We traveled on foot, in the dead of winter when the snow was very deep, and the first day broke the road for seven miles. . . . On the evening of the next day we wallowed through snowdrifts for a mile . . . and on the way I got one of my ears frozen. . . .

The following day we walked fifteen miles through deep

snow to Belfast, and, after being refused lodging for the night by eight families, were kindly entertained by a Mr. Thomas Teppley.[14]

Despite the hardships, missionaries continued to accept their calls and serve willingly, sometimes under almost miraculous circumstances. Heber C. Kimball accepted a call to England, though he was suffering from excruciating back pain. His wife, Vilate, recalled:

> A short time previous to my husband's starting . . . he was prostrated on his bed from a stitch in his back, which suddenly seized him while chopping and drawing wood for his family, so that he could not stir a limb without exclaiming, from the severeness of the pain. Joseph Smith hearing of it came to see him, bringing Oliver Cowdery and Bishop Partridge with him. They prayed for and blessed him, Joseph being mouth, beseeching God to raise him up, &c. He then took him by the right hand and said, "Brother Heber, I take you by your right hand, in the name of Jesus Christ of Nazareth, and by virtue of the holy priesthood vested in me, I command you, in the name of Jesus Christ, to rise, and be thou made whole." He arose from his bed, put on his clothes, and started with them, and went up to the temple, and felt no more of the pain afterwards.[15]

First Mission of the Twelve

The greatest emphasis on missionary work came after the calling of the Quorum of Twelve Apostles and the First Quorum of the Seventy in February 1835. Less than three months after they were organized, the Twelve went on a mission through the Eastern States. Parley P. Pratt wrote of circumstances related to his call:

> I was instructed to prepare for a mission . . . with my brethren of the quorum. I now returned home to New Portage, and began to make preparations for my mission, but the state of my affairs was such that it seemed almost

impossible for me to leave home; my wife was sick, my aged mother had come to live with me, and looked to me for support—age and infirmity having rendered my father unable to do for himself or family. I was also engaged in building a house, and in other business, while at the same time I was somewhat in debt, and in want of most of the necessaries of life.

Under these embarrassed circumstances, I hesitated for a while whether to attempt to perform the mission assigned me, or stay at home and finish my building and mechanical work. While I pondered these things . . . I was called very suddenly to administer to a brother. . . . I kneeled down to pray, but in the midst of my prayer we were interrupted by the cry of *fire! fire!! fire!!!* We sprang from our knees, and ran towards my house, which was all in a blaze, being an unfinished, two story frame building, open to the fresh breeze and full of shavings, lumber, shingles, etc. . . .

The building, tools, boards, shingles, building materials, all were consumed in a few moments. Thus closed all my hesitation; my works of that nature were now all completed, and myself ready to fill my mission. One gave me a coat; another a hat; a third, house room; a fourth, provisions; while a fifth forgave me the debts due to them; and a sixth bade me Godspeed to hasten on my mission.

Taking an affectionate leave of my family and friends in New Portage, I repaired to Kirtland, ready to accompany my brethren.[16]

With each of the Twelve making personal sacrifices, it was characteristic that they make one more sacrifice before they left: they got up and gathered at Elder Johnson's tavern to leave on their missions at two o'clock in the morning.[17] They then apparently walked briskly twelve miles to Fairport Harbor, where, in answer to prayer, "the Lord in his mercy provided a boat for us at the very moment we arrived," according to Elder Pratt.[18] They boarded the steamship *Sandusky* shortly after sunrise and sailed a few minutes later.

The Twelve started out together and later separated to travel individually and in pairs. The rigors of this five-month mission took their toll on the apostles. They covered considerable distances; for example, Brigham Young traveled 3,264 miles into New York, Canada, and New England. They also faced great hardships. Heber C. Kimball related: "A considerable portion of this mission was performed on foot, and I suffered severely from fatigue and blistered feet, which were sometimes so sore I could not wear my boots nor proceed without. I was frequently threatened and reviled by unbelievers, and had great difficulty in finding places to sleep and procuring food to eat."[19]

On their return trip to Kirtland, the Twelve all met in Buffalo. According to Elder Kimball, "We went on board the steamer *United States,* and proceeded as far as Dunkirk, where she ran aground and sprung a leak; she made her way for Erie, where she arrived with difficulty, but we were under the necessity of running upon a sand bar, to save the boat from sinking, we re-shipped and arrived at Fairport; we reached Kirtland the same evening, Sept. 27."[20]

Though they experienced many hardships, the Twelve were also blessed in their missionary efforts. A typical example is that of Heber C. Kimball and Luke Johnson:

> In Hewton [they] were turned away from twelve houses, where they had solicited entertainment. At midnight they put up at an inn, retiring supperless to bed, as they had but one shilling with which to pay for their lodging. A walk of six miles before breakfast next morning brought them to Esquire David Ellsworth's where they were warmly welcomed and hospitably entertained. The Apostles blessed the kind souls who thus administered to their wants, and who, on bidding them farewell, gave them money, wished them God-speed and wept at their departure. About one year later the whole family embraced the Gospel.[21]

Sacrifices and Blessings

As husbands, fathers, and brothers left homes to share the gospel with others, their families were often left to fend for themselves. However, both missionaries and families shared intense faith that they would be sustained by the Lord, regardless of illness, poverty, and other trials. For example, when Heber C. Kimball and Orson Hyde left for missions to England, Elder Hyde left his wife with a three-week-old baby. Elder Kimball described the agony that he felt at being separated from his own family:

> The idea of being appointed to such an important mission was almost more than I could bear up under. I felt my weakness and was nearly ready to sink under it, but the moment I understood the will of my heavenly Father, I felt a determination to go at all hazards, believing that he would support me by his almighty power, and although my family were dear to me, and I should have to leave them almost destitute, I felt that the cause of truth, the gospel of Christ, outweighed every other consideration.[22]

Robert B. Thompson, who accompanied Elder Kimball, described his companion's anguish:

> The door being partly open I entered and felt struck with the sight which presented itself to my view. I would have retired, thinking I was intruding, but I felt riveted to the spot. The father [Heber C. Kimball] was pouring out his soul to [God] that he would grant unto him a prosperous voyage across the mighty ocean, and make him useful wherever his lot should be cast, and that he who careth for the sparrows, and feedeth the young ravens when they cry, would supply the wants of his wife and little ones in his absence. He then, like the patriarchs, and by virtue of his office, laid his hands upon their heads individually, leaving a father's blessing upon them, and commending them to the care and protection of God, while he should be engaged preaching the gospel in foreign lands. . . . [H]is emotions were great, and he was obliged to stop at intervals, while the big tears rolled down his cheeks, an index to the feelings which reigned in his bosom. My heart was not stout enough to refrain; in spite of myself I wept and mingled my tears with theirs at the same time. I felt thankful that I had the privilege of contemplating such a scene. I realized that nothing could induce that man to tear himself

from so affectionate a family group—from his partner and children who were so dear to him—but a sense of duty and love to God and attachment to his cause.[23]

Vilate and the children accompanied Heber to the steamship at Fairport. She wrote:

> At nine o'clock in the morning of this never-to-be-forgotten-day . . . Heber bade adieu to his brethren and friends and started without purse or scrip to preach the gospel in a foreign land. He was accompanied by myself and children, and some of the brethren and sisters, to Fairport. Sister Mary Fielding, who became afterwards the wife of Hyrum Smith, gave him five dollars, with which Heber paid the passage of himself and Brother Hyde to Buffalo. They were also accompanied by her and Brother Thompson and his wife (Mary Fielding's sister), who were going on a mission to Canada.[24]

Before Elder Kimball left for England, Joseph Smith had a vision, which he described to his associate: "I saw the 12, apostles of the Lamb, who are now upon the earth who hold the keys of this last ministry, in foreign lands, standing together in a circle much [fatigued], with their clothes tattered and feet [swollen], with their eyes cast downward, and Jesus standing in their midst, and they did not behold him, the Saviour looked upon them and wept."[25]

On his mission to England, Heber learned a lesson from this vision: when people are nearest to the Lord, Satan exerts a greater influence on them to keep them from the Lord. The evening before his first baptism in England, legions of evil spirits appeared in the bedroom. Heber reported: "I perspired exceedingly, my clothes becoming as wet as if I had been taken out of the river. I felt excessive pain, and was in the greatest distress for some time. I cannot even look back on the scene without feelings of horror; yet by it I learned the power of the adversary, his enmity against the servants of God, and got some understanding of the invisible world. We distinctly heard those spirits talk and express their wrath and hellish designs against us.

However, the Lord delivered us from them, and blessed us exceedingly that day."[26]

Heber later asked Joseph Smith the meaning of this evil onslaught. He wondered if he might have done something wrong to cause it, but the Prophet reassured him. "No, Brother Heber, at that time you were nigh, unto the Lord; there was only a veil between you and Him, but you could not see Him. When I heard of it, it gave me great joy, for I then knew that the work of God had taken root in that land. It was this that caused the devil to make a struggle to kill you." Joseph then related some of his own experiences with the evil one and said, "The nearer a person approaches the Lord, a greater power will be manifested by the adversary to prevent the accomplishment of His purposes."[27]

Meanwhile, Elder Kimball's prayers were answered at home. His daughter, Helen Mar Whitney, said, "In the absence of my father the Lord was true to his promise. My father's prayer, that he had made upon the heads of his wife and little ones whom he had left poor and destitute, was answered. Kind friends came forward to cheer and comfort them, and administer to their wants."[28]

Families were sustained and missionaries and their loved ones received great blessings. Such was the case in April 1836, when Parley P. Pratt was called to go to Canada. He hesitated to leave because he was in debt, and Thankful, his wife, was chronically ill. Parley recounts what happened next:

> I had retired to rest one evening at an early hour, and was pondering my future course, when there came a knock at the door. I arose and opened it, when Elder Heber C. Kimball and others entered my house, and being filled with the spirit of prophecy, they blessed me and my wife, and prophesied as follows:
>
> "Brother Parley, thy wife shall be healed from this hour, and shall bear a son, and his name shall be Parley; and he shall be a chosen instrument in the hands of the Lord to inherit the priesthood and to walk in the steps of his father. He shall do a great work in the earth in ministering the

Word and teaching the children of men. Arise, therefore, and go forth in the ministry, nothing doubting. Take no thoughts for your debts, nor the necessaries of life, for the Lord will supply you with abundant means for all things."[29]

The blessing that Thankful would bear a son was particularly startling because in ten years of marriage she had been unable to conceive. However, Parley hesitated no longer, for his faith reassured him that the blessing would be fulfilled, and within a few days he left on his mission, which was very successful. Of particular significance, he converted and baptized John Taylor, who would later become President of the Church. Parley was exultant upon his return home two months later when he found that his wife, who had been ill for seven years, had been healed. He was also given money sufficient to take care of most urgent debts. He immediately returned to Canada, accompanied by Thankful, to complete his mission. And less than a year later Thankful gave birth to the promised son. The birth was a bittersweet experience, however, for she died just three hours later. Parley poignantly wrote of his grief:

> My dear wife had now lived to accomplish her destiny; and when the child was dressed, and she had looked upon it and embraced it, she ceased to live in the flesh. . . . A few days previous to her death she had a vision in open day while sitting in her room. . . . It also intimated to her that she should have the privilege of departing from this world of sorrow and pain, and of going to the Paradise of rest as soon as she had fulfilled the prophecy in relation to the promised son. This vision was repeated on the next day at the same hour. . . . She was overwhelmed with a joy and peace indescribable, and seemed changed in her whole nature from that time forth. She longed to be gone, and anticipated the time as a hireling counts the days of his servitude, or the prisoner the term of his imprisonment.
>
> She was buried in the churchyard near the Temple in Kirtland, Ohio. Many hundreds attended the funeral and wept sorely for she was extensively known. Her trials, for the gospel's sake, while her husband had been absent from

88

time to time on distant missions, her lingering sickness of years, her barrenness, her miraculous cure, her conception of the promised child, were all matters of note in the Church far and near. But she had gone behind the veil to rest, where the wicked cease from troubling and the weary are at rest; while I was left to toil and struggle alone. My grief, and sorrow, and loneliness I shall not attempt to describe. . . .

She was an affectionate and dutiful wife, and exemplary Saint. . . .

Farewell, my dear Thankful, thou wife of my youth, and mother of my firstborn; the beginning of my strength — farewell.[30]

Missionary Work in the Kirtland Area

Not all of the missionary work took place at some distance from Kirtland. Many conversions were made closer to home. Mary Elizabeth Rollins Lightner, a young girl in Kirtland who attended a meeting in 1831 on the Morley Farm, recorded her conversion story:

We learned that Brother Morley had the book [Book of Mormon] in his possession — the only one in that part of the country. I went to his house just before the meeting was to commence and asked to see the Book. . . . As I looked at it, I felt such a desire to read it, that I could not refrain from asking him to let me take it home and read it, while he attended meeting. . . . He finally said, "Child, if you will bring this book home before breakfast tomorrow morning, you may take it." He admonished me to be very careful, and see that no harm came to it. If any person in this world was ever perfectly happy in the possession of any coveted treasure I was when I had permission to read that wonderful book. . . .

When I got into the house, I exclaimed, "Oh, Uncle, I have got the 'Golden Bible'." . . . We all took turns reading it until very late in the night — as soon as it was light enough to see, I was up and learned the first verse in the book. When I reached Brother Morley's . . . he remarked, "I guess you did not read much in it." I showed him how far we had read. He was surprised, and said, "I don't believe you can tell me one word of it." I then repeated the first verse, also the outline of the history of Nephi. He gazed at me in surprise, and said, "child, take this book home and finish it, I can wait."[31]

Most of the baptisms were performed in the Chagrin River in a large pool created where the river was dammed to provide power for the grist mill. One of the most "chilling" baptisms was that of Dr. Willard Richards, a physician from Massachusetts, who was baptized by his cousin Brigham Young on December 31, 1836. "Heber C. Kimball and others spent the afternoon in cutting the ice to prepare for the baptism," he wrote.[32]

Ebenezer Robinson, who worked in the printing office adjoining the office of the First Presidency, was baptized in the river in October 1835. In his journal, he used the editorial term "we" in describing how he summoned the courage to interrupt a meeting of the First Presidency and remind them that the Prophet had promised to baptize him:

> We then went to the printing office together, he to his council room which adjoined the room where we worked, and we to our work in the printing office. We worked until well on to the evening, feeling very anxious all the time, for it seemed that we could not live over night without being baptized; after enduring it as long as we could, went to the door of their room, and gently opened it, (a thing we had never presumed to do before.) As soon as Mr. Smith saw us he said, "yes, yes, brethren, Brother Robinson wishes to be baptized, we will adjourn and attend to that."
>
> We repaired to the water, (the Chagrin river which flows through Kirtland,) and, after a season of prayer, Brother Joseph Smith, jr., baptized us by immersion, and as we arose from the water it seemed that everything we had on left us, and we came up a new creature, when we shouted aloud, "Glory to God." Our heart was full to overflowing,

and we felt that we had [been] born again in very deed, both of water and of the spirit.[33]

Lorenzo Snow was baptized in the Chagrin River in June 1836 by John Boynton, one of the Twelve Apostles. He experienced an overwhelming conversion by the Holy Ghost two or three weeks after his baptism when he went to a grove near his home and prayed:

> I had no sooner opened my lips in an effort to pray, than I heard a sound, just above my head, like the rustling of silken robes, and immediately the Spirit of God descended upon me, completely enveloping my whole person, filling me, from the crown of my head to the soles of my feet, and O, the joy and happiness I felt! No language can describe the almost instantaneous transition from a dense cloud of mental and spiritual darkness into a refulgence of light and knowledge, as it was at that time imparted to my understanding. I then received a perfect knowledge that God lives, that Jesus Christ is the Son of God, and of the restoration of the holy Priesthood, and the fulness of the Gospel. It was a complete baptism—a tangible immersion in . . . the Holy Ghost; and even more real and physical in its effects upon every part of my system than the immersion by water; dispelling forever, so long as reason and memory last, all possibility of doubt or fear. . . .
>
> I *knew* that [the Lord] had conferred on me what only an omnipotent being can confer—that which is of greater value than all the wealth and honors worlds can bestow.[34]

9

NEW SCRIPTURES COME FORTH

"There was never any hesitation reviewing, or reading back. . . . As he dictated [the words], so they stood. . . . I was present to witness the dictation of several communications."
(Parley P. Pratt.)

Less than one month after Joseph Smith arrived in Kirtland, the Lord revealed to him: "Ye are not sent forth to be taught, but to teach the children of men . . . and ye are to be taught from on High." (D&C 43:15-16.) From that point, the Prophet and the Church literally were "taught from on High." Intense spiritual activity burst forth in revelations and manifestations, which later became the major part of the Doctrine and Covenants.

Virtually all of Joseph Smith's translation of the Bible, in which he received instruction from the Lord, occurred in the Kirtland area. When he prayed about biblical passages and doctrines, the Lord responded by giving revelation after revelation. In addition, through ancient Egyptian mummies acquired in Kirtland came papyrus rolls that the Prophet translated. These translations, comprising additional writings from the ancient patriarchs Abraham and Joseph, are a major portion of an additional book of scripture, the Pearl of Great Price. From such divine sources, Joseph Smith identified and solidified the Church's doctrinal foundation during the years the Church was headquartered in Kirtland. During those years, he received eighty-four separate revelations. Sixty-five of these revelations appear in the Doctrine and Covenants and represent almost half of this volume of scripture.

Among the numerous topics given by revelation in Kirtland, revelations that formulated much of the Church's doctrinal foundation, are these:

Christ's mission	Role of parents
Millennium	Accountability of children
Resurrection	Baptism
Welfare principles	Definition of priesthood
Revelation	Priesthood offices
Satan's role and mission	and duties
Consecration of properties	Priesthood keys
Stewardship	Oath and covenant of
Seeking signs	priesthood
Moral conduct	Missionary work
Forgiveness	Life after death
Church courts	Second coming
Tithing	Destiny of Satan
Debt	Word of Wisdom
Priesthood authority	Godhead
Voice of warning	Preexistence
God's dealing with mankind	Creation of worlds
Eternal progression	Constitution
Judgment	Law of the land
Destiny of the Church	Patriarchal blessings
Role of a prophet	Sabbath day

Within three days of his arrival in Kirtland, the Prophet began to receive revelations. On February 9, 1831, in the presence of elders, the Lord gave a revelation specified as "embracing the law of the Church" (Doctrine and Covenants 42), which included instruction on such subjects as moral conduct, charity, consecration, discipline, new members, and transgressors. The revelation was given in two parts. The first part, comprising seventy-three verses, was "given by Jesus Christ to the Church in the presence of twelve Elders." The remaining forty-six verses

THE CHURCH OF JESUS CHRIST OF LATTER-DAY SAINTS

SEMINARY

CERTIFICATE OF COURSE COMPLETION

The Church Educational System awards this certificate of course completion to

Nathan Miller

for fulfilling the requirements of the *Doctrine and Covenants*
course of study. Issued ___May 18, 2003___

Marlin P. Elvers

Seminary Representative

Exemplary Attendance

were given a few days later.[1] Other early laws of the Church dealt with economic matters, health, the role of a prophet and how and to whom revelation would be given to the Church.

A vision that is considered to have had more impact upon Church doctrine than any other revelation, now known as section 76 of the Doctrine and Covenants, was given in the John Johnson home in Hiram in February 1832 as a result of the Prophet's inquiries to the Lord while translating the Bible. At the time Joseph was being assisted in the work by Sidney Rigdon. "While we were doing the work of translation which the Lord had appointed unto us," Joseph recorded, "we came to the twenty-ninth verse of the fifth chapter of John." (D&C 76:15.) In his history, the Prophet elaborates about the questions Elder Rigdon and he were contemplating before the vision was given:

> Upon my return from [the] Amherst conference, I resumed the translation of the Scriptures. From sundry revelations which have been received, it was apparent that many important points touching the salvation of man, had been taken from the Bible, or lost before it was compiled. It appeared self-evident from what truths were left, that if God rewarded every one according to the deeds done in the body the term "Heaven," as intended for the Saints' eternal home[,] must include more kingdoms than one. Accordingly, on the 16th of February, 1832, while translating St. John's Gospel, myself and Elder Rigdon saw the following vision.[2]

In this vision, not only did Joseph Smith and Sidney Rigdon see the throne of God, but their understanding was also expanded concerning death, the Resurrection, the judgment of God, the differing heavens, and the characteristics of those who will inhabit those heavens. About a dozen men were present in the room while Joseph and Sidney experienced the vision. An eyewitness, Philo Dibble, wrote:

> Joseph would, at intervals, say: "What do I see?" as one might say while looking out the window and beholding

what all in the room could not see. Then he would relate what he had seen or what he was looking at. Then Sidney replied, "I see the same." Presently Sidney would say "what do I see?" and would repeat what he had seen or was seeing, and Joseph would reply, "I see the same."

This manner of conversation was repeated at short intervals to the end of the vision, and during the whole time not a word was spoken by any other person. Not a sound nor motion made by anyone but Joseph and Sidney, and it seemed to me that they never moved a joint or limb during the time I was there, which I think was over an hour, and to the end of the vision.

Joseph sat firmly and calmly all the time in the midst of a magnificent glory, but Sidney sat limp and pale, apparently as limber as a rag, observing which, Joseph remarked, smilingly, "Sidney is not used to it as I am."[3]

The most significant message of the revelation concerns the state of man after death. According to some early Mormon journals, the doctrine given conflicted with the prevailing notions of heaven and hell that were being taught by ministers of that day. Brigham Young, in referring to this teaching, observed that initially he "did not reject it." He further stated:

> When God revealed to Joseph Smith and Sidney Rigdon that there was a place prepared for all, according to the light they had received and their rejection of evil and practice of good, it was a great trial to many, and some apostatized because God was not going to send to everlasting punishment heathens and infants, but had a place of salvation, in due time, for all, and would bless the honest and virtuous and truthful, whether they ever belonged to any Church or not.[4]

The Word of Wisdom

Another significant revelation is known as the Word of Wisdom, which constitutes the Lord's law of health and directs the

Saints to abstain from the use of "hot drinks" (accepted to mean coffee and tea), alcohol, and tobacco. In explaining how this revelation came about, Brigham Young described conditions at the School of the Prophets, which met under Joseph Smith's tutelage in Kirtland:

> When they [members of the School of the Prophets] assembled together in this room [schoolroom] after breakfast, the first they did was to light their pipes, and, while smoking, talk about the great things of the kingdom, and spit all over the room, and as soon as the pipe was out of their mouths a large chew of tobacco would then be taken. Often when the Prophet entered the room to give the school instructions he would find himself in a cloud of tobacco smoke. This, and the complaints of his wife at having to clean so filthy a floor, made the Prophet think upon the matter, and he inquired of the Lord relating to the conduct of the Elders in using tobacco, and the revelation known as the Word of Wisdom was the result of his inquiry.[5]

Zebedee Coltrin, who was present when the revelation was received, reported, "The Prophet Joseph was in an adjoining room . . . and came in with that Revelation in his hand. Out of the twenty two members that were there assembled, all used tobacco more or less, except two, Joseph read the Revelation and when they heard it they all laid aside their pipes and use of tobacco."[6]

Witnesses to the Revelations Testify

Many of the revelations were given when elders of the Church were present, usually united in prayer and seeking answers to gospel questions. A scribe recorded the heavenly instructions. The revelation known as the "Preface to the Book of Commandments," which is now section 1 of the Doctrine and Covenants, was received at a special conference on the Johnson farm November 1, 1831. Minutes indicate that the revelation came in the afternoon of the first day of conference and was "received by inspiration."[7] This was such a moving experience that ten men who were present "arose in turn and bore witness to the truth of the Book of Commandments. After which br. Joseph Smith jr arose & expressed his feelings & gratitude concerning the Commandment & Preface."[8]

The testimony of these brethren was so important that the Lord revealed the following statement, to be signed by them testifying to the world that they knew the Book of Commandments was from Him:

> The testimony of the witnesses to the book of the Lord's commandments, which He gave to His Church through Joseph Smith, Jun., who was appointed by the voice of the Church for this purpose; we therefore feel willing to bear testimony to all the world of mankind, to every creature upon the face of all the earth and upon the islands of the sea, that the Lord has borne record to our souls, through the Holy Ghost, shed forth upon us, that these commandments were given by inspiration of God, and are profitable for all men, and are verily true. We give this testimony unto the world, the Lord being our helper; and it is through the grace of God, the Father, and His Son, Jesus Christ, that we are permitted to have this privilege of bearing this testimony unto the world, that the children of men may be profited thereby.[9]

Ten persons were present when the "olive leaf" (section 88 of the Doctrine and Covenants) was revealed. Frederick G. Williams, one of those who were with the Prophet in the translating room, recorded, "We all bowed down before the Lord, after which each one arose and spoke in his turn his feelings, and determination to keep the commandments of God." A revelation concerning the duty of the elders was subsequently given that afternoon and the following morning, after which the meeting was closed "by prayer in harmony with the brethren and gratitude to our heavenly Father for the great manifestation of his holy Spirit."[10]

Newel K. Whitney, in whose store this revelation was received, witnessed and recorded revelations both at the store and in his nearby home. He later formally testified to the truth of the revelations: "The Book [Doctrine & Covenants] was then presented to Newel K. Whitney Bishop of Kirtland, who reviewed it & testified that he had examined . . . [it], and the revelations contained in it he knew were true, for God had testified to him by his holy Spirit, for many of them were given under his roof & in his presence through President Joseph Smith Junr. the Prophet of [the] Lord."[11]

Parley P. Pratt, who was often present when revelations were given, observed:

> Each sentence was uttered slowly and very distinctly, and with a pause between each, sufficiently long for it to be recorded, by an ordinary writer, in long hand.
>
> This was the manner in which all [Joseph Smith's] written revelations were dictated and written. There was never any hesitation, reviewing, or reading back, in order to keep the run of the subject; neither did any of these communications undergo revisions, interlinings, or corrections. As he dictated them so they stood, so far as I have witnessed; and I was present to witness the dictation of several communications of several pages each.[12]

Orson Pratt, present when section 51 of the Doctrine and Covenants was revealed, observed that "no great noise or physical manifestation was made; Joseph was as calm as the morning sun. . . . Joseph's face was exceedingly white, and seemed to shine."[13]

Others noted similar changes in the Prophet's appearance while he was receiving revelations, especially in his face. Though Philo Dibble did not himself see the vision of the heavens as it was revealed in the Johnson home, he testified, "I saw the glory and felt the power,"[14] and that Joseph "seemed to be dressed in an element of glorious white, and his face shone as if it were transparent."[15]

Brigham Young, another witness, explained the source of this change in countenance: "Those who were acquainted with him knew when the Spirit of revelation was upon him, for his countenance wore an expression peculiar to himself while under that influence. He preached by the Spirit of revelation, and taught in his council by it, and those who were acquainted with him could discover it at once, for at such times there was a peculiar clearness and transparency in his face."[16]

A similar change in facial expression was manifest at times when Joseph Smith was speaking under the influence of the Spirit. Edward Stevenson, as a boy of fourteen, heard the Prophet speak in Michigan and wrote: "He began relating his vision. . . . His countenance seemed to me to assume a heavenly whiteness."[17]

Doctrines of the Church were not man-made theology, but were revealed by God to the modern-day prophet Joseph Smith. This new bursting forth of revelations was witnessed by scribes and other participants. These new doctrines required people to change their old perspectives of religion. Some members could not accept the revealed doctrines and left the Church. Regardless, truth is truth, as the Lord emphasized: "Search these commandments, for they are true and faithful, and the prophecies and promises which are in them shall all be fulfilled. What I the Lord have spoken, I have spoken, and I excuse not myself; and though the heavens and the earth pass away, my word shall not pass away, but shall all be fulfilled." (D&C 1:37-38.)

Joseph Smith Translates the Bible

Part of the schooling period was closely related to Joseph Smith's translation of the Bible. In retrospect, it appears that the knowledge and instruction he received while completing the translation were as important as the translation itself. Many revelations and doctrines were given when his mind was stimulated while reading and studying the Old and New Testaments. After he presented his questions to the Lord in prayer, instructions and doctrines were revealed. Dr. Robert J. Matthews, who has done significant research into the Prophet's translation, has concluded:

The real *purpose* of the Bible translation was not so much to have a new corrected edition of the Bible, but rather, to bring the Prophet to a greater understanding of the gospel. Consequently, the real product is not so much a Bible itself, but the doctrines that were revealed in the process. Consequently, the Prophet's work with the Bible is an indispensible element in the unfolding of the gospel and the building of the dispensation of the fulness of times. . . .

The Prophet worked on the Bible translation primarily between June 1830 and July 1833. This is also the same period of time during which most of the doctrinal revelations now published in the Doctrine and Covenants were received. This is not *coincidence,* but rather it is *consequence.*[18]

Although the Prophet used the term "translation of the Bible," Elder B. H. Roberts commented: "It would be more proper to say 'revision of the Bible' than 'translation' of it; as the Prophet did not at any time pretend to a knowledge of the ancient languages that would enable him to translate from the Hebrew or the Greek as 'translation' is commonly understood. But what he did was to revise the English text of the Bible under the inspiration of God; and that led him not only to give different renderings of various passages, but also to supply missing parts."[19]

The translation was a high priority for the Prophet. In 1831 he underscored the importance of the work in remarks at a conference of high priests, telling them that "except the Church receive the fulness of the scriptures that they would yet fall."[20] These crucial revelations could not be given to the Prophet until he petitioned the Lord with questions and immersed himself in the translating effort. As a result, however, he did not have time to support his family. As a consequence, it was necessary for the Church to support the Smith family during this period. In February 1831, about three days after the Prophet arrived in Kirtland, the Lord through revelation commanded the Saints to build a home for the Prophet. (D&C 41:7.)

Explaining the critical nature of the work and the need for temporal assistance so he could concentrate on the translation,

Joseph declared at a general conference in October 1831 that "the promise of God was that the greatest blessings which God had to bestow should be given to those who contributed to the support of his family while translating the fulness of the Scriptures." Before the conference adjourned, Oliver Cowdery "begged the privilege" to propose to the conference that elders be sent out to the branches of the Church to "obtain means for the support of br. Joseph Smith jr. & those appointed to assist him in writing & copying the fulness of the Scriptures."[21]

The translation of the Bible was a primary activity in three places where Joseph resided: the Morley farm, the Johnson home, and an upstairs room at Newel K. Whitney's store. He completed the work on July 2, 1833, while he was at the Whitney store.

Within a few hours the members of the First Presidency — Joseph Smith, Sidney Rigdon, and Frederick G. Williams — were preparing to leave on missions. There was a sense of urgency and even eagerness to teach the gospel. Sidney wrote in a letter to the Saints in Missouri, "[We are] going off immediately . . . to proclaim the Gospel; we think of starting tomorrow. Having finished the translation of the Bible, a few hours since, and needing some recreation, we know of [no] way we can spend our time more to divine acceptance than in endeavoring to build up his Zion in these last days, as we are not willing to idle any time away which can be spent to useful purposes."[22]

The Egyptian Mummies

In the summer of 1835, a man named Michael H. Chandler, who lived in Philadelphia, brought to Kirtland four Egyptian mummies and some ancient scrolls of papyri that he had been displaying in various cities in the United States. The mummies had been discovered on the west bank of the Nile River across from the ancient city of Thebes by Antonio Lebolo, an Italian who was licensed by the French government to deal in artifacts. In 1830, following Lebolo's death in Italy, eleven of the mummies and some of the ancient papyri were shipped to the United States; and in the spring of 1833 they were claimed by Chandler,

Lebolo's nephew. A man at the customs house told Chandler that no one in Philadelphia could translate the papyrus, but he referred Chandler to Joseph Smith, who "possesses some kind of power or gifts, by which he had previously translated similar characters."[23]

Orson Pratt later described what happened:

> Mr. Chandler presented to him [Joseph Smith] the ancient characters, asking him if he could translate them. The prophet took them and repaired to his room and inquired of the Lord concerning them. The Lord told him they were sacred records. . . . And he also enquired of the Lord concerning some few characters which Mr. Chandler, gave him by way of a test, to see if he could translate them. The Prophet Joseph translated these characters and returned them, with the translation to Mr. Chandler.[24]

When Joseph provided Chandler with a translation of some of the characters, Chandler gave him the following statement:

> KIRTLAND, July 6, 1835.
> This is to make known to all who may be desirous, concerning the knowledge of Mr. Joseph Smith, Jun., in deciphering the ancient Egyptian hieroglyphic characters in my possession, which I have, in many eminent cities, showed to the most learned; and, from the information that I could ever learn, or meet with, I find that of Mr. Joseph Smith, Jun., to correspond in the most minute matters.
> MICHAEL H. CHANDLER,
> Traveling with, and proprietor of,
> Egyptian mummies.[25]

Chandler subsequently settled near Kirtland, in Parkman, Ohio.

Oliver Cowdery gave a vivid description of the records: "Upon the subject of the Egyptian records, or rather the writings of Abraham and Joseph, may I say a few words. This record is beautifully written in papyrus with black, and a small part, red

103

ink or paint, in perfect preservation. The characters are such as you find upon the coffins of mummies, hieroglyphics and etc. with many characters or letters exactly like the present, though perhaps not quite so square form of the Hebrew without points."[26]

A certificate signed by six Philadelphia doctors described the mummies and also the writing: "The features of some of the mummies are in perfect expression. The papyrus covered with black or red ink, or paint, in excellent preservation, are very interesting."[27]

Early in July 1835 Joseph Smith began translating the papyri, with William W. Phelps and Oliver Cowdery serving as his scribes. He wrote, "Much to our joy found that one of the rolls contained the writings of Abraham, another the writings of Joseph of Egypt."[28] Witnesses to the translating process testify that it was done by inspiration.

Orson Pratt, witnessing the translating process, testified: "I saw his [Joseph Smith's] countenance lighted up as the inspiration of the Holy Ghost rested upon him, dictating the great and most precious revelations now printed for our guide. I saw him translating by inspiration, the Old and New Testaments, and the inspired Book of Abraham from Egyptian Papyrus."[29]

The Prophet translated the scrolls at home until January 1836, when the upper west room in the temple was designated as a translating room.

During the translation, Joseph "engaged in translating an alphabet to the Book of Abraham, and arranging a grammar of the Egyptian language as practiced by the ancients."[30] Unexpected knowledge came as a by-product of these efforts, for he stated that he learned principles of astronomy from the writings of Abraham and "many things concerning the dealing of God with the ancients, and the formation of the planetary system."[31]

The artifacts were later put on display in the translating room in the temple. Wilford Woodruff, who visited the room, said: "We . . . viewed four Egyptian mummies and also the Book of Abraham written by his own hand and not only the hieroglyphics but also many figures that this precious treasure contains are calculated to make a lasting impression upon the mind which is not to be erased."[32]

The Book of Abraham, which the Prophet translated from the ancient papyrus, made a significant contribution to the Saints' understanding of such important gospel teachings as the Creation, premortal life and the plan of salvation, and events that took place in the Garden of Eden. It was subsequently accepted by the Church as scripture and published as a part of one of the standard works: the Pearl of Great Price.

10

APPEARANCES OF THE FATHER AND THE SON

"This is the testimony . . . which we give of him: That he lives! For we saw him, even on the right hand of God."
(Joseph Smith and Sidney Rigdon.)

Essential to launching a new dispensation of the gospel was a sure knowledge of the Father and the Son given to the Prophet Joseph Smith and other Church leaders. The Church in Kirtland was developed by the Lord through a prophet and other leaders who had personal knowledge of Him, and a major part of this schooling involved firsthand knowledge and understanding of Deity. Such knowledge, given through numerous appearances or visions of the Father and/or the Son, assured the Saints that God exists and that Christ is a living personage. Following appearances of the Father and the Son in the Whitney store, the Prophet said, "Brethren, now you are prepared to be the Apostles of Jesus Christ, for you have seen both the Father and the Son, and know that They exist and that They are two separate Personages."[1]

The visions and appearances of Deity in the Kirtland area that have been documented number at least into the teens and took place at four separate sites. Several witnesses also included descriptions of the heavenly beings.

Joseph Smith, Lyman Wight, and Harvey Whitlock received a vision of both God the Father and his Son, Jesus Christ, in the log schoolhouse on the Isaac Morley farm during a conference held from June 3 to 6, 1831. Levi Hancock recorded that the Prophet was speaking to the elders when he "stepped out on the floor and said, 'I now see God, and Jesus Christ at his right hand, let them kill me, I should not feel death as I am now.' "[2]

John Whitmer, the official Church historian and recorder, wrote of this same appearance:

> The spirit of the Lord fell upon Joseph in an unusual manner. . . . After he had prophesied he laid his hands upon Lyman Wight [and ordained him] to the High Priesthood. . . . And the spirit fell upon Lyman, and he prophesied, concerning the coming of Christ. . . . He saw the heavens opened, and the Son of man sitting on the right hand of the Father. Making intercession for his brethren, the Saints. He said that God would work a work in these last days that tongue cannot express, and the mind is not capable to conceive. The glory of the Lord shone around.[3]

Zebedee Coltrin, who was also present, said that an evil power seized Harvey Whitlock. "Joseph rebuked the power that had seized [Harvey], and it left him, and he testified, as Lyman [Wight] had done, that he saw the heavens open, and Jesus standing on the right hand of the Father."[4]

On February 16, 1832, in an upper room of the John Johnson home at Hiram, Joseph Smith and Sidney Rigdon received a glorious vision in which they beheld the Father and the Son as well as "the holy angels, and them who are sanctified before his throne." (D&C 76:21.) The Prophet recorded:

> The Lord touched the eyes of our understandings and they were opened, and the glory of the Lord shone round about. And we beheld the glory of the Son, on the right hand of the Father, and received of his fulness; and saw the holy angels, and them who are sanctified before his throne, worshiping God, and the Lamb, who worship him forever and ever. And now, after the many testimonies which have been given of him, this is the testimony, last of all, which we give of him: That he lives! For we saw him, even on the right hand of God; and we heard the voice bearing record that he is the Only Begotten of the

Father—That by him, and through him, and of him, the worlds are and were created, and the inhabitants thereof are begotten sons and daughters unto God. (D&C 76:19-24.)

At this time, both Joseph Smith and Sidney Rigdon were permitted to see in vision the fall of Lucifer, which gave them an understanding of Lucifer's role as well as the role of our Savior, Jesus Christ.

The Father and the Son each appeared in the Newel K. Whitney store about the time the Prophet formally organized the office of the First Presidency on March 18, 1833.[5] That day was depicted as a day of revelation and vision, for angels and other heavenly messengers were also seen. Following the ordination of the Presidency, the Prophet recorded:

I exhorted the brethren to faithfulness and diligence in keeping the commandments of God, and gave much instruction for the benefit of the Saints, with a promise that the pure in heart should see a heavenly vision; and after remaining a short time in secret prayer, the promise was verified; for many present had the eyes of their understanding opened by the Spirit of God, so as to behold many things. . . . Many of the brethren saw a heavenly vision of the Savior, and concourses of angels, and many other things, of which each one has a record of what he saw.[6]

One participant, John Murdock, experienced a vision of the Savior similiar to that of John the Revelator:

The visions of my mind were opened, and the eyes of my understanding were enlightened, and I saw the form of a man, most lovely! The visage of his face was sound and fair as the sun. His hair, a bright silver grey, curled in most majestic form, His eyes, a keen penetrating blue, and the skin of his neck a most beautiful white, and He was covered from the neck to the feet with a loose garment, pure white, whiter than any garment I have ever before seen. His countenance was most penetrating, and yet most lovely! And while I was endeavoring to comprehend the whole personage, from head to feet, it slipped from me, and the Vision was closed up. But it left on my mind the impression of love, for months, that I never before felt, to that degree.[7]

Zebedee Coltrin related that he also saw the Savior, following which he saw God the Father, who "was surrounded as with a flame of fire, which was so brilliant that I could not discover anything else but His person. I saw His hands, His legs, his feet, his eyes, nose, mouth, head and body in the shape and form of a perfect man. . . . This appearance was so grand and overwhelming that it seemed I should melt down in His presence, and the sensation was so powerful that it thrilled through my whole system and I felt it in the marrow of my bones."[8]

Probably no other place was as sacred to the early Saints as the Kirtland Temple. Even Moses, who many dispensations earlier had stood on "holy ground," appeared to the Prophet here. (D&C 110:11.) The many revelations, visions, and appearances of Deity and other messengers truly sanctified and made the temple holy. The faithful Saints sacrificed and worked despite poverty and tribulation to prepare themselves for the Prophet's promise that they would see the Savior in the temple.

On January 21, 1836, one of the most glorious visions in recorded history occurred as Joseph Smith and about three dozen other men were assembled in the temple. Present were the First Presidency, Joseph Smith Sr., a scribe, the bishoprics of both Kirtland and Missouri, and members of the Kirtland and the Missouri high councils. The Prophet wrote that after spiritual anointings and blessings, the Presidency "laid their hands upon me, and pronounced upon my head many prophecies and blessings. . . .

> The heavens were opened upon us and I beheld the celestial kingdom of God, and the glory thereof, whether in the body or out I cannot tell. I saw the transcendent beauty of the gate through which the heirs of that kingdom will enter, which was like unto circling flames of fire; also the blazing throne of God, whereon was seated the Father and the Son.

I saw the beautiful streets of that kingdom, which had the appearance of being paved with gold. . . .

Many of my brethren . . . saw glorious visions also. Angels ministered unto them as well as to myself, and the power of the Highest rested upon us, the house was filled with the glory of God, and we shouted Hosanna to God and the Lamb.[9]

On April 3, 1836, Joseph Smith and Oliver Cowdery were privileged to see the Savior in an overwhelming confirmation of his acceptance of their efforts to build and dedicate the temple. The Prophet wrote:

We saw the Lord standing upon the breastwork of the pulpit, before us; and under His feet was a paved work of pure gold in color like amber. His eyes were as a flame of fire; the hair of His head was white like the pure snow, His countenance shone above the brightness of the sun, and His voice was as the sound of the rushing of great waters, even the voice of Jehovah, saying: I am the first and the last, I am He who liveth, I am He who was slain, I am your advocate with the Father.[10]

Many other visions and appearances of the Lord were experienced in the Kirtland Temple by individuals who had sacrificed and labored for its completion. Orson Pratt recalled, "In that house the veil was taken away from the eyes of many of the servants of God and they beheld his glory."[11] According to one estimate, "hundreds of others" had such experiences.[12] Joseph Smith promised, "All who are prepared, and are sufficiently pure to abide the presence of the Savior, will see him in the solemn assembly [in the temple]."[13]

Many accounts are available in journals and official publications that testify of sacred experiences during this pentecostal period. Large numbers were present during some of these spiritual manifestations. Among them are the following:

January 21, 1836. In the presence of about ten Church leaders, Joseph Smith "saw the Twelve . . . and Jesus standing in their midst. . . . The Savior looked upon them and wept." Later, in a meeting of about thirty some "saw the face of the Savior."[14]

January 28, 1836. Some one hundred Melchizedek Priesthood members — high priests, seventies, and elders — were assembled when Zebedee Coltrin "saw the Savior extended before him, as upon the cross, and a little after, crowned with glory upon his head above the brightness of the sun."[15] Those present also heard Joseph Smith exclaim aloud, "I behold the Savior, the Son of God."[16]

March 30, 1836. With three hundred priesthood leaders assembled in the temple, "the Savior made his appearance to some, while angels ministered to others."[17]

In addition to these visions in the temple, others testified that God spoke to them. Warren Snow, while on a mission to England many years later, declared: "I have seen the power of God manifested. . . . I remember when receiving my endowments in the Temple at Kirtland, I heard the voice of God as plain as I hear my own, and this testimony I have borne for thirty-one years."[18]

The Savior's presence was felt by many who were not privileged to see him in Kirtland. Mary Elizabeth Rollins Lightner described one such experience that occurred at the Morley farm in 1831:

> Said he [Joseph Smith,] "There are enough here to hold a little meeting." Joseph looked around very solemnly. It was the first time some of them had ever seen him. They got a board and put it across two chairs to make seats. Martin Harris sat on a little box at Joseph's feet. They sang and prayed. Joseph got up and began to speak to us. As he began to speak very solemnly and very earnestly all at once his countenance changed and he stood mute. Those who looked at him that day said there was a search light within him, over every part of his body. I never saw anything like it on the earth. I could not take my eyes off of him. He got so white that anyone who saw him would have thought he was transparent. I remember I thought I could almost see the bones through the flesh. I have been

through many changes since, but that is photographed on my brain. I shall remember it and see in my mind's eye as long as I remain upon the earth. He stood some minutes. He looked over the congregation as if to pierce every heart. Said he: "Do you know who has been in your midst?" One of the Smiths said "an angel of the Lord." Martin Harris said: "[I]t was our Lord and Savior, Jesus Christ." Joseph put his hands down on Martin and said: "God revealed that to you. Brothers and Sisters, the spirit of God has been in your midst. The Savior has been here this night and I want to tell you to remember it. There is a vail over your eyes for you could not endure to look upon Him." . . . Then he knelt down and prayed. I have never heard anything like it before or since. I felt that he was talking to the Lord and that power rested down upon us in every fiber of our bodies, and we received a sermon from the lips of the representative of God.[19]

The dispensation of the fulness of times was launched by the Father and Son themselves, and they personally prepared Joseph Smith and others for their leadership roles in the restored church. Like Moses, who was told, "put off thy shoes . . . [for] the place whereon thou standest is holy ground" (Exodus 3:5), these modern leaders truly stood on holy ground in "the Ohio."

11

SCHOOLING A PEOPLE

"Teach ye diligently and my grace shall attend you. . . . Seek learning, even by study and also by faith." (D&C 88:78, 118.)

A spiritual schooling of the Church transpired throughout the Kirtland years. The foreshadowing of this schooling began immediately after the arrival of the Prophet in 1831, when revelation after revelation burst forth upon the Saints. Plans for a printing operation to disseminate revelations and teachings were begun in a meeting in 1832. Later that year the Saints were commanded to establish a "school of the prophets." Although the emphasis would initially be on doctrine and spiritual instruction, other subjects, such as penmanship, arithmetic, English grammar, and geology, would be added later.

On January 22, 1833, the School of the Prophets was organized at the Newel K. Whitney store, the first of three locations for the school in Kirtland. Joseph and Emma Smith had moved into quarters in the store in late 1832, and soon afterwards, a schoolroom was prepared. Levi Hancock, a carpenter, was hired to build a desk for the Prophet and enclose the room. In payment for his services, he was allowed to trade at the store, but he refused, saying, "I told him [the Prophet] I would pay for all I purchased and I did do it."[1]

Brigham Young described the room: "The first School of the Prophets was held in a small room situated over the Prophet Joseph's kitchen. . . . In the rear of this building [the Whitney store] was a kitchen, probably ten by fourteen feet, containing rooms and pantries. Over this kitchen was situated the room in which the Prophet received revelations and in which he instructed his brethren. The brethren came to that place for hundreds of miles to attend school in a little room probably no larger than eleven by fourteen."[2]

At first, about twenty to twenty-five leaders participated in the school, but later hundreds of people were involved. Secular as well as doctrinal topics were discussed and taught. In the revelation known as the Olive Leaf (section 88 of the Doctrine and Covenants), the Lord said that the purpose of the school was for "instruction in all things." (D&C 88:127.) Later he urged Saints to "study and learn, and become acquainted with all good books, and with languages, tongues, and people." (D&C 90:15.) He further challenged:

> Teach ye diligently . . . of things both in heaven and in the earth, and under the earth; things which have been, things which are, things which must shortly come to pass; things which are at home, things which are abroad; the wars and the perplexities of the nations, and the judgments which are on the land; and a knowledge also of countries and of kingdoms — that ye may be prepared in all things . . . to magnify the calling . . . and the mission with which I have commissioned you. . . .
>
> Seek ye diligently and teach one another words of wisdom; yea, seek ye out of the best books words of wisdom; seek learning, even by study and also by faith. (D&C 88:78-80, 118.)

The School of the Prophets was regarded as a sacred gathering place. Even when it was in the Whitney store, the Lord referred to it as "mine house," "the house of God," "the house of the Lord," and "a sanctuary, a tabernacle of the Holy Spirit." (D&C 88:134-37.) The Prophet said the school would qualify those who attended to be "messengers of Jesus Christ."[3] When the school was first organized, the members, in order to gain entrance, gave a sacred salutation that identified them as worthy to participate. After entering, they received the ordinance of washing of feet. As written in the Doctrine and Covenants, section 88, the Lord said, "Ye shall not receive any among you into this school save he is clean from the blood of this generation;

and he shall be received by the ordinance of the washing of feet." (D&C 88:138-39.) The Lord instructed Joseph Smith on how to perform the ordinance. When the ordinance was instituted, many gifts of the Spirit were witnessed. Lucy Mack Smith, the Prophet's mother, wrote:

> Joseph took all the male portion of our family into the . . . school room [of the School of the Prophets] and administered to them the ordinance of washing of feet; after which the Spirit fell upon them, and they spake in tongues, and prophesied. The brethren gathered together to witness the manifestations of the power of God. At that time I was on the farm a short distance from the place where the meeting was held, and my children being anxious that I should enjoy the meeting, sent a messenger in great haste for me. I went without delay, and shared with the rest, the most glorious out-pouring of the Spirit of God, that had ever before taken place in the Church.[4]

To prepare for the school, the students usually fasted, breaking the fast at the close of the instruction period by partaking of the sacrament. Records indicate that the sacrament was "administered at times when Joseph appointed, after the ancient order; that is, warm bread to break easy was provided, and broken into pieces as large as [a] fist."[5]

Several names were used interchangeably for the school: "School of the Prophets," "School of the Elders," and "School of Mine Apostles." Sessions were held during winter, when there was less work to be done on farms and elders were not traveling as much on missionary assignments. During the winter of 1834-35, the school moved from the Whitney store to the newly completed schoolhouse/printing office near the temple. A historian, Lyndon W. Cook, gives an overview of the 1834-35 school term:

> About the first of November 1834, arrangements were made to resume the instruction of the Elders in the Kirtland area for the coming winter. A special room, on the ground floor of the newly finished printing office in Kirtland was

117

designated as the school room. Classwork began in early December 1834 and continued until late March 1835, nearly sixteen weeks. A school board (also known as the Kirtland School Committee) consisting of Joseph Smith, Sidney Rigdon, Oliver Cowdery, and Frederick G. Williams directed the operation and instruction of the school. Though the purpose of instruction was aimed at better preparing the Elders for the ministry, the initial enrollment included nearly fifty adolescents. The resultant overcrowding forced the school board to dismiss the younger students in favor of the Elders. The study of penmanship, arithmetic, English grammar, and geography complemented the theological discussions.[6]

In January 1835, Joseph Smith began preparing a series of lectures on theology for presentation at the School of the Prophets. These seven lectures were subsequently published in the first seventy-five pages of the Doctrine and Covenants under the title "Lectures on Faith." They were not, however, considered as revelations from the Lord. When the Doctrine and Covenants was submitted to the priesthood quorums for acceptance on August 17, 1835, John Smith, speaking on behalf of the Kirtland high council, "bore record that the revelations in said book were true, and that the lectures were judiciously arranged and compiled, and were profitable for doctrine." He stated that they were not considered as revelations.[7] Today they are printed separately, not with the Doctrine and Covenants.

The 1835-36 school term commenced on November 2, 1835, and on January 18, 1836, the School of the Prophets moved into the temple. One of the subjects that year was Hebrew, taught by Joshua Seixas, an instructor at a seminary in Hudson, Ohio. He was hired for seven weeks at a salary of $320.00 and was given an office in the building. Forty-five students initially enrolled for the a series of one-hour lectures. By February 4, additional classes were created. Joseph Smith was elated with the course. He wrote in his diary:

> Spent the day at school. The Lord blessed us in our studies. This day we commenced reading in our Hebrew

Bibles with much success. It seems as if the Lord opens our minds in a marvelous manner, to understand His word in the original language; and my prayer is that God will speedily endow us with a knowledge of all languages and tongues, that His servants may go forth for the last time the better prepared to bind up the law, and seal up the testimony.[8]

As many as 150 attended sessions of the school held in the winter of 1836-37 in the temple. The increase of the Church members' knowledge and understanding did not go unnoticed among nonmember observers. James H. Eells of Elyria, Ohio, made a critical examination of the Saints in Kirtland and wrote the following letter in March 1836:

> The Mormons appear to be very eager to acquire education. Men, women and children lately attended school, and they are now employing Mr. Seixas, the Hebrew teacher, to instruct them in Hebrew; and about seventy men in middle life, from twenty to forty years of age, are most eagerly engaged in the study. They pursue their studies alone until twelve o'clock at night, and attend to nothing else. Of course many make rapid progress. I noticed some fine looking and intelligent men among them. Some in dress and deportment have all the appearance of gentlemen. . . . They are by no means, as a class, men of weak minds. . . .
>
> The rise and progress . . . shows religious teachers the importance of having sound instruction imparted along with high excitement, that men may have some other evidence on which their faith rests.[9]

The Beginnings of Home Teaching

In Kirtland, members of the priesthood were assigned to visit the homes of the Saints and teach them. In a revelation received in April 1830, nine months before Joseph Smith went to Kirtland, the Lord outlined some of the duties of priesthood holders. The duties of a priest, he declared, were "to preach, teach, expound, exhort, . . . and visit the house of each member, and exhort them to pray vocally and in secret and attend to all family duties." (D&C 20:47.) William Cahoon, one of the earliest Ohio converts, later recalled his experience as home teacher to the Prophet's family:

> I was called and ordained to act as a teacher to visit the families of the Saints. I got along very well till I found that I was obliged to call and pay a visit to the Prophet. Being young, only about seventeen years of age, I felt my weakness in visiting the Prophet and his family in the capacity of a teacher. I almost felt like shrinking from duty. Finally I went to his door and knocked, and in a minute the Prophet came to the door. I stood there trembling, and said to him:
>
> "Brother Joseph, I have come to visit you in the capacity of a teacher, if it is convenient for you."
>
> He said, "Brother William, come right in, I am glad to see you; sit down in that chair there and I will go and call my family in."
>
> They soon came in and took seats. He then said, "Brother William, I submit myself and family into your hands," and then took his seat. "Now Brother William," said he "ask all the questions you feel like."
>
> By this time all my fears and trembling had ceased, and I said, "Brother Joseph, are you trying to live your religion?"
>
> He answered "Yes."
>
> I then said "Do you pray in your family?"
>
> He said "Yes."
>
> "Do you teach your family the principles of the gospel?"
>
> He replied "Yes, I am trying to do it."
>
> "Do you ask a blessing on your food?"
>
> He answered "Yes."
>
> "Are you trying to live in peace and harmony with all your family?"
>
> He said that he was.
>
> I then turned to Sister Emma, his wife, and said "Sister Emma, are you trying to live your religion? Do you teach your children to obey their parents? Do you try to teach them to pray?"

To all these questions she answered "Yes, I am trying to do so."

I then turned to Joseph and said, "I am now through with my questions as a teacher; and now if you have any instructions to give, I shall be happy to receive them."

He said "God bless you, Brother William; and if you are humble and faithful, you shall have power to settle all difficulties that may come before you in the capacity of a teacher."

I then left my parting blessing upon him and his family, as a teacher, and took my departure.[10]

First Conference of the Church in Ohio

Additional schooling for the Saints came through the influence and power of the Holy Ghost. On June 3, 1831, a small group of priesthood leaders participated in such schooling at the Church's first conference in Ohio, held at the Morley farm. Several persons recorded their experiences and feelings as spiritual instructions were given.

Jared Carter wrote, "Brother Joseph notwithstanding he is not naturally talented for a speaker yet, he was filled with the power of the holy ghost so that he spoke as I never heard man speak for god by the power of the holy ghost spoke in him and marvelous was the display of the power of the spirit among the Elders present."[11]

Satan also manifested his power, as recorded by John Whitmer, Church historian: "While the Lord poured out His Spirit upon His servants, the devil took a notion to make known his power. He bound Harvey Whitlock and John Murdock so that they could not speak, and others were affected but the Lord showed to Joseph, the seer, the design of the thing; he commanded the devil in the name of Christ, and he departed, to our joy and comfort."[12]

Members of the congregation, having witnessed the manifestation of power, left the conference with a more sure knowledge of the divinity of the Church. Some went on missions to bear that witness to other people and nations; some stayed to build up the Church in the areas where they lived.

The Kirtland Printing Office

Perhaps one of the most important things that spiritually strengthened the Saints in Kirtland was being able to have revelations and other communications available in Church publications. Early journals tell how members or investigators stayed up all night to read borrowed books or publications. Many did not have money to purchase them or could not get them because of the limited supply. The Church's publishing capability became a key to instructing the members.

On November 1, 1831, leaders meeting in a conference at the Johnson home in Hiram decided to establish a printing firm. They also decided on a name for the Church's first publication, *The Evening and Morning Star*. At a conference of high priests on May 4, 1833, a committee was appointed to raise money to build "a schoolhouse, for the accommodation of the Elders, who should come together to receive instruction preparatory for their missions, and ministry."[13]

That July the Church received word that a printing press being used by the Saints in Missouri had been destroyed. The Prophet reacted by saying, "Another printing office must be built." Subsequently, in a revelation given August 2, 1833, the Lord commanded that a building be constructed for a printing press: "The second lot . . . shall be dedicated unto me for the building of a house unto me, for the work of the printing of the translation of my scriptures, and all things whatsoever I shall command you." (D&C 94:10.) The revelation also directed that a "house for the Presidency" be built. (D&C 94:3.) The latter was never built, but on October 10, a decision was made to build one building for multiple purposes: to house both the First Presidency's office and a printing press, as well as provide space for the School of the Prophets and other meetings.

On October 1, Oliver Cowdery left for New York with eight hundred dollars to purchase another printing press. When he returned to Kirtland with a press and other equipment in December, a temporary printing office was established in the John Johnson inn. He wrote to William W. Phelps and John Whitmer on January 21, 1834, that "our office is yet in the brick building, though we expect in the spring to move on the hill near the Methodist-Meeting house."[14] This move was not completed until the latter part of November 1834. The printing operation, which was named the "Literary Firm," printed a number of books and publications during the four years it operated. Among the publications issued from the press were the following, which are listed chronologically:

1. *The Evening and Morning Star.*

This periodical was printed in Missouri from June 1832 until July 1833, when the Church's press there was destroyed. The paper was subsequently printed in Kirtland from December 1833 until about September 1834. Issues that had originally been printed in Missouri were reprinted in Kirtland in January 1835. Many of Joseph Smith's writings and the revelations given to him were printed in the paper, which helped the Saints to better understand the doctrines of the Church and their individual responsibilities. Some revelations, in fact, were printed in this periodical but were not included in the first edition of the Doctrine and Covenants.

After the paper was reestablished in Kirtland, it was published monthly "by F. G. Williams and Co., O. Cowdery, Editor" with a subscription price of one dollar per year "in advance."[15]

2. *The Latter-day Saints Messenger and Advocate.*

First printed in October 1834, the *Messenger and Advocate,* a monthly, had the same basic purpose as the *Evening and Morning Star*. In it were writings to the world, warnings, revelations, and explanations of revelations.

Readers were urged to purchase subscriptions, and as missionaries went out to their fields of labor, they also sold subscriptions. Erastus Snow reported that during his mission, he had been "absent 8 months and 14 days and traveled in all 1600 miles and preached 220 times," and had obtained twenty subscriptions to the *Messenger and Advocate*.[16] Oliver Cowdery served as editor until February 1837 and was succeeded by his brother, Warren Cowdery, who edited the paper through its final edition in September 1837.

3. *The first Church hymnal.*

In July 1830 Emma Smith was directed, in a revelation given through her husband, the Prophet, to select hymns for a hymnal. In the revelation, the Lord declared, "My soul delighteth in the song of the heart; yea, the song of the righteous is a prayer unto me, and it shall be answered with a blessing upon their heads." (D&C 25:12.)

Records of a meeting of the high council on September 14, 1835, indicate that "it was further decided that Sister Emma Smith proceed to make a selection of Sacred Hymns, according to the revelation; and that President W. W. Phelps be appointed to revise and arrange them for printing."[17]

Many of the hymns selected were printed in the *Evening and Morning Star* and in the *Messenger and Advocate.* The hymnal, which was completed in February 1836, measured three inches by four inches. There was no musical score; hymns were sung to various tunes, and congregations sometimes used different tunes for the same hymns.

4. *The Northern Times.*

A monthly political newspaper, the *Northern Times* was initially intended as a "Democratic" paper that supported Andrew Jackson's administration. It was first published in February 1835 and continued for about a year.

5. *The Doctrine and Covenants.*

With 101 revelations, publication of the Doctrine and Covenants had begun by June 1835. By August it was ready for binding, and in mid-September 1835 the first copies were received from a bookbinder in Cleveland and sold for one dollar each. The preface stated that the book contained "the leading items of the religion which we have professed to believe."[18] The seven Lectures on Faith, which were delivered by the Prophet in Kirtland during the winter of 1834-35, were included in this first edition.

6. *The Book of Mormon.*

Ownership of the printing office was transferred in June 1836 from the "Literary Firm" to a firm named Oliver Cowdery and Co. Sometime between then and the first of February 1837, the firm published the second edition of the Book of Mormon. Upon completion of that printing project, Oliver Cowdery sold his interest in the firm to Joseph Smith and Sidney Rigdon.

7. *The Elders' Journal.*

Joseph Smith edited the *Elders' Journal,* a monthly newspaper, which was published in Kirtland in October and November 1837 by Thomas B. Marsh. After the Prophet departed from Kirtland in January 1838, arrangements were made to continue the publication in Far West, Missouri. Only two more issues were published in July and August 1838 in Missouri, and then the publication was discontinued.

The Church in Kirtland was continually faced with financial problems, which thwarted many of the printing efforts. In an effort to reduce the costs of printing and binding, the Church operated its own equipment as much as possible. Oliver Cowdery was sent to New York again in November 1835 to purchase bookbinding materials, after heavy expenses were incurred when the Doctrine and Covenants was bound in Cleveland. But such cost-saving measures failed to solve the financial problems, and finally Joseph Smith and Sidney Rigdon, the only two remaining owners of the printing business, were forced to sell it. In May 1837 William Marks purchased the office, with contractual rights to rent or lease the equipment, which he sub-leased to the former owners until November. But Marks's ownership was short-lived. "The Elders' Journal No. 2 for November was the last paper printed at Kirtland," the Prophet wrote. "Our printing establishment was attached to satisfy an unjust judgment of the county court, and soon after the whole printing apparatus and office were burned to the ground."[19]

12

"A Storehouse Unto This Church"

"Let the bishop appoint a storehouse unto this church; . . . and let all things both in money and in meat, which are more than is needful for the wants of this people, be kept in the hands of the bishop." (D&C 51:13.)

In February 1831, within three days after Joseph Smith arrived in Kirtland, the Lord began organizing for the temporal needs of the Church by calling Edward Partridge to "spend all his time" as "bishop unto the church." (See D&C 41:9.) This highest office in the Aaronic Priesthood was designated in the first revelation given in Kirtland. Immediately afterward, welfare principles were revealed that placed the bishop at the heart of the temporal welfare of the Church and its members. A law of consecration and stewardship was revealed and a "united order" established.

Upon being called as the first bishop of the Church, Partridge left his hatter's shop in Painesville to devote full-time service to the Church. He was promptly directed to go to Missouri; consequently, it took about a year before he could find a buyer for his hatter's shop.

In December 1831, Newel K. Whitney was called to be the first bishop in Ohio. (See D&C 72:8.) When the call came, he told the Prophet, "Brother Joseph, I can't see a Bishop in myself." Joseph answered, "Go and ask the Lord about it." As Newel prayed alone in his room, he heard a voice that said, "Thy strength is in me."[1] This assurance gave him confidence to fulfill the calling, and from this and other reassurances, he developed a conviction that the Lord, not any man, directs His church.

Welfare Principles Are Established

From February to June 1831, several revelations were given through Joseph Smith in which the Lord revealed some basic welfare principles for the Church:

"Behold, thou wilt remember the poor, and consecrate of thy properties for their support." (D&C 42:30.)

"Inasmuch as ye impart of your substance unto the poor, ye will do it unto me." (D&C 42:31.)

"For I will consecrate of the riches of those who embrace my gospel among the Gentiles unto the poor of my people." (D&C 42:39.)

"But it is not given that one man should possess that which is above another." (D&C 49:20.)

"Appoint unto this people portions, every man equal according to his family, according to his circumstances and his wants and needs." (D&C 51:3.)

"Let every man deal honestly, and be alike among this people, and receive alike, that ye may be one, even as I have commanded you." (D&C 51:9.)

"Let all things . . . which are more than is needful . . . be kept in the hands of the bishop." (D&C 51:13.)

"Wo unto you rich men, that will not give your substance to the poor, for your riches will canker your souls." (D&C 56:16.)

"Wo unto you poor men, whose hearts are not broken, whose spirits are not contrite, . . . whose eyes are full of greediness, and who will not labor with your own hands!" (D&C 56:17.)

"Every man shall be made . . . a steward over his own property . . . as much as is sufficient for himself and family." (D&C 42:32.)

"If there shall be properties . . . more than is necessary for their support . . . it shall be kept to administer to those who have not." (D&C 42:33.)

"The residue shall be kept in my storehouse, to administer to the poor and the needy." (D&C 42:34.)

"Ye must visit the poor and the needy and administer to their relief." (D&C 44:6.)

"Remember in all things the poor and the needy, the sick and the afflicted, for he that doeth not these things, the same is not my disciple." (D&C 52:40.)

These principles became the basis for several economic laws, such as the law of consecration and stewardship, that were implemented by the Church in the 1830s. They remain the basis of the current Church welfare plan.

The principles were vital in supporting and sustaining needy members who were making financial sacrifices for the Church. Almost everything the members had or acquired went toward the Church: to build the temple and other buildings, to purchase property, to support the printing of the scriptures and Church periodicals, and to assist the Saints in both Ohio and Missouri.

Those who accepted missionary calls often left families at home who needed assistance. The Lord said he "held the Church bound to provide for the families."[2] In order to fulfill these commandments, the Saints adopted the welfare principles and shared their material means.

"The Family" and the Welfare Plan

Prior to Joseph's arrival in Kirtland, a number of families, influenced by Sidney Rigdon, were persuaded to join on Isaac Morley's farm a group that was known as "the family," "the common-stock family," or "the big family."

Members of the group, filled with a desire to follow strictly Christian principles, attempted to live the New Testament teaching to hold "all things common." (Acts 2:44.) Lyman Wight wrote: "In conformity to this covenant I moved [in February [1830] to Kirtland, into the house with Bro. Morley. We commenced our labors together with great peace and union. We were soon joined by eight other families. Our labors were united both in farming and mechanism, all of which was prosecuted with great vigor. We truly began to feel as if the millenium was close at hand."[3]

Despite Morley's generosity and good intentions, this attempt to share one's resources fully with everyone else was neither practical nor scriptural. Two early journal accounts depict the type of problems experienced. John Whitmer wrote: "The disciples had all things common, and were going to destruction very fast as to temporal things; for they considered from reading the scripture that what belonged to a brother belonged to any of the brethren. Therefore, they would take each other['']s clothes and other property and use it without leave. . . . They did not understand the scriptures."[4] Levi Hancock recalled:

> Brother Harvey Redfield took us to Brother Isaac Morley['']s who was a cooper by trade and one of the most honest, patient men I ever saw. The company he maintained looked large enough to bring on a famine. I do not know if they lived on him all the time or not.
>
> While I was in the room at "Father Morley's" as we all called him, this same Hermon [Heman] Bassett [Basset] came to me and took my watch out of my pocket and walked off as though it was his. I thought he would bring it back soon but was disappointed as he sold it. I asked him what he meant by selling my watch.
>
> "Oh," said he, "I thought it was all in the family."
>
> I told him I did not like such family doing and I would not bear it.[5]

Law of Consecration and Stewardship

Five days after Joseph Smith received the revelation calling Edward Partridge to serve as bishop, he received another revelation concerning a law of consecration and stewardship. One specific instruction was: "Thou shalt not take thy brother's garment; thou shalt pay for that which thou shalt receive of thy brother." (D&C 42:54.) As a result, the Prophet said that the plan of "common stock" as practiced by "the family" on the

Morley farm was "abandoned for the more perfect law of the Lord."[6]

The law of consecration and stewardship, as practiced by the Church from 1831 to 1833, required that the Saints convey all of their real and personal property to the bishop. Each person was then given stewardship over whatever resources were needed for support of the individual's family, according to needs and circumstances. Surplus profits were returned to the bishop, which he distributed where they were needed. Later changes in the law permitted private ownership of property, with only the surplus deeded to the bishop.

The law of consecration and stewardship was not an easy principle for many of the Saints to accept and live. Although the law was mainly practiced in Missouri, the first attempt to live it was near Kirtland in Thompson, Ohio. The difficulty in living the law is exemplified by events that took place when members of the Colesville Branch in New York arrived in the Kirtland area and went to live on Leman Copley's farm in Thompson.

In May 1831, Joseph Smith received a revelation concerning how the members were to conduct their temporal affairs while in Thompson. They were told to consecrate their property to the Lord through Bishop Partridge, who would then "appoint unto this people their portions, every man equal according to his family, according to his circumstances and his wants and needs." (D&C 51:3.) When Bishop Partridge attempted to implement the law of consecration, however, conflicts arose. Though Leman Copley was willing at first to share his farm, within two months he rescinded his offer, leaving many of the Saints without a home.

Newel Knight and other elders went to Joseph Smith for guidance, and the Prophet subsequently received a revelation in which he was told that inasmuch as the law of stewardship and consecration "has been broken, even so it has become void and of none effect." (D&C 54:4.) The members of the Colesville Branch were told to join the Saints who were gathering in Missouri. Joseph Knight Jr. recalled, "We had to leave his [Copley's] farm and pay sixty dollars damage for fitting up his houses and planting his ground."⁷ The group left for Missouri on July 3, 1831.

Leman Copley left the Church and did considerable damage by testifying falsely against Joseph Smith in a lawsuit in Chardon, Ohio, in 1834. In the spring of 1836, after the Kirtland Temple was completed, Copley returned to the Prophet, confessed his wrongdoing, and asked for forgiveness, which the Prophet said "was readily granted," adding that Copley "wished to be received into the Church again, by baptism, and was received according to his desire."⁸

Though the law of consecration and stewardship, a divine law, was not practiced for long, its basic principles and spirit allowed the Church to be established more firmly in Kirtland and the members to survive intense economic difficulties.

The United Order

In March 1832, Joseph Smith received a revelation instructing the Church to "stand independent above all other creatures beneath the celestial world." (D&C 78:14.) In an earlier revelation, the Lord had directed that a storehouse be established and "all things both in money and in meat, which are more than is needful for the wants of this people, be kept in the hands of the bishop." (D&C 51:13.) Now the Lord directed that "the storehouse for the poor of my people" be established in order that the Saints be "equal in the bonds of heavenly things, yea, and earthly things also. . . . For if ye are not equal in earthly things ye cannot be equal in obtaining heavenly things." (D&C 78:3, 5-6.)

As a result, the "united order" was implemented to help the Saints live the law of consecration, and two storehouses were established, one in Independence and the other in Kirtland. In Kirtland the storehouse was known as Newel K. Whitney and Co.

The major business properties of the united order consisted of a store and an ashery owned by Newel K. Whitney. Within three months after the order was established, the Whitney store was designated as the bishop's storehouse. The ashery produced potash for the use of the Saints as well as for commercial sale.

As part of the united order, in March and April 1833 the Church purchased from Peter French a farm and two businesses being operated on it. The land would be used for the temple and home sites. One of the businesses, the Peter French Tavern, served as a public house and hotel. This was the place where the Church's first printing operation in Kirtland began in December 1833. At this site, the first patriarchal blessing was given, the first Patriarch to the Church was called, and the mummies of Michael Chandler were displayed, and from it the Twelve Apostles left on their first mission. When the united order was disbanded, the building was given to John Johnson and became known as the Johnson Inn.

Also located on the French farm was a brick kiln, which was intended to be used to manufacture brick for the temple.

Another business that was operated as part of the united order was a tannery, which Ezra Thayer was authorized, at a meeting of high priests on April 2, 1833, to purchase from Arnold Mason in Kirtland.[9]

The initial partners of the united order, or "United Firm," were Joseph Smith, Newel K. Whitney, and Sidney Rigdon. Other partners were added later, but the membership never exceeded twelve. After the order was dissolved on April 23, 1834, the assets were divided among the partners, as specified in section 104 of the Doctrine and Covenants.

13

ZION'S CAMP: A FORGING PROCESS

"We did not fear. . . . for God was with us . . . [and] the faith of our little band was unwavering. We know that angels were our companions for we saw them."
(Joseph Smith.)

Although the initial objective of Zion's Camp was to help restore their lands to the beleaguered Saints in Missouri, the army's long march also became a forging process that produced stalwart Church leaders. Zion's Camp was first discussed at the home of Joseph Smith on February 24, 1834, when the Kirtland high council met to "giv[e] an audience or hearing to Lyman Wight and Parley P. Pratt, delegates from the Church in Missouri."[1]

Elders Pratt and Wight, who had left their families in Missouri without protection from mob violence and persecution, had come to solicit help and guidance from the leadership of the Church. Parley described his desperate journey from Jackson County to Kirtland: "I was at this time entirely destitute of proper clothing for the journey; and I had neither horse, saddle, bridle, money nor provisions to take with me; or to leave with my wife, who lay sick and helpless most of the time. Under the circumstances I knew not what to do. Nearly all had been robbed and plundered, and all were poor." A man named Higbee, "moved by the Spirit," gave him a horse and saddle. Sidney A. Gilbert, whose store had been "broken up, and his goods plundered and destroyed by the mob," gave him some material, which some women made into a suit, and Brother Gilbert furnished a coat.

"Faith and the blessings of God had cleared up our way to accomplish what seemed impossible," he continued. "We were soon ready, and on the first of February we mounted our horses, and started in good cheer to ride one thousand or fifteen hundred miles through a wilderness country. We had not one cent of money in our pockets on starting. We travelled every day, whether through storm or sunshine, mud, rain or snow."[2]

Lyman Wight, Parley's companion on this mission, also placed his faith in the Lord. Before he left, it was reported, "his wife lay by the side of a log in the woods, with a child three days old and he had three days' provisions on hand."[3]

The Church's commitment in Missouri had begun about three years earlier, on July 20, 1831, when Joseph Smith and other Church leaders had assembled in Jackson County. At that time Joseph received a revelation in which the Lord declared, "The land of Missouri . . . is the land which I have appointed and consecrated for the gathering of the saints. Wherefore, this is the land of promise, and the place for the city of Zion. . . . Behold, the place which is now called Independence is the center place." (D&C 57:1-3.) He also revealed that a temple was to be built there. Sidney Gilbert was appointed to purchase land throughout the area and to establish a store so he could sell goods and with the profits buy additional property. William W. Phelps was to establish a printing business, and Oliver Cowdery was to assist him as an editor.

When Church members heard about the revelation, they migrated to Jackson County in great numbers. Within two years some one thousand members had gathered to Independence.

This great influx of newcomers concerned the citizens of Independence, who were highly suspicious of the Church's migration, purpose, and plans. In July 1833, two years after Missouri was designated as the land of promise, the older settlers banded together and demanded that the Mormons leave Jackson County. Local authorities banned the Church's newspaper, ordered that the printing office discontinue operations, and mandated that stores and businesses operated by Mormons close immediately. When the Saints refused to abide by these directions, violent mobs began harassing them and plundering their property, in an effort to drive them from Missouri. One mobber boasted that 203 Mormon homes had been burned. Among the buildings destroyed were the home of W. W. Phelps, which housed the printing press; the Gilbert and Whitney store, a dozen homes near the Big Blue River, and Sidney Gilbert's home.

Individuals were also humiliated and threatened. An angry mob dragged Bishop Edward Partridge and Charles Allen to the public square and stripped them of their clothes, smeared their bodies with tar containing lime or some other flesh-eating substance, and then put feathers on them. Two Mormons were seized near the banks of the Big Blue River and pummeled with stones and clubs. In the skirmish that resulted, one person was killed and four others were wounded.

The violence and feelings of hate and fear finally drove the Mormons from Jackson County. Forced to surrender their arms, they had no way to defend themselves. It was a matter of leave and live or stay and die. In the wintry days of November 1833, hundreds of members were forced to flee from their homes. The destitute immigrants lined both sides of the Missouri River. Journal accounts portray tragic pictures of forlorn fugitives who, having lost everything they owned, had no protection from the unrelenting cold and the vicious mobs.

The Prophet Joseph Smith, deeply affected by these reports, wrote to the Missouri Saints that the suffering "awakens every sympathy of our hearts; it weighs us down; we cannot refrain from tears."[4] Lucy Mack Smith wrote that when Joseph heard of the problems in Missouri, "he burst into tears and sobbed aloud, 'Oh my brethren! my brethren. . . . Would that I had been with you, to have shared your fate.' "[5]

Zion's Camp Is Organized

On the day Parley P. Pratt and Lyman Wight arrived in Kirtland from Missouri, Joseph Smith received a revelation (D&C 103) that directed him to gather the young and middle-

aged men and lead them to Missouri. The revelation stated that
five hundred men should travel to Missouri to redeem the land;
however, if five hundred could not be found, fewer — even one
hundred — should go. (D&C 103:32-33.) When the Prophet presented the revelation to the high council, they approved it unanimously, and some thirty or forty men volunteered immediately.[6]

Thus, Zion's Camp was formed to restore homes and businesses to Church members in Independence, Missouri. Corres-
pondence and meetings with the governor of Missouri indicated
that he would support reinstating the Mormons to their properties.

Preparations had to be hurried so the first group of Zion's
Camp could leave Kirtland by May 1. Church leaders worked
feverishly during March and April to recruit members for the
camp, raise money, and gather clothing to be taken to the Missouri Saints. By the time the camp was ready to march, 207 men
had been recruited. The thousand-mile journey began as two
groups of men left Kirtland, planning to meet at New Portage,
Ohio, about sixty miles away. The first group left on May 1.
Wilford Woodruff, who was part of that group, wrote: "The
Prophet asked those who were ready, to go as far as New Portage
and there await the arrival of those who would follow later. I
left in company with about twenty men with baggage wagons.
At night we pitched our tents. Climbing to the top of the hill,
I looked down upon the Camp of Israel. There I knelt upon the
ground and prayed. I rejoiced and praised the Lord that I had
lived to see some of the tents of Israel pitched, and a company
gathered by the commandment of God to go up and help to
redeem Zion."[7]

Joseph Smith was in charge of the second group, which left
four days later. He wrote: "Having gathered and prepared clothing and other necessaries to carry to our brethren and sisters,
who had been robbed and plundered of nearly all their effects;
and having provided for ourselves horses, and wagons, and
firearms, and all sorts of munitions of war of the most portable
kind for self-defense . . . I started with the remainder of the

company from Kirtland. . . . My company from Kirtland consisted of about one hundred men, mostly young men, and nearly all Elders, Priests, Teachers or Deacons. As our wagons were nearly filled with baggage, we had mostly to travel on foot."[8]

The anti-Mormon *Painesville Telegraph* reported on the departure of the small army:

> Gen. Joe Smith took upon his line of march from this county on Monday inst. with a large party of his fanatical followers, for the seat of war. — This expedition has been a long time in active preparation. Soon after the outrages committed upon the members of the sect last Nov. in Missouri, the prophet here sent forth his general order, which he pretended was a revelation from God, for all his able bodied men to repair to the scene of difficulty. His preachers were sent forth to all parts of the country among their proselytes, with a printed copy of the revelation in their pockets. . . . They have made every effort to stir up the holy zeal of the "warriors, my young men, and they that are of middle age also," to the combat. . . . For several months past they have been collecting munitions of war for the crusade. Dirks, knives, swords, pistols, guns, power-horns, &c. &c. have been in good demand in this vicinity.[9]

Joseph Smith rendezvoused with the first group and merged them on May 7 in New Portage. He wrote:

> I continued to organize the company, appoint such other officers as were required, and gave such instructions as were necessary for the discipline, order, comfort and safety of all concerned. I also divided the whole band into companies of twelve, leaving each company to elect its own captain, who assigned each man in his respective company his post and duty, generally in the following order: Two cooks, two firemen; two tent men, two watermen, one runner, two wagoners and horsemen, and one commissary. We purchased flour and meal, baked our own bread, and cooked our own food, generally, which was good, though sometimes scanty; and sometimes we had johnny-cake, or

corn-dodger, instead of flour bread. Every night before retiring to rest, at the sound of the trumpet, we bowed before the Lord in the several tents, and presented our thank-offerings with prayer and supplication; and at the sound of the morning trumpet, about four o'clock, every man was again on his knees before the Lord, imploring His blessing for the day.[10]

The March to Missouri

Historian Milton V. Backman Jr., who has researched the Kirtland period extensively, has described the long march of Zion's Camp:

> In many respects the daily routine of Zion's Camp was similar to that of other armies. Since the wagons were loaded with supplies, nearly every able-bodied person walked along the muddy and dusty trails, many of them carrying knapsacks on their backs and guns in their arms. They marched from morning till late afternoon or early evening, when they would make camp, generally near a body of water. Guards would be posted around the encampment at night. There was little time for relaxation, for when the men were not busy marching, caring for their animals, or preparing meals, they were drilling and preparing for action when they reached their destination.
>
> In other respects, Zion's Camp was not like an ordinary army. These men were heading west in compliance with what they believed to be a commandment of the Lord, and they were being led by a prophet of God. During the journey their commander-in-chief preached the doctrines of the kingdom to them. Every morning and evening the soldiers offered prayers in their tents. On Sunday, the men would usually rest and hold meetings, where they would hear sermons and partake of the sacrament.[11]

As the small army approached Jackson County, Parley P. Pratt and Orson Hyde were sent ahead to Missouri Governor Dunklin asking that he carry out his promises to the Saints and call out the militia to restore the Saints' property and protect them. While he expressed concern for the plight of the Mormons, he refused their request. Other attempts were made to resolve the disputes peaceably, but these also failed.

On June 19, while Zion's Camp was making camp for the night on elevated land between Little Fishing and Big Fishing rivers, five armed men rode into their camp and told them that they would "see hell before morning." These men bragged that 130 men from Richmond and 70 from Clay County were joining with about two hundred men from Jackson County to enforce their threats.[12]

Wilford Woodruff described what happened then:

When the five men entered the camp there was not a cloud to be seen in the whole heavens, but as the men left the camp there was a small cloud like a black spot appeared in the north west, and it began to unroll itself like a scroll, and in a few minutes the whole heavens were covered with a pall as black as ink. This indicated a sudden storm which soon broke upon us with wind, rain, thunder and lightning and hail. Our beds were soon afloat and our tents blown down over our heads. We all fled into a Baptist meeting-house. As the Prophet Joseph came in shaking the water from his hat and clothing he said, "Boys, there is some meaning to this. God is in this storm." We sang praises to God, and lay all night on benches under cover while our enemies were in the pelting storm. It was reported that the mob cavalry who fled into the schoolhouse had to hold their horses by the bridles between the logs, but when the heavy hail storm struck them they broke away, skinning the fingers of those who were holding them. The horses fled before the storm and were not found for several days. It was reported that the captain of the company in the schoolhouse said it was a strange thing that they could do nothing against the Mormons but what there must be some hail storm or some other thing to hinder their doing anything, but they did not feel disposed to acknowledge that God was fighting our battles.[13]

Because of the violent storm, the mob scattered and the battle failed to materialize. A few days later, the army was attacked by an enemy perhaps even more deadly than another army: an epidemic of cholera. Seventy persons were stricken, and thirteen died. The Prophet subsequently disbanded the group on July 3. Most of the men prepared to return to Kirtland. Others went to mission fields, while some stayed in Missouri.

As conflicting reports about Zion's Camp reached Kirtland, the Saints there became alarmed. Rumors abounded. The local newspaper in Chardon reported: "*A Mormon Battle.* — A letter has been received, by a gentleman in this neighborhood, direct from Missouri, stating that a body of well armed Mormons, led on by their great prophet, Joe Smith, lately attempted to cross the river into Jackson county. A party of the citizens of Jackson county opposed their crossing, and a battle ensued, in which Joe Smith was wounded in the leg, and the Mormons obliged to retreat; that Joe Smith's limb was amputated, but he died three days after the operation."[14]

Until the Prophet arrived back in Kirtland, almost three weeks later, Emma Smith could not be sure if he was dead or alive. To dispel rumors of his death, Joseph Smith visited the editor who had initiated the story, but the editor refused to believe he was not really dead. George A. Smith, who was with the Prophet, said that the editor felt "assured he had published the true state of the case."[15]

Zion's Camp's Accomplishments

Though Zion's Camp did not succeed in restoring their land to members of the Church in Missouri, it did have great value in preparing its participants for Church leadership. The men prayed together, were taught by the Prophet, and witnessed miracles and spiritual manifestations. And in spite of their trials, they developed strong faith in the Lord. Joseph Smith wrote: "Notwithstanding our enemies were continually breathing threats of violence, we did not fear, neither did we hesitate to prosecute our journey, for God was with us, and His angels went before us, and the faith of our little band was unwavering. We know that angels were our companions, for we saw them."[16]

At a meeting of priesthood leaders in Kirtland some time later, the Prophet declared: "Brethren, some of you are angry with me, because you did not fight in Missouri; but let me tell you, God did not want you to fight. He could not organize His kingdom with twelve men to open the Gospel door to the nations of the earth, and with seventy men under their direction to follow in their tracks, unless he took them from a body of men who had offered their lives, and who had made as great a sacrifice as did Abraham."[17]

The men chosen for the Quorum of the Twelve Apostles and the First Quorum of Seventy came principally from those who had offered their lives for the gospel in Zion's Camp. Nine of the original Twelve Apostles, called in 1835, were members of Zion's Camp, as were all seventy members of the First Quorum of Seventy. Their commitment was proven.

In an address to the Saints in the Salt Lake Valley nineteen years later, Brigham Young summarized his feelings about his experience in Zion's Camp: "When I returned from that mission . . . a brother said to me, 'Brother Brigham, what have you gained by this journey?' I replied, "Just what we went for; but I would not exchange the knowledge I have received this season for the whole of Geauga County; for property and mines of wealth are not to be compared to the worth of knowledge."[18]

And in 1869, Elder Wilford Woodruff declared: "We gained an experience that we never could have gained in any other way. We had the privilege of beholding the face of the prophet, and we had the privilege of travelling a thousand miles with him, and seeing the workings of the Spirit of God with him, and the revelations of Jesus Christ unto him and the fulfillment of those revelations. . . . Had I not gone up with Zion's Camp I should not have been here to-day."[19]

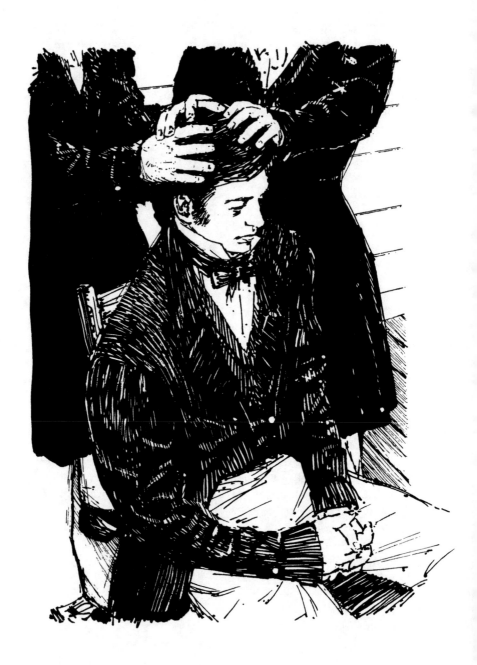

14

THE RESTORATION OF OFFICES AND ORGANIZATION

"It [is] the will of God that those who went to Zion . . . should be ordained to the ministry, and go forth to prune the vineyard." (Joseph Smith.)

Within three days of his arrival in Kirtland in 1831, Joseph Smith, now holding the keys of the priesthood, called Edward Partridge to be the first bishop of the Church. Within five months of his arrival, he organized the office of high priest. Within the first two years, he organized and ordained the First Presidency (three presiding high priests). In December 1833 the office of Patriarch was added. The seventies and Twelve Apostles were added in 1835. Each step was directed by the Lord and built on the same structure used two thousand years ago in Christ's original church.

A vision given to Joseph Smith preceded and was the basis for the organization of the quorums of the Twelve and the seventy. The Prophet, alluding to this vision several times, emphasized that he saw the order of the Church organization. He also saw the " 'order of the Seventy' . . . and the manner in which the Twelve should be chosen."[1]

From 1831-35, as Joseph Smith moved to each new residence, the headquarters of the Church also moved: to the Morley farm, the Johnson farm, the Whitney store, and the Prophet's home near the temple. Revelations received during this period gave important counsel pertaining to the Melchizedek Priesthood. For example, the "oath and the covenant" of the priesthood encouraged all men to magnify their priesthood callings and promised eternal possessions to those who were obedient.

High Priests Are Ordained

The first high priests of this dispensation were ordained at the Church's first conference in Ohio in June 1831. Among the twenty-three men ordained were many of the the leaders of the Church, including Joseph Smith Jr., Oliver Cowdery, David Whitmer, Hyrum Smith, Sidney Rigdon, Martin Harris, and Joseph Smith Sr. Levi Hancock's journal has a description of the conference:

> The Fourth of June came and we all met in a little string of buildings under the hill near Isaac Morleys in Kirtland, [Geauga] County, Ohio. Then we all went to a school house on the hill about one fourth of a mile ascending nearly all the way. The building was built of logs. It was filled with slab benches. Here the Elders were seated and the meeting was opened as usual. . . . Joseph put his hands on Harvey Whitlock and ordained him to the high priesthood. . . . Then he ordained Jacob Scott and some others to the High Priesthood.[2]

At a second conference in Orange on October 25, 1831, additional high priests were ordained. Joseph Smith addressed those who were ordained high priests and promised them: "If we will but cleanse ourselves and covenant before God, to serve Him, it is our privilege to have an assurance that God will protect us at all times."[3]

Several of those assembled then bore testimony and committed themselves and all they had to the Lord. The testimonies were summarized in minutes of the meeting, including the following:

> Br. Sidney Rigdon said[,] I bear testimony that God will have a pure people who will give up all for Christ's sake and when this is done they will be sealed up unto eternal life. . . .

146

Br. Orson Hyde said that he covenanted to give all to the Lord and be for his glory. . . .

Br. Wm. E. McLellin said that he had the greatest reason to rejoice of any present and that he also would be subject to the will of God even unto death. . . .

Br. Martin Harris . . . also covenanted to give all for Christ's sake.

Br. John Smith said that he felt through grace to do the will of the Lord notwithstanding his extreme old age, also felt to covenant to give all to the Lord. . . .

Br. David Whitmer said that he felt to declare to this conference that he had consecrated all that was his to the Lord, and also was desirous to do all for the glory of God.

Br. Simeon Carter . . . testified that the Book of Mormon was true.[4]

The First Presidency Is Organized

On March 18, 1833, in the Newel K. Whitney store, the First Presidency was organized as directed by revelation (section 90 of the Doctrine and Covenants), with a president—Joseph Smith—and two counselors. The counselors' position was to be "equal with [Joseph Smith's] in holding the keys of this last kingdom." (D&C 90:6.)[5]

At this meeting, great spiritual manifestations took place. The Prophet recorded: "Elder Rigdon expressed a desire that himself and Brother Frederick G. Williams should be ordained to the offices to which they had been called, viz., those of the Presidents of the High Priesthood, and to be equal in holding the keys of the kingdom with Brother Joseph Smith, Jun., according to the revelation given on the 8th of March, 1833. Accordingly I laid my hands on Brothers Sidney and Frederick, and ordained them to take part with me in holding the keys of this last kingdom, and to assist in the Presidency of the High Priesthood, as my Counselors."[6]

The Patriarch and Patriarchal Blessings

On December 18, 1833, while the elders were assembled at the John Johnson inn to dedicate the printing office, Joseph

Smith Sr. was called and ordained as Patriarch to the Church by his son, Joseph Smith Jr., and Oliver Cowdery, Sidney Rigdon, and Frederick G. Williams.[7]

The first patriarchal blessings of this dispensation were also bestowed at the meeting. Since the Prophet Joseph Smith held the keys of all the authority in the Church, he gave the first blessings. Those who received blessings on this occasion were Oliver Cowdery, Joseph Smith Sr., and Lucy Mack Smith, as well as the Prophet's brothers, Hyrum, Samuel, and William.[8]

Numerous journals indicate that the Prophet's father, as Patriarch to the Church, actively bestowed blessings throughout the Kirtland period. Lorenzo Snow testified to the inspiration through which the blessings were given:

> I listened with astonishment to him telling the brethren and sisters their parentage, their lineage, and other things which I could not help but believe he knew nothing about, save as the Spirit manifested them unto him. After listening to several patriarchal blessings pronounced upon the heads of different individuals with whose history I was acquainted, and of whom I knew the Patriarch was entirely ignorant, I was struck with astonishment to hear the peculiarities of those persons positively and plainly referred to in their blessings. I was convinced that an influence, superior to human prescience, dictated his words.[9]

The High Council

The first high council was organized on February 17, 1834, in Joseph Smith's home. This meeting was so important that Joseph Smith spent the following day, February 18, reviewing and correcting the minutes. Carefully guarding against error, he presented them to the council and "urged the necessity of prayer, that the Spirit might be given, that the things of the Spirit might be judged thereby." The minutes, read three times, were then unanimously adopted and received as a "form and constitution of the High Council."[10]

The minutes indicate that the high council was chosen from twenty-four high priests who were present. The Prophet said the council was appointed by revelation to settle important difficulties that might arise in the Church, particularly those which could not be settled by the Church or the bishop's council to the satisfaction of the parties involved. The procedures "for the purpose of settling important difficulties" were also defined. (D&C 102:2.)

The Kirtland Stake

The organization of the first stake, the Kirtland Stake, is assumed to have been simultaneous with the organization of the first high council. On February 18, 1834, Joseph Smith and his two counselors in the First Presidency, Sidney Rigdon and Frederick G. Williams, were set apart to preside over the high council, which meant that they also were to preside over the stake. The establishment of a stake had long been expected, for the term *stake* had been used in revelations beginning in 1831. In 1832, the Lord said that Zion's "stakes must be strengthened" and "I have consecrated the land of Kirtland . . . for a stake to Zion." (D&C 82:13-14.) In 1833, the Lord referred to the Kirtland Stake in two revelations. Since the high council was organized in 1834, the long-awaited stake certainly had come into being by that time.

The Twelve Apostles

Organization of the Melchizedek Priesthood continued as the Twelve Apostles were named in the schoolroom on February 14, 1835. Joseph Young described going with his brother, Brigham, to Joseph Smith's home the previous Sunday, February 8, 1835, when the Prophet related a vision to them:

"Brethren, [the Prophet said,] I have seen those men who died of the cholera in our camp; and the Lord knows, if I get a mansion as bright as theirs, I ask no more." At this revelation he wept, and for some time could not speak. When he had relieved himself of his feelings, in describing the vision, he resumed the conversation, and addressed himself to Brother Brigham Young. He said to him, "I wish you to notify all the brethren living in the branches, within a reasonable distance from this place, to meet at a general conference on Saturday next. I shall then and there appoint twelve Special Witnesses, to open the door of the Gospel to foreign nations, and you" said he, (speaking to Brother Brigham,) "will be one of them.". . . Agreeable to his request to Elder Brigham Young, the branches were all notified, and a meeting of the brethren in general conference was held in Kirtland, in the new school house under the printing office, on the following Saturday, February 14th.[11]

Before the apostles were chosen, Joseph Smith explained that the conference was called "because God had commanded it" and it had been made known to him (Joseph) through a vision.[12] He then asked those who had gone to Missouri with Zion's Camp to be seated together in a section apart from the others, explaining that "it was the will of God that those who went to Zion, with a determination to lay down their lives, if necessary, should be ordained to the ministry, and go forth to prune the vineyard."[13]

Joseph Smith then talked about choosing the Twelve and asked the brethren if they would be satisfied to have "the Spirit of the Lord dictate in the choice of the Elders to be Apostles."[14] Those present concurred, and Lyman E. Johnson, Brigham Young, Heber C. Kimball, Orson Hyde, David W. Patten, Luke S. Johnson, William E. McLellin, John F. Boynton, Orson Pratt, William Smith, Thomas B. Marsh, and Parley P. Pratt were named to serve as the first apostles in this dispensation. They were set apart by the three men who had been witnesses to the Book of Mormon — Oliver Cowdery, David Whitmer, and Martin Harris — and the ordination was confirmed by the First Presidency. Orson Hyde, one of these original apostles, later said:

> Joseph said to me, although I was young, weak, inexperienced, especially in public speaking, and ignorant of many important things which we now all understand, that I should be one of this Twelve. It seemed to me a very great saying. I looked upon the Twelve Apostles who lived in ancient days with a great deal of reverence — as being almost

superhuman. They were, indeed, great men — not by virtue of the flesh, nor their own natural capacities, but they were great because God called them. When Joseph told me that I would be one of the Twelve, I knew all things were possible with God, but it seemed to me that I would have to be altogether changed to occupy such a great position in the Church and Kingdom of our God.[15]

The First Quorum of the Seventy

Joseph Smith's history indicates that on Saturday, February 28, 1835, the Church met in council to select certain individuals to be ordained as seventies from "the number of those who went up to Zion with me in the camp."[16] Seven men were named to be presidents of the quorum of the seventies, and they, along with sixty-three others, constituted the quorum. All had participated in Zion's Camp. Joseph Young, who was one of the presidents of the seventies, recorded the startling way his call came to him. The Prophet asked Brother Young to come to his home, and there he was told, "Brother Joseph, the Lord has made you President of the Seventies."[17] The Prophet instructed the seventies "to constitute traveling quorums, to go into all the earth, whithersoever the Twelve Apostles shall call them."[18] Thus, the seventies were called to do missionary work.

Caroline Crosby, whose husband was one of those called, wrote: "I well recollect the sensations with which my mind was actuated when I learned the fact that my husband had been called and ordained to the Melchisedek priesthood and would undoubtedly be required to travel and preach the gospel to the nations of the earth. I realized in some degree the immense responsibility of the office, and besought the Lord for grace and wisdom to be given him that he might be able to magnify his high and holy calling."[19]

Support of Priesthood Holders

Wives and families of priesthood holders often made considerable sacrifices by carrying extra burdens so their husbands and fathers could attend to their Church callings. The men went on missions, constructed the temple and other buildings, went to Missouri on Zion's Camp, and attended frequent meetings. In their absence, women often had to provide income for their families, perform chores around the home that might normally be done by their husbands, and assume responsibility for rearing children and making family decisions.

Elizabeth Ann Whitney, whose husband, as bishop to the Church in Ohio, was frequently away from home, epitomized the attitude of these early mothers. She wrote: "During all these absences and separations from my husband I never felt to murmur or complain in the least . . . yet I was more than satisfied to have him give all, time, talents and ability into the service of the Kingdom of God; and the change in our circumstances and associations which were consequent upon our embracing the Gospel, never caused me a moment's sorrow. I looked upon it as a real pleasure to give all for the sake of my faith in the religion of Jesus, considering all as nought in comparison with the example of our blessed Savior."[20]

Church Administration Headquarters

Since Joseph Smith presided over the Church, the headquarters literally moved when he moved until permanent office space could be secured.

At the Isaac Morley farm, where the Smith family resided in 1831, welfare principles were revealed and put into practice, the priesthood and a branch of the Church were organized, and a number of conferences were held. The farm was also the scene of several revelations and other spiritual manifestations.

At the John Johnson farm in Hiram, where the family moved in September 1831, the Prophet worked on his translation of the Bible. Fifteen revelations were received there, including section 1 (also known as the preface) of the Doctrine and Covenants, and the Prophet received visions of Deity and of the eternal worlds.

At least eight special conferences were held in Hiram, and journals mention many meetings at the Johnson home. Lorenzo Snow recorded that at one meeting, "Joseph Smith was standing

in the door of Father Johnson's house, looking into the bowery,"
where some 150 or 200 people had gathered.[21]

The upper story of the Newel K. Whitney store, into which
the Prophet moved in September 1832, served as Church headquarters for about eighteen months. The initial command to build
the Kirtland Temple and much of the subsequent planning occurred there. A survey of the high council minutes reveals that
at least eighteen meetings and conferences were held in the
store between December 3, 1832, and June 21, 1833. At the
Whitney store building, Joseph received seventeen revelations
that were compiled into the Doctrine and Covenants, continued
his translation of the Bible, conducted the School of the Prophets, and organized the First Presidency. Great spiritual outpourings occurred there, including visions of the Father and the
Son. The store also served as the first bishop's storehouse.

Joseph Smith's home on the hill, near the temple, was the
next Church headquarters. Minutes record that various council
meetings were held there, including meetings of the Twelve
Apostles, high priests, elders, and high council, as well as many
individual and impromptu gatherings. It is believed that six
revelations were received there, including directives to organize
the first high council, initiate Zion's Camp, and dissolve the
united order. The Egyptian mummies and papyrus scrolls were
exhibited in this home, and hundreds flocked to view them.
Translation of the scrolls also commenced here.

The schoolhouse/printing office was completed in November
1834, and this building finally provided an office outside the
Prophet's home. Following that, in 1836 the west room on the
top story of the temple was reserved for the Prophet's "translating room" and office until the end of the Kirtland period.

15

BUILDING A HOUSE
OF THE LORD

*"Had it not been for the assurance that
God had spoken, . . . an attempt towards building that temple, under the
then existing conditions, would have
been . . . . pronounced preposterous."
(Eliza R. Snow.)*

From a command of God, the Saints began the seemingly
impossible feat of building the Kirtland Temple — a modern
"house of God." (D&C 88:119.)[1] Construction of the
temple, the main priority of the Church between 1833 and 1836,
presented challenges of gigantic proportions to the Saints, who
lacked both the necessary manpower and money. According to
Eliza R. Snow, "At that time . . . the Saints were few in number,
and most of them very poor; and, had it not been for the assurance that God had spoken, and had commanded that a house
should be built to his name, of which he not only revealed the
form, but also designated the dimensions, an attempt towards
building that Temple, under the then existing circumstances,
would have been, by all concerned, pronounced preposterous."[2]

Neither the Church nor its poverty-stricken members had
ever undertaken such a task. The cost of the building, estimated
at about $40,000, was a staggering sum for the 1830s.[3] Relative
to the meager resources of the Saints at the time, the Kirtland
Temple is probably the most costly temple ever constructed by
the Church. In addition, there were only a handful of experienced builders among the Saints, and certainly none had constructed anything as huge and complex as the temple.

155

The Saints also faced great opposition from the community. Townspeople thought it foolhardy for them to build such a structure, and some vowed "that the walls should never be erected."[4] The Lord, however, promised support, declaring, "It is my will that you should build a house. If you keep my commandments you shall have power to build it." (D&C 95:11.)

Brigham Young acknowledged that the Church members were "too few in numbers, too weak in faith, and too poor in purse, to attempt such a mighty enterprise. But by means of all these stimulants, a mere handful of men, living on air, and a little hominy and milk, and often salt or no salt when milk could not be had; the great Prophet Joseph, in the stone quarry, quarrying rock with his own hands; and the few then in the Church, following his example of obedience and diligence wherever most needed; with laborers on the walls, holding the sword in one hand to protect themselves from the mob, while they placed the stone and moved the trowel with the other."[5]

A non-Mormon historian, writing about the temple in 1965, said, "The Kirtland Temple stands as a monument to Joseph Smith and to those faithful souls. . . . It appears a miracle the temple was constructed and a second miracle it was not harmed in all the years since it was built. . . . Members of the Church of Christ constructed a temple lovelier perhaps than Smith's fondest hopes, for they were inspired by almost superhuman exertion of body and brilliance of mind, by their devotion to Smith and to the visions and revelations experienced by him."[6]

Joseph Smith, given both the commandment and the promise, expressed the intensity of his determination in a letter written to William W. Phelps on January 11, 1833: "You will see that the Lord commanded us, in Kirtland, to build a house of God, and establish a school for the Prophets. This is the word of the Lord to us, and we must, yea the Lord helping us, we will obey. . . . He has promised us great things; yea, even a visit from the heavens to honor us with His own presence."[7]

The Lord Provides the Plan

On December 27, 1832, the Prophet received a commandment to "establish a house of prayer, a house of fasting, a house of faith, a house of learning, a house of glory, a house of order, a house of God." (D&C 88:119.) In a subsequent revelation, on June 1, 1833, the Lord directed him to build the temple "after the manner which I shall show unto three of you" (D&C 95:14), meaning Joseph Smith, Sidney Rigdon, and Frederick G. Williams, members of the First Presidency.

Truman O. Angell (who was architect of the Salt Lake Temple), recorded in his journal President Williams's description of how the temple plan was revealed: "Joseph received the word of the Lord for him to take his two counsellors Williams and Rigdon and come before the Lord, and He would show them the plan or model of the House to be built. We went upon our knees, called on the Lord, and the Building appeared within viewing distance: I being the first to discover it. Then all of us viewed it together. After we had taken a good look at the exterior, the building seemed to come right over us, and the Makeup of this Hall seemed to coincide with what I there saw to a minutia."[8]

In a letter to John Taylor in 1885, Truman O. Angell confirmed the fact that the temple had been seen in vision: "F.G. Williams came into the Temple about the time the main hall 1st floor was ready for dedication. He was asked, how does the house look to you. He answered that it looked to him like the model he had seen. He said President Joseph Smith, Sidney Rigdon and himself were called to come before the Lord and the model was shown them. He said the vision of the Temple was thus shown them and he could not see the difference between it and the House as built."[9] He further stated in his journal that "the leading mechanic" recommended to Joseph Smith that the seats in the building be rearranged. The Prophet responded by saying he had seen them in vision and insisted that the original plans be carried out.[10]

Brigham Young drew a parallel with Moses and Solomon and emphasized that without this direct vision, Joseph Smith "could not know what was wanting, having never seen one [a temple], and not having experienced its use."[11]

At a meeting in Kirtland, Joseph Smith asked the brethren

for their views about how the temple was to be constructed. Lucy Mack Smith described their responses: "Some were in favor of building a frame house, but others were of a mind to put up a log house. Joseph reminded them that they were not building a house for a man, but for God; 'and shall we, brethren,' said he, 'build a house for our God, of logs? No, I have a better plan than that. I have a plan of the house of the Lord, given by himself; and you will soon see by this, the difference between our calculations and his idea of things.' "[12]

The Work Begins

Although the Prophet had been commanded by the Lord to build the temple, overwhelming problems and other priorities delayed construction. On June 1, 1833, the Lord chastized the Church for not having made greater progress on the sacred edifice. (See D&C 95:1-6.) Needless to say, activity started immediately. The ground was broken on June 5. Lucy Mack Smith wrote: "Joseph took the brethren with him, for the purpose of selecting a spot for the building to stand upon. The place which they made choice of was situated in the north-west corner of a field of wheat, which was sown by my sons the fall previous, on the farm upon which we were then living. In a few minutes the fence was removed, and the standing grain was levelled, in order to prepare a place for the building and Hyrum commenced digging a trench for the wall, he having declared that he would strike the first blow upon the house."[13]

Less than two months later, on July 23, 1833, twenty-four Church leaders met to lay the cornerstones "after the order of the Holy Priesthood."[14] The First Presidency laid the stone on the southeast corner, and the remaining three cornerstones were laid by other leaders.

The major activity in Kirtland from July 1833 through March 1836 centered around construction of the temple. According to the Prophet's mother, the Saints "had to endure great fatigue and privation, in consequence of the opposition they met with from their enemies, and which was so great, that they were compelled to keep a guard around the walls much of the time until they were completed. They 'gave no sleep to their eyes, nor slumber to their eyelids, until they found a place for the Lord, a habitation for the mighty God of Jacob.' . . . There was but one mainspring to all our thoughts and actions, and that was, the building of the Lord's house.''[15]

Initially the brethren desired to construct the temple out of brick. One of the main reasons they purchased the Peter French farm was "on account of the facilities found there for making brick."[16] Benjamin F. Johnson wrote that "the purpose of building the Temple of brick was abandoned as a stone quarry at easy distance was opened to obtain the rock for its construction."[17] Evidently to create the desired effect, the finished walls were marked to have the appearance of brick.

The Stannard Stone Quarry, two miles away, provided most of the stone for the temple. When construction began, Joseph Smith, Hyrum Smith, Brigham Young, Lorenzo D. Young, and Reynolds Cahoon rode south to visit the quarry and make sure the stone was suitable for the temple walls, which would be two feet thick and more than sixty feet high. Lorenzo's wagon was then loaded with stones and taken back to the construction site.

Joseph Smith himself helped quarry the stone. Heber C. Kimball told how, when the brethren returned to Kirtland from the march of Zion's Camp, "Joseph said, 'Come, brethren, let us go into the stone quarry and work for the Lord.' And the Prophet went himself, in his tow frock and tow breeches and worked at quarrying stone like the rest of us. Then, every Saturday we brought out every team to draw stone to the temple, and so we continued until that house was finished."[18]

Everyone who had a team was enlisted to carry stone to the temple site. Elder Kimball reported that "those who had no teams went to work in the stone quarry and prepared the stones for drawing to the house. President Joseph Smith jr. being our foreman in the quarry. The Presidency, High Priests, and Elders all alike assisting. —Those who had teams assisted in drawing the stone to the house. These all laboring one day in the week, brought as many stones to the house as supplied the masons through the whole week. We continued in this manner until the walls of the house were reared."[19]

Obtaining sufficient wood for the temple was a problem because a vast quantity was needed quickly. Much of the freshly cut wood from neighboring forests had to be dried and seasoned before it could be cut and used. In order to expedite the drying and seasoning process, a board kiln was built in the flats. The board kiln was apparently located adjacent to the sawmill so that when the wood was ready, it could be cut.

The kiln, which required heat and evidently open flame, caught fire frequently. The Prophet recorded in his diary on December 10, 1835, "The board kiln had taken fire, and on our return we found the brethren engaged in extinguishing the flames. After laboring about one hour against this destructive element, we succeeded in conquering it, and probably saved about one-fourth part of the lumber. I do not know the amount of loss the committee have sustained, but it must have been considerable, as there was much lumber in the kiln. There were about two hundred brethren engaged on this occasion; they displayed much activity and interest, and deserve much credit."[20]

Three days later he wrote, "To day the board kiln, took fire again,"[21] and the next day he recorded that he met "to make ar[r]angements to guard against fire, and organized a company for this purpose."[22]

Because the Saints could not overcome problems with the kiln, they did not have enough seasoned wood for the temple and finally had to contract with a non-Mormon Kirtland businessman to furnish lumber.

Construction of the temple required vigorous labor by the workers, who often labored into the night and had to rely on others to provide them with sufficient clothing and food. Daniel Tyler recalled:

How often have I seen those humble, faithful servants of the Lord, after toiling all day in the quarry, or on the building, when the walls were in course of erection, weary and faint, yet with cheerful countenances, retiring to their

homes with a few pounds of corn meal that had been donated. And, in the case of those who lacked a cow to give
a little milk, the corn meal was sometimes, for days together, all that they and their families had to subsist upon.
When a little flour, butter or meat came in, they were lux-
uries. Sometimes a little New Orleans molasses, not as good
as our sorghum, would be donated; but oftener the hands
had to seek a job elsewhere to get a gallon or so, and then
return to the labor on the temple.[23]

Because of the height of the building — 110 feet to the dome
of the steeple — the builders erected a scaffolding so they could
raise the walls and construct the interior. Such work was dangerous, and Daniel Tyler described the results of one accident:

I think it was Father Fisher, who, by some accident, fell
from the scaffold, and was disabled for performing manual
labor. He could manage, by the labor of his boys, to get a
little corn; but corn bread alone was dry food. He went to
the Prophet and asked him what he should do, and was
told to get up a subscription paper and present to those
who were best able to donate, and raise money enough to
buy a cow, which would cost from ten to twelve dollars.
He did as directed, and received the full sum of seventy-
five cents. One person gave fifty and another twenty-five
cents. This so disgusted the Prophet that he preferred a
charge against them before the High Council "for a lack of
charity to the Church, and benevolence to the poor." One
of them made a humble acknowledgment, and the other
was disfellowshipped.[24]

The temple construction progressed fairly well except for
the winter of 1833, when work was suspended because there
was not enough wood, stone, or other necessary materials, and
the summer of 1834, when so many men went to Missouri with
Zion's Camp. The work was also sometimes suspended when
the winter weather was harsher than usual, especially before
the exterior walls were completed. Lorenzo Young described
the winter of 1835-36:

It was then the last of November, and the weather daily grew colder. A Brother Stillman assisted me a day or two, but said that he could not stand the cold, and quit the work. I continued, day after day, determined, if possible, to complete the job. When I got badly chilled I went into my house, warmed myself and returned again to the work.

I completed the task in the forepart of December, but was sick the last two days. I had caught a bad cold, had a very severe cough, and, in a few days was confined to my bed. My disease was pronounced to be the quick consumption. I sank rapidly for six or seven weeks. For two weeks I was unable to talk.[25]

The women in Kirtland contributed toward completing the temple by providing support for the workers. Heber C. Kimball reported:

Our women were engaged in spinning and knitting in order to clothe those who were laboring at the building, and the Lord only knows the scenes of poverty, tribulation, and distress which we passed through in order to accomplish this thing. My wife toiled all summer in lending her aid towards its accomplishment. She had a hundred pounds of wool, which, with the assistance of a girl, she spun in order to furnish clothing for those engaged in the building of the Temple, and although she had the privilege of keeping half the quantity of wool for herself, as a recompense for her labor, she did not reserve even so much as would make her a pair of stockings; but gave it for those who were laboring at the house of the Lord. She spun and wove and got the cloth dressed, and cut and made up into garments, and gave them to those men who labored on the Temple; almost all the sisters in Kirtland labored in knitting, sewing, spinning, etc., for the purpose of forwarding the work of the Lord.[26]

As the building neared completion, the women also made carpets and veils, or curtains, of white canvas that were mounted on rollers and hung from the ceiling. They could be dropped to divide the large rooms on the first and second floors into four separate, smaller rooms, and were also placed above the pulpits so they could be dropped for privacy. Joseph Smith wrote: "This afternoon the sisters met again at the Temple to work on the veil. Towards the close of the day I met with the Presidency and many of the brethren in the house of the Lord, and made some remarks from the pulpit upon the rise and progress of the Church of Christ of Latter-day Saints, and pronounced a blessing upon the sisters, for their liberality in giving their services so cheerfully, to make the veil for the Lord's House."[27]

Polly Angell, wife of the Church architect, said that the Prophet told them: "Well, sisters, you are always on hand. The sisters are always first and foremost in all good works. Mary was first at the resurrection; and the sisters now are the first to work on the inside of the temple."[28]

One apparently apocryphal story was that the women furnished their finest glass and crockery to be mixed with the stucco for the outside walls. And when it was finished, the temple did sparkle when the sun shone on it. The biography of Artemus Millet explained: "When the wall of the Temple was finished, [Artemus] sent men and boys to the different towns and places to gather old crockery and glass to put in the cement which [he] had invented. Not that glass and crockery had any adhesive property but it had its use. . . . Many ladies would smooth their hands over the plaster, which looked so smooth, then look at their hands and tell where the fine glass had cut them and made them bleed."[29]

Poverty and Tribulation

The temple wasn't completed without exacting a toll on the Saints. In the dedicatory prayer, the Prophet said, "For thou knowest that we have done this work through great tribulation; and out of our poverty we have given of our substance to build a house to thy name." (D&C 109:5.)

"Poverty" is a word used many times in journals and accounts of the members in Kirtland. Benjamin F. Johnson said that when the work commenced, "There were but few saints in Kirtland, and those all of the poorer class. . . . There was not a scraper and hardly a plow that could be obtained among the Saints."[30] Another account noted, "Joseph Smith and Brigham Young worked on that building day after day; also, many others did so. They did not have molasses to eat with their johnny cake. Sometimes they had shoes, and sometimes not; sometimes they would have tolerable pants, and, sometimes, very ragged ones."[31]

Heber C. Kimball originally felt that to build the temple would be almost impossible because of the poverty: "When I got to Kirtland the brethren were engaged in building the house of the Lord. The commandment to build the house, and also the pattern of it was given in a revelation to Joseph Smith jr., Sidney Rigdon, and Frederick G. Williams, and was to be erected by a stated time. The church was in a state of poverty and distress, in consequence of which it appeared almost impossible that the commandment could be fulfilled, at the same time our enemies were raging and threatening destruction upon us."[32]

Not only was the Church poor, but it was also in debt. Joseph Smith revealed his deep concern for the Church's debts in writing to Missouri in December 1833: "It will be impossible for us to render you any temporal assistance, as our means are already exhausted, and we are deeply in debt, and know of no means whereby we shall be able to extricate ourselves."[33]

Since nearly everyone worked on the temple, most financial reserves were used to sustain the workers. Special mission calls were issued for men to solicit funds from members of the Church in other areas. In May 1834 Jared Carter was sent east to obtain funds, and a year later Phineas Young was sent to Michigan. Christopher Crary, a non-Mormon businessman in Kirtland, said that "property of all kinds was sent in." He told of purchasing from the Church a horse and yoke of oxen that had been donated to the temple fund.[34] Though many contributions were collected, at least fourteen thousand dollars had to be borrowed to finance the temple.[35]

Despite the poverty and tribulation, however, the Lord answered the prayers of the Saints, sometimes in their darkest hours. Heber C. Kimball told of Sidney Rigdon's intense petitions: "Looking at the sufferings and poverty of the Church, he frequently used to go upon the walls of the building both by night and day and frequently wetting the walls with his tears, crying aloud to the Almighty to send means whereby we might accomplish the building."[36]

Oliver Huntington, the Prophet's bodyguard, tells how one prayer was answered:

> At a time when Joseph Smith was guarded day and night by his brethren from mob violence, that he might perform his necessary business labors and get the necessary night's rest and that his life should be safe; he was in a log house at night. Several brethren were with him and were making arrangements as to who should stand guard that night.
>
> Joseph was listening to the prayer of a little boy in the room adjoining. The boy prayed for the Prophet, that he might be secure and safe from his enemies, the mob, that night.
>
> When the boy had done praying, Joseph turned to his brethren and told them all to go to bed and all sleep and rest themselves that night, for God had heard and would answer that boy's prayer. They all went to bed and slept safely until morning undisturbed.[37]

In addition to answering prayers for protection, the Lord also answered prayers for financial assistance. At a time of the Saints' greatest need, the Lord directed wealthy Church members, such as John Tanner and Artemus Millet, to go to Kirtland, and there they sacrificed their means freely to save the temple from foreclosure.

Unseen forces also protected the Saints and their efforts. In January 1836, prior to completion of the temple, Joseph Smith reported: "Elder Roger Orton saw a mighty angel riding upon a horse of fire, with a flaming sword in his hand, followed by five others, encircle the house, and protect the Saints, even the Lord's annointed, from the power of Satan and a host of evil spirits, which were striving to disturb the Saints."[38]

Many accounts tell of persecution and mob violence. Heber C. Kimball wrote from firsthand experience: "While we were building the Temple, in Kirtland, . . . we were persecuted and were under the necessity of laying upon the floor with our firelocks by our sides to sustain ourselves, as there were mobs gathering all around to destroy us, and prevent us from building the Temple. And when they were driven, every man that was in the church, arose, and we took our firelocks, to reinstate our brethren, and in the night we laid upon the floor; we laid upon Brother Joseph's floor, and upon Sidney Rigdon's floor, so as to be ready to keep our enemies at bay."[39]

Joel Hills Johnson said that the Saints had "but very few friends" while they also had "thousands of enemies who were holding their secret meetings to devise plans to thwart and overthrow all of our arrangements. . . . We were obliged . . . to keep up night watches to prevent being mobbed, and our work being overthrown."[40]

In December 1833 the Prophet wrote to Church members in Missouri: "The inhabitants of this county threaten our destruction, and we know not how soon they may be permitted to follow the example of the Missourians; but our trust is in God, and we are determined, His grace assisting us, to maintain the cause and hold out faithful unto the end."[41]

Blessings for the Faithful Saints

In early March 1835, while the temple walls were still being erected, a spiritual meeting was called for the purpose of blessing those who were assisting in the building. Even though much work remained, the Prophet felt a blessing was needed for the faithful who had consecrated themselves to the work. One hundred nineteen faithful brethren were blessed one by one under the hands of the First Presidency. These individual blessings also provided motivation to the individuals to complete the temple.

Benjamin Johnson was the last person to be blessed. He was young—only seventeen years old—and in poor health. Four of his brothers and sisters had also been ill and died of consumption. Although Benjamin had not worked on the temple, he fervently desired a blessing. He recalled:

Oh! how I did yearn for a blessing! And as the last blessing, apparently, was given, the Prophet earnestly looked towards the door where I was standing, and said to his brother Hyrum, "Go and see if there is not one more yet to be blessed." Brother Hyrum came to the door, and seeing me, put his hand upon my shoulder and asked me if I had not worked upon the Temple. I said, "No sir," but it seemed like passing a sentence upon my fondest hopes. He then asked if I had done nothing towards it. I then thought of a new gun I had earned and given as a donation, and of the brick I had helped to make. I said, "I did give often." "I thought," he said, "there was a blessing for you," and he almost carried me to the stand. The Prophet blessed me, with a confirmation of all his father had sealed upon me, and many more also. I felt then that the Lord had respect for my great desire. Even to be the youngest and last to be blessed seemed to me a high privilege. When the Prophet had looked towards the door, I felt as though he would call for me, though I could not see how I had merited so high a privilege. But so it was, and my joy was full.[42]

With faith and with the Lord sustaining them, the Church members accomplished the miracle. Overcoming mob action and hostility, extreme poverty, and other hardships, they completed the temple in a remarkably short time—just over two and one-half years. The temple was completed in March 1836. The house of the Lord was ready to be dedicated.

16

"A PENTECOST AND A TIME OF REJOICING"

"I have seen the power of God as it was on the day of Pentecost. . . . I saw the Lord. . . . The angels of God rested upon the Temple and we heard their voices singing heavenly music." (Zebedee Coltrin.)

The year 1836 saw the completion and dedication of the Kirtland Temple, with overwhelming spiritual manifestations and restoration of divine keys of authority. Pentecostal events of that year, when the heavens were opened to the Saints, followed a sequential pattern. These sacred manifestations came after disciplined schooling, methodical organization, and difficult trials. The Saints met the prerequisites necessary for their spiritual rewards by consecrating their worldly goods and their efforts to the Lord's work.

In addition to the physical preparation and sacrifices for the temple, the Prophet also prepared the Saints spiritually. He told the Twelve Apostles, "Great blessings await us at this time, and will soon be poured out upon us, if we are faithful in all things." Therefore, he said, "Be prepared in your hearts, be faithful in all things. . . . We must be clean every whit."[1]

Church leaders prepared the Saints to expect heavenly manifestations. Sidney Rigdon, Newel K. Whitney, and Oliver Cowdery, in a letter to John A. Boynton, declared: "Within that house God will pour out his spirit in great majesty and glory and encircle his people with fire more gloriously and marvel-

169

ously than at Pentecost because the work to be performed in the last days is greater than was in that day."[2]

Thus prepared for their "endowment from on high," which the Lord had promised by revelation (D&C 105:33), these modern disciples experienced visions and other spiritual manifestations. As attested in journals, letters, and histories, their experiences, similar to those of ancient prophets, enhanced their faith and gave them great joy and gratitude.

Joseph Smith called this period "a pentecost . . . a year of jubilee, and time of rejoicing."[3] Daniel Tyler testified, "All felt that they had a foretaste of heaven . . . and we wondered whether the millenium had commenced."[4] Orson Pratt declared that "the people were blessed as they never had been blessed for generations and generations."[5] Commemorating these spiritual experiences, William W. Phelps wrote the words to a song, "We'll sing & we'll shout with the armies of heaven: Hosanna, hosanna to God and the Lamb!"[6]

Lorenzo Snow enumerated blessings received in the temple during this pentecostal period: "There we had the gift of prophecy—the gift of tongues—the interpretation of tongues—visions and marvelous dreams were related—the singing of heavenly choirs was heard, and wonderful manifestations of the healing power, through the administrations of the Elders, were witnessed. The sick were healed—the deaf made to hear—the blind to see and the lame to walk, in very many instances. It was plainly manifest that a sacred and divine influence—a spiritual atmosphere pervaded that holy edifice."[7]

The Savior appeared in five different meetings held in the temple. Visions, including a vision of the Father and Son, were beheld at eight meetings, and the congregation saw heavenly beings or angels in nine meetings. In other sessions many Saints reported that they experienced such manifestations as the gift of tongues, the sounds of a mighty wind, a pillar of fire resting down upon the temple roof, prophesying, and the voices of angels. Over one thousand people attended these meetings, many of whom testified to having had sacred experiences and put their observations and feelings in letters and journals.

The Savior himself spoke of the far-reaching implications of these blessings when he appeared and accepted the temple in April 1836. He told Joseph Smith and Oliver Cowdery: "Yea the hearts of thousands and tens of thousands shall greatly rejoice in consequence of the blessings which shall be poured out, and the endowment with which my servants have been endowed in this house. And the fame of this house shall spread to foreign lands; and this is the beginning of the blessing which shall be poured out upon the heads of my people." (D&C 110:9-10.)

The magnitude of these manifestations compelled Joseph Smith to record: "It was a Pentecost and an endowment indeed, long to be remembered, for the sound shall go forth from this place into all the world, and the occurrences of this day shall be handed down upon the pages of sacred history, to all generations; as the day of Pentecost, so shall this day be numbered and celebrated as a year of jubilee, and time of rejoicing to the Saints of the Most High God."[8]

The pentecostal experiences in the temple commenced with an overpowering vision of Deity accompanied by the ministering of angels, communion with heavenly beings, and glorious visions given to key priesthood leaders. On January 21, 1836, Joseph Smith and others experienced a vision of the Father and Son at a meeting on the west end of the temple's upper story. Those present included Joseph Smith Sr., the First Presidency, the presidency of the Church in Missouri, the bishoprics in Kirtland and Missouri, and the Prophet's scribe, Warren Parrish, who recorded the event in Joseph Smith's diary. Section 137 of the Doctrine and Covenants contains an account of this vision:

> The heavens were opened upon us, and I beheld the celestial kingdom of God, and the glory thereof, whether in the body or out I cannot tell. I saw the transcendent beauty of the gate through which the heirs of that kingdom will enter, which was like unto circling flames of fire; also the blazing throne of God, whereon was seated the Father and the Son. I saw the beautiful streets of that kingdom, which had the appearance of being paved with gold.
>
> I saw Father Adam and Abraham; and my father and

my mother; my brother Alvin, that has long since slept; and marveled how it was that he had obtained an inheritance in that kingdom, seeing that he had departed this life before the Lord had set his hand to gather Israel the second time, and had not been baptized for the remission of sins.

Thus came the voice of the Lord unto me, saying: All who have died without a knowledge of this gospel, who would have received it if they had been permitted to tarry, shall be heirs of the celestial kingdom of God; also all that shall die henceforth without a knowledge of it, who would have received it with all their hearts, shall be heirs of that kingdom; for I, the Lord, will judge men according to their works, according to the desire of their hearts.

And I also beheld that all children who die before they arrive at the years of accountability are saved in the celestial kingdom of heaven. (D&C 137.)

In his journal, after describing others whom he saw in his vision, including members of the Twelve, Joseph concluded: "Many of my brethren who received the ordinance with me saw glorious visions also. Angels ministered unto them as well as to myself, and the power of the Highest rested upon us, the house was filled with the glory of God, and we shouted Hosanna to God and the Lamb."[9]

On April 3, 1836, Oliver Cowdery and Joseph Smith saw and received priesthood keys from ancient prophets who held those keys: Moses, Elias, and Elijah. This restoration of keys and authority was so significant the ancient prophet Malachi had prophesied of it. (See Malachi 4:5-6.)

It was necessary that these Old Testament prophets bestow power and authority upon the Church so the kingdom of God could once again be established upon the earth. The Prophet explained how the heavens opened to Oliver Cowdery and him:

Moses appeared before us, and committed unto us the keys of the gathering of Israel from the four parts of the earth, and the leading of the ten tribes from the land of the north.

After this, Elias appeared, and committed the dispensation of the gospel of Abraham, saying that in us and our seed all generations after us should be blessed.

After this vision had closed, another great and glorious vision burst upon us, for Elijah the prophet, who was taken to heaven without tasting death, stood before us, and said: Behold, the time has fully come, which was spoken of by the mouth of Malachi—testifying that he [Elijah] should be sent, before the great and dreadful day of the Lord come—

To turn the hearts of the fathers to the children, and the children to the fathers, lest the whole earth be smitten with a curse—

Therefore, the keys of this dispensation are committed into your hands; and by this ye may know that the great and dreadful day of the Lord is near, even at the doors. (D&C 110:11-16.)

Joseph Smith later emphasized the importance of Malachi's prophecy by saying that the word *turn* in the prophecy should be translated "bind, or seal." He said that the objective of Elijah's visit was to deliver the binding or sealing keys or authority so that members of the Church could receive "all the ordinances, baptisms, confirmations, washings, anointings, ordinations, and sealing powers . . . in behalf of all their progenitors who are dead." Emphasizing their eternal stewardship, he counseled the Saints "to save their dead, seal their posterity." Joseph boldly underscored Elijah's mission and the purpose of temples when he stated, "The question is frequently asked 'Can we not be saved without going through with all those ordinances, &c.?' I would answer, No, not the fullness of salvation."[10] The three prophets bestowed on Joseph Smith and the latter-day apostles the same authority held by the apostles in the time the Savior was on the earth. This authority, direct from God through his prophets, set the restored church apart from all other churches. It was not a new man-made church but a church with original, divine, eternal authority, restored from the original church in Jerusalem by Jesus Christ himself.

Many journals of the Saints testify that the year 1836 was

173

PENTECOSTAL SEASON OF THE KIRTLAND TEMPLE (17 JANUARY – 1 MAY 1836)

Date	Type Meeting	Number Present (a)	Gift of Tongues	Sound of Mighty Wind	Visions	Pillar of Fire	Vision or Appearance of the Savior	Heavenly Beings or Angels	Ministering of Angels	Prophesying	Voices of Angels	Vision of Father and Son
January 17	Large Congregation	(b)	X	X								
January 21	Priesthood Leadership	30			X		X	X	X	X		X
January 22	General Authorities	47	X		X			X	X		X	
January 28	Priesthood	100	X		X	X	X	X		X		
February 6	Priesthood	(b)			X					X		
March 27	Temple Dedication	1000	X		X	X		X				
March 27	Priesthood	416	X	X	X			X		X	X	
March 29	General Authorities	47								X		
March 30	Priesthood	300					X	X	X	X		
April 3	Joseph Smith, Oliver Cowdery	2					X	X				
April 6	Priesthood	600	X	X	X			X	X	X		
May 1	Seventies and Elders	(b)			X			X		X		

(a) On some occasions, not all present directly witnessed the events.
(b) Records do not indicate exact numbers present.

indeed the "year of jubilee," a "time of rejoicing," when communication with the heavens was constant and real.

Zebedee Coltrin testified: "In the Kirtland Temple I have seen the power of God as it was on the day of Pentecost, and cloven tongues of fire have rested on the brethren, and they have spoken in other tongues as the Spirit gave them utterance. I saw the Lord high and lifted up. The angels of God rested upon the Temple and we heard their voices singing heavenly music."[11]

Orson Pratt, called to the temple with missionaries and leaders from all over the country, said that in "that sacred edifice,

> God was there, his angels were there, the Holy Ghost was in the midst of the people, the visions of the Almighty were opened to the minds of the servants of the living God; the v[e]il was taken off from the minds of many; they saw the heavens opened; they beheld the angels of God; they heard the voice of the Lord; and they were filled from the crown of their heads to the soles of their feet with the power and inspiration of the Holy Ghost, and uttered forth prophecies in the midst of that congregation, which have been fulfilling from that day to the present time.[12]

One particularly overpowering meeting in the temple was held on January 28, 1836, when Joseph Smith organized and anointed the high priests, elders, and seventies quorums. He recorded: "Elder Roger Orton saw a mighty angel riding upon a horse of fire. . . . President William Smith, one of the Twelve, saw the heavens opened, and the Lord's host protecting the Lord's anointed. . . . I retired to my home, filled with the Spirit, and my soul cried hosanna to God and the Lamb, through the silent watches of the night; and while my eyes were closed in sleep, the visions of the Lord were sweet unto me, and His glory was round about me."[13]

Apparently speaking of this same meeting, Harrison Burgess testified:

> The Lord blessed His people abundantly in that Temple with the Spirit of prophecy, the ministering of angels, vi-

175

sions, etc. I will here relate a vision which was shown to me. It was near the close of the endowments. I was in a meeting for instruction in the upper part of the Temple, with about a hundred of the High Priests, Seventies and Elders. The Saints felt to shout "Hosannah!" and the Spirit of God rested upon me in mighty power and I beheld the room lighted up with a peculiar light such as I had never seen before. It was soft and clear and the room looked to me as though it had neither roof nor floor to the building and I beheld the Prophet Joseph and Hyrum Smith and Roger Orton enveloped in the light: Joseph exclaimed aloud, "I behold the Savior, the Son of God." Hyrum said, "I behold the angels of heaven." Brother Orton exclaimed, "I behold the chariots of Israel." All who were in the room felt the power of God to that degree that many prophesied, and the power of God was made manifest, the remembrance of which will remain with me while I live upon the earth.[14]

Prescindia Huntington's records tell of pentecostal events in two temple meetings:

I was in the temple with my sister Zina. The whole of the congregation were on their knees, praying vocally, for such was the custom at the close of these meetings when Father Smith presided; yet there was no confusion; the voices of the congregation mingled softly together. While the congregation was thus praying, we both heard, from one corner of the room above our heads, a choir of angels singing most beautifully. They were invisible to us, but myriads of angelic voices seemed to be united in singing some song of Zion, and their sweet harmony filled the temple of God.

We were also in the temple at the pentecost. In the morning Father Smith prayed for a pentecost, in opening the meeting. That day the power of God rested mightily upon the saints. There was poured out upon us abundantly the spirit of revelation, prophe[c]y and tongues. The Holy Ghost filled the house; and along in the afternoon a noise was heard. It was the sound of a mighty rushing wind.[15]

Eliza R. Snow also described a meeting in which Joseph Smith Sr. prayed for "a pentecost." She describes his strict preparation for a fast and the fulfillment of his prayer:

> On fast days, Father Smith's constant practice was to repair to the temple very early, and offer up his prayers before sunrise, and there await the coming of the people; and so strictly disciplined himself in the observance of fasting, as not even to wet his lips with water until after the dismissal of the meeting at four P.M. One morning, when he opened meeting, he prayed fervently that the spirit of the Most High might be poured out as it was at Jerusalem, on the day of pentecost—that it might come "like a mighty rushing wind." It was not long before it did come, to the astonishment of all, and filled the house. It appeared as though the old gentleman had forgotten what he had prayed for. When it came, he was greatly surprised, and exclaimed, "What! is the house on fire?"[16]

Prescindia Huntington described one other experience that occurred during a meeting she had not attended:

> A little girl came to my door and in wonder called me out, exclaiming, "The meeting is on the top of the meeting house!" I went to the door, and there I saw on the temple angels clothed in white covering the roof from end to end. They seemed to be walking to and fro; they appeared and disappeared. The third time they appeared and disappeared before I realized that they were not mortal men. Each time in a moment they vanished, and their reappearance was the same. This was in broad daylight, in the afternoon. A number of the children in Kirtland saw the same.
>
> When the brethren and sisters came home in the evening, they told of the power of God manifested in the temple that day, and of the prophesying and speaking in tongues. It was also said, in the interpretation of tongues, "That the angels were resting down upon the house."[17]

17

THE TEMPLE IS DEDICATED

"I have accepted this house, and my name shall be here; and I will manifest myself to my people in mercy in this house." (D&C 110:7.)

The long-awaited day had finally arrived. On Sunday, March 27, 1836, the Kirtland Temple was dedicated to the Lord.

Joseph Smith estimated that by seven o'clock that morning, more than one thousand persons waited near the temple doors. Over the next hour, a number of Church leaders and ushers entered the building. Finally, at eight o'clock, the temple doors opened, and about one thousand people crowded into the main hall. The doors were closed when all available space was occupied. Hundreds could not enter the building. To accommodate the overflow, Joseph Smith directed that a meeting be held in the schoolhouse west of the temple. After that room was filled to capacity, many still remained outside, so the temple windows were opened to allow those outside to listen, if possible. A repeat of the dedicatory services was also scheduled for the following Thursday.

The dedicatory services began at nine o'clock with Sidney Rigdon, a counselor in the First Presidency, reading Psalms 96 and 24. A choir then sang the hymn "Ere Long the Veil Will Rend in Twain," after which President Rigdon offered the invocation. This was followed by a song by the congregation, "O Happy Souls, Who Pray Where God Appoints to Hear." Then President Rigdon spoke for two and a half hours, using as his text Matthew, chapter 8, verses 18 to 20. He emphasized the Savior's comment that "the foxes have holes, and the birds of

179

the air have nests, but the Son of man hath not where to lay his head."[1] According to Eliza R. Snow, although it was a lengthy sermon, it was eloquent and moving. "At one point," she said, "as he reviewed the toils and privations of those who had labored in rearing the walls of that sacred edifice, he drew tears from many eyes, saying, there were those who had wet those walls with their tears, when, in the silent shades of the night, they were praying to the God of heaven to protect them, and stay the unhallowed hands of ruthless spoilers, who had uttered a prophecy, when the foundation was laid, that the walls should never be erected."[2]

Following President Rigdon's talk, Joseph Smith was sustained as a prophet and seer first by the priesthood quorums and then by the congregation. This part of the service concluded with the choir and congregation standing to sing "Now Let Us Rejoice in the Day of Salvation." An intermission of about fifteen or twenty minutes followed, during which most people remained in the building. The service then continued with another song, "This Earth Was Once a Garden Place," also known as "Adam-ondi-Ahman." After a few brief remarks by Joseph Smith, the congregation sustained various officers of the Church and then sang another song, "How Pleased and Blessed Was I."

Joseph Smith then read the dedicatory prayer, which had been revealed to him. This prayer, recorded in section 109 of the Doctrine and Covenants, contains a petition that the Kirtland Temple "may be a house of prayer, a house of fasting, a house of faith, a house of learning, a house of glory, a house of order, a house of God. . . .

"That we may be found worthy, in thy sight, to secure a fulfilment of the promises which thou hast made unto us, thy people. . . .

"That thy glory may rest down upon thy people, and upon this thy house, which we now dedicate to thee, that it may be sanctified and consecrated to be holy, and that thy holy presence may be continually in this house;

"And that all people who shall enter upon the threshold of

the Lord's house may feel thy power, and feel constrained to acknowledge that thou hast sanctified it, and that it is thy house, a place of thy holiness." (D&C 109:8, 11-13.)

Following the dedicatory prayer, the choir sang a hymn written by William W. Phelps. This hymn proclaimed their experiences as they sang and shouted "with the armies of heaven":

> The Spirit of God like a fire is burning!
> The latter-day glory begins to come forth;
> The visions and blessings of old are returning;
> The angels are coming to visit the earth. . . .
>
> The Lord is extending the Saints' understanding—
> Restoring their judges and all as at first;
> The knowledge and power of God are expanding;
> The veil o'er the earth is beginning to burst. . . .
>
> We'll call in our solemn assemblies, in spirit,
> To spread forth the kingdom of heaven abroad,
> That we through our faith may begin to inherit
> The visions and blessings and glories of God. . . .
>
> How blessed the day when the lamb and the lion
> Shall lie down together without any ire;
> And Ephraim be crowned with his blessing in Zion,
> As Jesus descends with His chariot of fire!
>
> We'll sing and we'll shout with the armies of heaven—
> Hosanna, hosanna to God and the Lamb!
> Let glory to them in the highest be given,
> Henceforth and forever: amen and amen![3]

After the song, the quorums accepted the dedicatory prayer and the sacrament was passed to members of the Church. Then Joseph Smith, Don Carlos Smith, Oliver Cowdery, Frederick G. Williams, and David Whitmer bore their testimonies. After some remarks by Hyrum Smith and Sidney Rigdon and a short prayer by Sidney Rigdon, the congregation gave the Hosanna Shout, shouting three times, "Hosanna, hosanna, hosanna to God and the Lamb." Each series of hosannas ended with three amens. Brigham Young then arose and spoke briefly in tongues while

David W. Patten interpreted, and David W. Patten delivered a short exhortation in tongues. At about four o'clock, the Prophet concluded the seven-hour dedicatory service by blessing the congregation.

Spiritual Powers Are Manifested

Many participants in the dedicatory service reported a rich outpouring of spiritual manifestations. Benjamin Brown testified that "there the Spirit of the Lord, as on the day of Pentecost, was profusely poured out. . . . We had a most glorious and never-to-be-forgotten time. Angels were seen by numbers present."[4] Many mentioned hearing heavenly singing and others witnessed visions and appearances of heavenly beings. Eliza R. Snow testified that a babe in arms participated in the Hosanna Shout. Summarizing this extraordinary event, she said, "As marvelous as that incident may appear to many, it is not more so than other occurrences on that occasion."[5] It was reported that hundreds spoke in tongues, prophesied, or saw visions. A heavenly messenger, identified by Joseph Smith as Peter, the ancient apostle,[6] was seen entering the temple and sat near Frederick G. Williams and Joseph Smith Sr. Heber C. Kimball described him as being tall, with "black eyes, white hair, and stoop shouldered; his garment was whole, extending to near his ankles; on his feet he had sandals. He was sent as a messenger to accept of the dedication."[7]

This day, comparable to the biblical day of Pentecost, was a glorious and memorable day. Eliza R. Snow recorded: "The ceremonies of that dedication may be rehearsed, but no mortal language can describe the heavenly manifestations of that memorable day. Angels appeared to some, while a sense of divine presence was realized by all present, and each heart was filled with "joy inexpressible and full of glory."[8]

Indelible impressions were made even upon children. Sylvia Cutler Webb said,

One of my earliest recollections was the dedication of the Temple. My father took us up on his lap and told us why we were going and what it meant to dedicate a house to God. And although so very young at that time, I clearly remember the occasion. I can look back through the lapse of years and see as I saw then Joseph the Prophet, standing with his hands raised towards heaven, his face ashy pale, the tears running down his cheeks as he spoke on that memorable day. Almost all seemed to be in tears. The house was so crowded the children were mostly sitting on older people's laps; my sister sat on father's, I on my mother's lap. I can even remember the dresses we wore. My mind was too young at that time to grasp the full significance of it all, but as time passed it dawned more and more upon me, and I am very grateful that I was privileged to be there.[9]

That evening, in a priesthood meeting in the temple, additional manifestations were given. George A. Smith describes them: "There were great manifestations of power, such as speaking in tongues, seeing visions, administration of angels. Many individuals bore testimony that they saw angels, and David Whitmer bore testimony that he saw three angels passing up the south aisle, and there came a shock on the house like the sound of a mighty rushing wind, and almost every man in the house arose, and hundreds of them were speaking in tongues, prophecying or declaring visions, almost with one voice."[10]

Joseph Smith also described the evening meeting: "All the congregation simultaneously arose, being moved upon by an invisible power; many began to speak in tongues and prophesy; others saw glorious visions; and I beheld the Temple was filled with angels, which fact I declared to the congregation. The people of the neighborhood came running together (hearing an unusual sound within, and seeing a bright light like a pillar of fire resting upon the Temple), and were astonished at what was taking place."[11]

Angels also were seen outside the temple, and heavenly singing was heard coming from the roof. Oliver Cowdery testified: "The Spirit was poured out—I saw the glory of God, like a great cloud, come down and rest upon the house, and fill the same like a mighty rushing wind. I also saw cloven tongues, like as of fire rest upon many, (for there were 316 present), while they spake with other tongues and prophesied."[12]

On the day of dedication, the Lord rewarded his valiant people for building the Kirtland Temple so that "the Son of Man might have a place to manifest himself to his people." (D&C 109:5.) When the Lord told the Church to move to "the Ohio," he promised that they would be given "a blessing such as is not known among the children of men." (D&C 39:15.) Numerous accounts attest that the divine promise was fulfilled, and unparalleled spiritual manifestations were the rewards.

Christ Appears and Accepts the Temple

Possibly no other manifestation was as welcome and rewarding as the appearance of Christ when he accepted the temple during a meeting there on Sunday, April 3, 1836, one week after the dedication. The Prophet wrote:

> In the afternoon, I assisted the other Presidents in distributing the Lord's Supper to the Church, receiving it from the Twelve, whose privilege it was to officiate at the sacred desk this day. After having performed this service to my brethren, I retired to the pulpit, the veils being dropped, and bowed myself, with Oliver Cowdery, in solemn and silent prayer. After rising from prayer, the following vision was opened to both of us—
>
> The veil was taken from our minds, and the eyes of our understanding were opened.
>
> We saw the Lord standing upon the breastwork of the pulpit, before us; and under his feet was a paved work of pure gold, in color like amber.
>
> His eyes were as a flame of fire; the hair of his head was white like the pure snow; his countenance shone above the brightness of the sun; and his voice was as the sound of the rushing of great waters, even the voice of Jehovah, saying:
>
> I am the first and the last; I am he who liveth, I am he who was slain; I am your advocate with the Father.

Behold, your sins are forgiven you; you are clean before me; therefore, lift up your heads and rejoice.

Let the hearts of your brethren rejoice, and let the hearts of all my people rejoice, who have, with their might, built this house to my name.

For behold, I have accepted this house, and my name shall be here; and I will manifest myself to my people in mercy in this house.

Yea, I will appear unto my servants, and speak unto them with mine own voice, if my people will keep my commandments, and do not pollute this holy house.

Yea the hearts of thousands and tens of thousands shall greatly rejoice in consequence of the blessings which shall be poured out, and the endowment with which my servants have been endowed in this house.

And the fame of this house shall spread to foreign lands; and this is the beginning of the blessing which shall be poured out upon the heads of my people. Even so. Amen.[13]

This vision apparently took place in the Melchizedek Priesthood pulpits, at the second pulpit from the top on the west end of the main auditorium. What a confirmation to the Saints! The Savior himself accepted their efforts and promised that he would manifest himself to them in this temple.

An Endowment Is Bestowed

The sacred purposes for which the temple was built, however, were far more significant than the dedication ceremony or the many pentecostal experiences. The long-awaited endowment could now be bestowed upon individual members. In remarks to the Twelve Apostles, Joseph Smith taught that ordinances performed in the temple would "unite our hearts, that we may be one in feeling and sentiment, and that our faith may be strong, so that Satan cannot overthrow us, nor have any power over us here. . . . You need an endowment, brethren," he said, "in order that you may be prepared and able to overcome all things." He promised them that "all who are prepared, and are sufficiently pure to abide the presence of the Savior, will see Him in the solemn assembly."[14]

Before the Ascension in the meridian of time, the Savior asked his disciples to "tarry" in Jerusalem. In Kirtland, he likewise instructed his disciples: "I command you to tarry, even as mine apostles at Jerusalem." The Lord promised both the ancient disciples and the Kirtland Saints that they would be endowed "with power from on high." (Luke 24:49; D&C 95:8-9.)

The disciples in both time periods had similar missions: to establish the Church and "to go into all the world to preach [the] gospel." (D&C 38:32; see also Matthew 28:19.) Both groups established new dispensations while enduring opposition, persecution, and poverty. In both times, the Lord blessed them with an overwhelming pentecostal outpouring and endowments of power. As they began their sacred missions, divine manifestations strengthened their testimonies and gave them knowledge that the Lord supported them and directed his work.

The Lord designated the Kirtland Temple as the place where the Saints would receive further instructions and a temple endowment. John Whitmer, Church historian, wrote that "the first Elders were to receive their endowment at Kirtland, Ohio in the house of the Lord built in that stake."[15] For five years, the Saints had prepared to receive the special blessing. In meetings prior to the dedication of the temple, brethren learned more about the promised endowment, which early Church sources indicate consisted of several parts. One part was a gift of knowledge and instruction; another consisted of ordinances and ceremonies, such as washings and anointings. Those who received the endowment were also promised "power from on high." Although the endowment given in the Kirtland Temple was later referred to as "a portion," "introductory," and "preparatory" and was not the full endowment given later, it was of great importance.[16]

Joseph Smith emphasized the significance of the endowment in a charge to the Twelve: "Remember, you are not to go to other nations till you receive your endowments. Tarry at Kirtland until you are endowed with power from on high. You need a fountain of wisdom, knowledge and intelligence such as you never had. . . . He can give you that wisdom, that intelligence, and that power, which characterized the ancient saints and now characterizes the inhabitants of the upper world."[17]

He encouraged leaders to prepare for the endowment through a cleansing of both spirit and body. They were cautioned, "Strive to be prepared in your hearts, be faithful in all things. . . . Do not watch for iniquity in each other, if you do you will not get an endowment, for God will not bestow it on such."[18]

Although the temple was used for public meetings and schooling, we know, from reviewing the Prophet's instruction and from the many journals kept by others, that sacred ordinances relating to the endowment were also performed in private sessions. For example, on April 6, 1836, four hundred priesthood holders "met together in the House of the Lord to attend to further ordinances; none being permitted to enter but official members who had previously received their washings and annointings."[19]

Many journal accounts attest to washings, anointings, and endowments being received in the temple. Here are some typical references from the time:

Wilford Woodruff: "This winter [1836] and the following spring, in some respects, may be regarded as one of the most interesting periods of the history of the Church, when we consider the endowments and teachings given in the temple."[20]

Daniel Tyler: "I had the inestimable blessing of receiving my endowments in the temple at Kirtland."[21]

Newel Knight: "I . . . commenced labor on the temple . . . until it was finished, and ready for the endowments. . . . I then received my anointings."[22]

George A. Smith: "I passed through the ordinances of endowments and received much instruction and many manifestations of the spirit."[23]

Artemus Millet: "I was then ordained an Elder, and got my Endowments in the Temple and in 1836 went on a mission."[24]

Heber C. Kimball: "I . . . received my washings and anointings . . . and . . . all the blessings and ordinances of endowment which were then administered."[25]

At the Pentecost in Jerusalem, large numbers of the people witnessed appearances of the resurrected Christ, spoke in tongues, and saw "cloven tongues like as of fire." (Acts 2:3.) They had visions, participated in healings, and beheld wonders and signs. Then they were sent out to be witnesses throughout the earth. So it was in Kirtland: modern disciples took part in the same kinds of spiritual manifestations. The keys, or power and authority, of this dispensation had been committed into the hands of the priesthood leaders and holders; now, having received the endowment, they were empowered to take the gospel message into all the world.[26]

Temple Rules and Regulations

The Saints regarded the Kirtland Temple as a sacred edifice that deserved reverence and respect by all who entered. To ensure reverence and proper conduct, rules and regulations were drawn up, in order, Joseph Smith said, "that due respect may be paid to the order of worship."[27] The "Rules and Regulations to be Observed in the House of the Lord in Kirtland" included these:

> 1st. No man shall be interrupted who is appointed to speak by the Presidency of the Church, by any disorderly person or persons in the congregation, by whispering, by laughing, by talking, by menacing gestures, by getting up and running out in a disorderly manner, or by offering indignity to the manner of worship. . . .
>
> 2nd. An insult offered to the presiding Elder of said Church shall be considered an insult to the whole body. . . .
>
> 3rd. All persons are prohibited from going up the stairs in times of worship.
>
> 4th. All persons are prohibited from exploring the house, except waited upon by a person appointed for that purpose.
>
> 5th. All persons are prohibited from going into the

several pulpits, except the officers who are appointed to officiate in the same.

6th. All persons are prohibited from cutting, marking or marring the inside or outside of the house with a knife, pencil, or any other instrument whatever, under pain of such penalty as the law shall inflict.

7th. All children are prohibited from assembling in the house, above or below, or any part of it, to play, or for recreation, at any time: and all parents, guardians, or masters, shall be amenable for all damage that shall accrue in consequence of their children's misconduct.

8th. All persons, whether believers or unbelievers, shall be treated with due respect by the authorities of the Church.

9th. No imposition shall be practiced upon any members of the Church, by depriving them of their rights in the house.[28]

Meetings in the Temple

Once the temple was completed, it became the scene of many meetings. Records tell of meetings of the First Presidency, Council of the Twelve, bishop's councils, high councils, seventies' councils, and elders' councils being held in the temple. These many meetings prompted Caroline Crosby, who came to Kirtland in 1836, to comment: "I enjoyed myself well with sister Thankful Pratt. . . . The brethren attended meetings almost every evening, which left us tog[e]ther considerably. When they all left us, she would look about her and say, "well it is you and I again, Sister Crosby."[29]

Wilford Woodruff spoke about attending a meeting on December 20, 1836, in which the Third Quorum of Seventy was organized, and noted that every Tuesday evening through that winter, the three seventies quorums met, with about one hundred seventies present on each occasion.[30]

Joseph Smith recorded: "On Monday evenings the quorum of High Priests meet in the west room of the attic story, where they transact the business of their particular quorum. On Tuesday evenings the Seventies occupy the same room. On Wednesday evenings the rooms are occupied by the quorum of Elders.

. . . The Twelve, the High Council and other quorums, generally meet each week to transact business.[31]

On Sundays, meetings were held in the morning and afternoon, and sometimes special Sunday evening services were held in the temple. Fast and testimony meetings, held on the first Thursday of each month, began at ten o'clock in the morning and continued until four o'clock in the afternoon. Curtains divided the main floor of the temple into four compartments so small, simultaneous sessions could be held. Usually about three o'clock the curtains were raised, and all in attendance continued to worship together. In 1837, the Prophet's father presided over the fast and testimony meetings.

Music played an important role in the temple meetings with both congregational singing and choirs to perform special numbers. Caroline Barnes Crosby recalled: "The brethren had meetings of some kind almost every evening in the week. Besides singing schools in which all ages took a part, from the young adult to the old gray heads. Consequently we also took a part with them, and met two evenings in a week. The choir was large."[32]

On Monday, January 4, 1836, Joseph Smith wrote in his journal that he "met this evening at the Temple, to make arrangements for a singing school. After some discussion, a judicious arrangement was made, a committee of six was chosen to take charge of the singing department."[33]

An early journal describes congregational singing and the need for singing instruction:

Church music was taught at singing schools. No one ever thought of taking his song book to church. After the reading of the hymn the leader pitched the tune and started off. The congregation — all that could sing — would join in, some a note or two too high, others as much too low, and most of them a little behind the leader. Uncultivated people did not mind the discord, and the congregation dispersed feeling spiritually refreshed. They had heard a good sermon, taken part in the worship, and were ready for the week's labors, anticipating a good time next Sabbath in airing their musical talents.[34]

Christ's words, "the fame of this house shall spread" (D&C 110:10), were fulfilled as Saints and nonmembers alike came to realize the monumental accomplishment of the Church in building the Kirtland Temple and the spiritual significance of it. It became a rallying point for the Saints from far and near. Some came from Missouri, where they were facing great hardships of their own, making great sacrifices and enduring a very difficult journey in order to visit the temple, which had much the same significance as the temple of old in Jerusalem. Oliver B. Huntington's feelings as his company arrived in Kirtland and caught sight of the magnificent building express what so many felt:

"O, what joy again came over every one of us as we came in sight of the temple. The Lords House, Solemnly exclaimed every one, as we were trudging along in a confused flock. It makes me think of tribes going up to Jerusalem to worship, [as] anciently."[35]

All this was in fulfillment of the earnest entreaty of the Prophet Joseph Smith as he offered the prayer of dedication for the temple:

"O hear us, O Lord! And answer these petitions, and accept the dedication of this house unto thee, the work of our hands, which we have built unto thy name; and also this church, to put upon it thy name. And help us by the power of thy Spirit, that we may mingle our voices with those bright, shining seraphs around thy throne, with acclamations of praise, singing Hosanna to God and the Lamb!" (D&C 109:78-79.)

18

THE KIRTLAND SAFETY SOCIETY BANK

"It seemed as though all the powers of earth and hell were combining their influence . . . to overthrow the Church at once." (Joseph Smith.)

Near the end of the Kirtland period, Joseph Smith and other Church leaders founded the Kirtland Safety Society Bank, which sold its first stock in October 1836. One year later, in November 1837, the bank closed. Some two hundred shareholders who had bought stock in the bank suffered losses, as did merchants, farmers and others in the community who had accepted the printed bank notes.

Placing in perspective the events that led to the bank's failure, it becomes evident that Joseph Smith had no control over those factors. The records show that he struggled to maintain his integrity throughout this difficult episode. Enemies of the Church used the bank in their efforts to force the Church out of Kirtland, destroying confidence in the bank and causing a run on its currency. Supposed friends and trusted associates fell to the temptations of overnight wealth and turned against the Prophet. Also, the bank was unfortunately spawned during a period of runaway inflation nationwide, which resulted in economic collapse and numerous bank failures.

Founding a bank in Kirtland in 1836 was a logical business decision. Other communities in the area, such as Ashtabula, Warren, and Ravenna, while not as large as Kirtland, had banks. A successful Church bank in Kirtland, it was believed, would encourage community development, keep money in the area, contribute to friendlier community relationships, and make funds more readily available than banks in other communities and/or nearby states.

Extreme financial needs and pressures also contributed toward the decision. In 1837 the Church's debt probably exceeded fifty thousand dollars. Sidney Rigdon estimated that thirteen thousand dollars were still owed for temple debts; six thousand dollars for aid to Missouri members; and an unspecified amount for the purchase of land.[1] Recent research indicates that the land-acquisition debt was perhaps as much as forty-six thousand dollars.[2] In April 1837 Joseph Smith wrote about the financial pressure:

> There are many causes of embarrassment, of a pecuniary nature now pressing upon the heads of the Church. They began poor; were needy, destitute, and were truly afflicted by their enemies; yet the Lord commanded them to go forth and preach the Gospel, to sacrifice their time, their talents, their good name, and jeopardize their lives; and in addition to this, they were to build a house for the Lord, and prepare for the gathering of the Saints. Thus it is easy to see this must [have] involved them [in financial difficulties]. They had no temporal means in the beginning commensurate with such an undertaking; but this work must be done; this place [Kirtland] had to be built up. Large contracts have been entered into for lands on all sides, where our enemies have signed away their rights. We are indebted to them.[3]

In a letter to the Church that year, the bishopric reviewed the financial plight, discussed the "heavy burden" placed upon the Kirtland Saints "in order that the foundation of the kingdom of God might be laid," and pointed out that when the Saints had no more money to contribute, they were forced to resort to borrowing money and pledging property. The letter referred to the financial "embarrassments of the stake of Kirtland" and paid tribute to Saints who borrowed money and "have thus exposed themselves to financial ruin in order that the work of the gathering might not fail."[4]

Following is an overview of key events in the Kirtland Safety Society Bank from its inception until its closure.

July-August 1836: Engraving sources are investigated.
On July 25, 1836, Joseph Smith and his brother Hyrum, Oliver Cowdery, and Sidney Rigdon went to New York and Boston to investigate sources for plates and dies for printing bank notes. They arrived in New York City on July 31 and remained there for three days.

October 1836: A safe is purchased.
In mid-October, Joseph Smith purchased an iron safe, apparently for the bank. The safe, measuring 25"x24"x29", had wheels attached to the bottom. It is now owned by the Western Reserve Historical Society.

October 18, 1836: Stock shares are sold.
Sidney Rigdon made the first stock purchase in the bank on this date, paying twelve dollars as an installment on two thousand shares of stock.[5] The stock ledger shows that most stock was purchased in installments. Bank officers requested payment in gold or silver. In all, two hundred people invested, with an average investment of twelve dollars (which represented about one-week's income in 1840). About twenty thousand dollars was invested in the bank.[6]

November 2, 1836: Articles of agreement are drawn up.
Articles of agreement were drawn for a banking institution, to be called the Kirtland Safety Society.[7] The purpose of the bank was "for the promotion of our temporal interests, and for the better management of our different occupations, which consist in agriculture, mechanical arts, and merchandising."[8] Sidney Rigdon was elected president and Joseph Smith, cashier.

November 1836: Oliver Cowdery goes to Philadelphia.
Shortly after the November 2 meeting, Oliver Cowdery went to Philadelphia to procure dies and plates for bank bills. He chose an engraving firm called Underwood, Bald, Spencer and

Huffy. The Prophet Joseph Smith said that he "succeeded at a great expense in procuring the plates and bringing them to Kirtland."[9] He returned about January 1 with printing plates and a supply of freshly printed bills. The name The Kirtland Safety Society Bank appeared on the notes because it was assumed that the state of Ohio would grant a charter.

December 1836: Petition for charter.
In early December, Orson Hyde went to Columbus, the Ohio state capital, with a petition for the legislature for an act of incorporation. "But because we were 'Mormons,' " he reported, "the legislature raised some frivolous excuse on which they refused to grant us those banking privileges."[10]

January 2, 1837: Anti-banking company is formed.
Since the Church assumed that the state would grant the bank charter, plates had been engraved, money had been printed with the bank's name, and about 60 percent of the stock had been sold. The bank officers called a meeting on January 2 to decide on a new course. Two-thirds of the members present annulled the old articles of agreement, new articles were drawn up, and a new name was adopted: Kirtland Safety Society Anti-Banking Company.

Although forming a bank without a state charter may seem unusual to one today, it was not at all unusual in 1837. Accounts in newspapers in 1837 indicate that such institutions, often called "anti-banks," were operating not only in Ohio but also in surrounding states, including Michigan and Pennsylvania, and anti-bank conventions were held in counties near Kirtland.

With the name changed, the firm felt it could operate without a charter, as similar institutions were operating in Ohio in the 1830s. Even as late as 1843, a state auditor's report showed that nine concerns were operating without charters. In reviewing the banking industry in Ohio in the 1830s, one author concluded that "commercial firms were encouraged to conduct banklike business, even without state bank charters, by Whigs and people in the soft-money wing of the Democratic Party. Uniform opposition to these quasi banks did not appear until after most banking establishments in Ohio encountered serious financial problems as a result of the economic turmoil that began in 1837."[11]

Despite choosing to operate without a charter, the Kirtland bank ran a legal risk. An 1816 Ohio law prohibited bank operations except for those duly incorporated by the legislature and imposed a thousand-dollar penalty on all persons with interest in such a bank. Attorneys, however, counseled Joseph Smith and other officers that the 1816 law had been implicitly repealed by the Ohio state legislature in 1824.[12] Political groups and even newspapers publicly proclaimed that the 1816 law was invalid. One newspaper declared that the statute "has long since become obsolete and inoperative."[13]

January 4, 1837: First bills reprinted.

The earliest date appearing on the Kirtland Safety Society Bank notes is January 4, 1837. On the notes, where possible, the word "Bank" was changed to "Anti-Banking Co." In the first few days of operation, bills in one, two, and three dollar denominations were issued,[14] but the three dollar bill was the only one on which the phrase "Anti-Banking Co." was successfully stamped.

January 6, 1837: The bank opens under new name.

Four days after the Anti-Banking Company was formed, the bank opened for trading. On this day Wilford Woodruff wrote in his diary:

> I visited the office of the Kirtland Safety Society & saw the first money that was issued by the Treasurer or Society[.] It was given to Brother Bump (in exchange for other notes) who was the first to Circulate it[.] I also he[a]rd President Joseph Smith jr. declare . . . that if we would give heed to the commandments the Lord had given this morning all would be well. May the Lord bless Brother Joseph with all the Saints & support the above named institution & Protect it so that every weap[o]n formed against it may be [broken] & come to nought while the Kirtland

Safety Society shall become the greatest of all institutions on EARTH.[15]

Holders of the bank bills, however, experienced difficulty circulating them, even in the first two weeks. One contemporary historical record reported:

> Mr. D. B. Hart, of Mentor, informs us that he received the first Mormon bill that was placed in circulation by this bank. He happened to be in Kirtland the Saturday evening preceding the Monday morning on which the bank was first opened for business, and, having a debt against some of the chief Mormon worthies, was, upon requesting payment, [preferred] one of the new Mormon ten-dollar bankbills. He received it, but the next Monday morning, finding it impossible to use it for any legitimate commercial ends, he presented it to the officers of the bank, demanding its redemption in something which should pass for a legal tender among his neighbors. They were very reluctant to oblige him, and, in fact, refused to do so until he threatened them with the law, when some one, not an officer of the bank, stepped up to him and [preferred] him a genuine ten-dollar bill in exchange for his spurious one.[16]

A chain reaction began in which bills of the bank were discounted—and as soon as noteholders had trouble redeeming the discounted bills, the bills became even more heavily discounted.

January 21, 1837: Payments in specie are suspended.

Just two weeks after the bank opened for trading, the officers decided to suspend all payments in specie (gold, silver, or bills or notes from other institutions). One reason for this decision was described by Warren Cowdery in a report in the *Messenger and Advocate:*

> Enemies . . . were willing to receive the bills, come and demand the specie on them, and when the notes become due that were given for bills at the bank, avail themselves of that clause of the statute which we have quoted to avoid

payment, still the officers of the bank continued to redeem their paper when presented. Previously to the commencement of discounting by the bank, large debts had been contracted for merchandize in New York and other cities, and large contracts entered into for real estate in this town, and adjoining towns, some of them had fallen due and must be met or incur forfeitures of large sums. — These causes, we are bound to believe, operated to induce the officers of the bank to let out larger sums than their better judgements dictated, which almost invariably fell into, or passed through the hands of those who sought our ruin. . . . Hundreds who were enemies, either came or sent their agents and demanded specie till the officers thought best to refuse payment. This fact was soon rumored abroad as upon the wings of the wind; some returned their bills with curses, and some with entreaties for their redemption according to the character, temper and disposition of the holders. Some contended that the bank was down and refused to take its paper, others contended that it was yet good or would soon be made good, and continued to use it and buy land and all kinds of property with it. Holders of the bills from abroad came and purchased property of people, in this place and paid in bills of our own bank, while others residing here were actively engaged in recommending the paper, and purchasing property abroad. Speculators and others continued to trade in the bills without any fixed marketable value, sometimes at one rate of discount and sometimes at another, till there was no reasonable hope that it would ever be all returned to the bank.[17]

Newspaper reports also warned the community that it was unlawful to trade the notes and that those trading them could be heavily fined. With heavy demand for specie payment for the bank notes, the bank's liquid reserves were wiped out. Although the estimated reserves were about fifteen thousand dollars, which should have been sufficient, there was a run on the bank,[18] resulting in the suspension of the specie payments. On January 24, three days after the suspension, Wilford Woodruff recorded: "We [were] threatened by a mob from Pa[i]nesville to visit us that night & demolish our Bank & take our property but they did not [appear] but the wrath of our enemies appears to be kindled against us . . . may the Lord show us mercy & deliver us from the hand of our enemies for Christ sake."[19]

Antagonism against the Church increased when merchants, farmers, and others in the community holding notes couldn't redeem them. However, still hoping to turn the situation around, Joseph Smith and other Church leaders asked members of the Church to buy stock in the bank. In the January *Messenger and Advocate* the Prophet said, "We invite the brethren from abroad, to call on us, and take stock in our Safety Society."[20]

February 10, 1837: Second charter application.

Still hoping to salvage the bank operation, Church leaders decided to apply again for a charter from the Ohio legislature. In this application, they requested that capital stock be reduced from the previous million-dollar proposal to only $300,000.[21] Though five influential non-Mormons supported this second application, it was rejected. Had a new charter been granted by the legislature, it would have accomplished at least two major purposes: it would have helped instill confidence in the bank notes, and it would have helped Joseph Smith and the Church avoid further legal problems.

February 1837: Lawsuits against leaders begin.

February 1837 marked the beginning of numerous lawsuits, arrests, and court appearances that lasted until Joseph Smith left Kirtland. Samuel D. Rounds, who filed the first lawsuits, was apparently acting in behalf of Grandison Newell, a wealthy Kirtland businessman and opponent of Joseph Smith and the Church. The first lawsuit filed by Rounds charged the bank officers with violating the 1816 Ohio statute, which prohibited banking except by authorized corporations. From February through July 1837, Joseph Smith was arrested six times and repeatedly appeared in court. Lawsuits against other bank officers ensued but eventually were dismissed except those against the chief officers of the bank, Sidney Rigdon and Joseph Smith.

May 1837: Nationwide banking panic.

A banking panic occurred not only in Kirtland but throughout the country in the spring of 1837, resulting in the collapse of many banks. Most banks in the country suspended payments in specie, just as the Kirtland Safety Society Bank did. Specie payments were suspended first by New York banks on May 10; northern city banks followed on May 11, and Ohio banks on May 17.[22] Dale W. Adams, in researching bank failures, concluded that "a number of the banks in Ohio and virtually all of the banks in Michigan failed in the late 1830s."[23]

Historian Samuel Eliot Morrison summarized the situation: "[Martin] Van Buren was no sooner seated in the White House than American mercantile houses and banks began to fail, and there were riots in New York over the high cost of flour. In May [1837], after almost every bank in the country had suspended specie payments, and the government had lost $9 million through the collapse of pet banks, the President summoned Congress for a special session. In the meantime, there was widespread suffering."[24]

Church leaders did all they could to help those who suffered because of the bank failure. Jonathan Crosby recalled:

> In the spring [1837] I went to work on a house for the Prophet Smith, there was several hands at work on the same building, we took Kirtland money for pay, but it would not pass only for a short time, and hard times came on, provisions high and the money would not [buy] it and the workmen all left, but myself, they went off in the country to get work, but I stayed and helped to work until everything was gone and we had nothing to eat. I then spent a day running about trying to [buy] with Kirtland money, but could get nothing. [I] went home sorrowful [and] sat down with my wife. Now what shall we do? Well, I said, in the morning I will go tell Sister Emma . . . how it is with us, and we won't starve in one night. It was then night.
>
> Just at that time Pres. Joseph Young and Wm. Cahoon came in and learning our poverty offered to lend us some

[flour] and potatoes for supper and breakfast. It was very thankfully received. The next morning I went back to work with a resolution to tell Sister Emma of our poverty and see if she would let us have some provision; well I went to work and did not go in to see her, but in about 2 or 3 hours she came in and brought a nice ham of bacon, and said I do not know how you are off for provision, but you have stopped and worked, while the others are all gone therefore I thought I would make a present of a ham of bacon. I thanked [her] very much, and told her of our destitute situation, well she said, I will let you have some [flour]. . . . Then, at night a company of 5 or 6 of the brethren with myself went down the [Chagrin] river 2 or 3 miles a fishing gone all night, catched a nice lot of fish, so we lived well again.[25]

June 1837: Shareholders withdraw from bank.

Despite the setbacks in obtaining a state charter and in suspending specie payment, the Prophet hoped for the bank's rescue. He continued to encourage the Saints to invest in the bank, and twice in April he warned that the bank couldn't succeed unless they accepted bank notes. By June he and other officers concluded that the odds against the bank's succeeding were too great. On June 8, ten stockholders, including the Prophet, transferred their stock to Oliver Granger and Jared Carter and withdrew from the bank. Joseph wrote:

I resigned my office in the "Kirtland Safety Society," disposed of my interest therein, and withdrew from the institution; being fully aware, after so long an experiment, that no institution of the kind, established upon just and righteous principles for a blessing not only to the Church but the whole nation, would be suffered to continue its operations in such an age of darkness, speculation and wickedness. Almost all banks throughout the country, one after the other, have suspended specie payment, and gold and silver have risen in value in direct ratio with the depreciation of paper currency. The great pressure of the money market is felt in England as well as America, and bread stuffs are everywhere high.[26]

By June 20, twenty-nine shareholders withdrew from the bank and transferred their stock to the new officers.[27]

Joseph Smith suffered overwhelming financial losses and embarrassments from the bank's failure. He had personally borrowed money to keep the bank open, so when the bank closed, his financial losses were greater than those of most investors; in fact, he suffered more financial losses than all other investors except one. His personal investment in bank stock totaled $1360. He had also borrowed money, about $4250, from two banks. In early 1837, in an attempt to repay the loans, he sold $5100 worth of land within a three-month period of time.[28]

August 1837: Joseph warns against bank bills.

Warren Cowdery, editor of the Church newspaper, wrote about the Church's management of the bank after the Prophet resigned and indicated that the financial mistakes made by Church leaders were unintentional:

> Respecting the man[a]gement of our banking institution, much has been said, and various opinions and conjectures offered by friends and foes. We are not bankers, bank stock holders, or financiers. We believe that banking . . . is as much a regular science, trade or business, as those of law, physics. . . .
>
> We are not prepared in our feelings to censure any man, we wish to extend that charity to others, which under similar circumstances we should claim at their hands. . . . Permit us also further to remark, that it is no more consistent with our feelings and our wishes, than our duty, to say *who* under the then existing circumstances would have done any better. Other men under far more propitious circumstances . . . have failed. . . . It is easy to see, when the deed is done, the die cast and the time gone by, where there were errors. . . . They may have been errors of the head and not of the heart.[29]

After Joseph resigned from the bank, Frederick G. Williams was appointed president and Warren Parrish became cashier. Against the advice of Joseph, they issued more bills, which drove down the already low value of the original bills, further agitating the community. Though Parrish and other bank officers were accused of dishonesty, fraud, and counterfeit coin distribution, they proceeded to print more money. At that point, the Prophet himself issued a public caution in the Church newspaper that the bills were worthless:

> To the brethren and friends of the Church of the Latter-day Saints: I am disposed to say a word relative to the bills of the "Kirtland Safety Society Bank." I hereby warn them to beware of speculators, renegades, and gamblers, who are duping the unwary and unsuspecting, by palming upon them those bills, which are of no worth here. I discountenance and disapprove of any and all such practices. I know them to be detrimental to the best interests of society, as well as to the principles of religion. [Signed] Joseph Smith, Jun.[30]

Aware of spurious practices occurring in the bank itself, George A. Smith stated: "Warren Parrish was the teller of the bank, and a number of other men who apostatized were officers. They took out of its vault, unknown to the President or cashier, a hundred thousand dollars, and sent their agents around among the brethren to purchase their farms, wagons, cattle, horses and every thing they could get hold of. The brethren would gather up this money and put it into the bank, and those traitors would steal it and send it out to buy again, and they continued to do so until the plot was discovered and payment stopped."[31]

Joseph Smith, suspecting that Parrish was embezzling bank funds, went to Frederick G. Williams — who was, in addition to a counselor in the First Presidency, a justice of the peace — for a warrant to search Parrish's trunk. According to Lucy Mack Smith, the Prophet's mother, the request "was flatly refused. 'I insist upon a warrant,' said Joseph, 'for if you will give me one, I can get the money, and if you do not, I will break you of your office.' 'Well, break it is, then,' said Williams, 'and we will strike hands upon it.' 'Very well,' said Joseph, 'from henceforth I drop you from my quorum, in the name of the Lord.' "[32]

Many of those who were defrauding the bank later formed a secret group to depose Joseph.

October 1837: Joseph and Sidney go to trial.

Joseph Smith and Sidney Rigdon were tried by jury in October 1837 on the February lawsuit by Samuel D. Rounds for having violated the 1816 law that prohibited banking except by authorized corporations. Evidence indicates the lawsuit was initiated by influential enemies of the Church. The Prophet and Sidney Rigdon felt they had a substantial legal case; nevertheless, each was found guilty and fined one thousand dollars plus costs. Joseph and Sidney appealed the fine.

November 1837: The bank closes its doors.

Although the last entry in the bank's stock ledger was made on July 2, 1837, the bank did not formally close until November. The new officers did not want to risk additional lawsuits. As a result of the closure, many persons lost their investments and left the Church. It has been estimated that the total losses were a little over forty thousand dollars. The average loss, therefore, would have been about one hundred dollars to two hundred dollars, or about one-fourth to one-half of an individual's yearly income in 1837 Kirtland.[33] This was a considerable sum for families in Kirtland. Christopher Crary wrote, "The failure of the Kirtland Bank left them in destitute circumstances, and with very ill feelings with those who had placed their money in the bank. Many, not strong in the faith, seceded. Among them, some who were supposed to have joined the church out of speculative motives, hoping to make money out of the concern. The quarrel became quite serious, resulting in the burning of the printing office."[34]

One faithful Kirtland Mormon, Oliver Huntington, described his father's entrapment in a mortgage held by Jacob Bump: "One year had not rolled away and brother Bump had denied the faith and refused to lift the mortgage, and father could not pay, having bestowed all his surplus money upon the bank and the poor, so when the bank broke we were broken and as poor as the best of the Mormons; well, we expected to become poor but not quite so quick."[35]

Knowing that Joseph Smith's losses were great, the non-member community emphasized his financial difficulties and used them to discredit him and the Church, thus hurting the image of the Church not only in Kirtland but in surrounding communities as well.

Aftermath of the Bank Failure

In January 1838 the sheriff was about to arrest the Prophet and take him into custody. Luke Johnson, the local constable, learning of the sheriff's intention, immediately went to Joseph's home and arrested him on a fifty dollar charge for another judgment, explaining that he had done so in order to prevent Joseph's arrest on a more serious charge.[36] This was the Prophet's final arrest in Kirtland.

Realizing that it was unsafe for him to remain in Kirtland, Joseph prepared to leave the area. Hepzibah Richards wrote to her brother Willard, "The lives of the Presidents have been seriously threatened. We do not dare to have Cousin B[righam Young] return to this place."[37]

The Prophet would undoubtedly have suffered fewer losses and escaped the mounting abuse had he left earlier. And even after being forced to leave, he spent considerable effort, until his death, to repay notes and loans. The fact that he and other founders of the bank repaid the bulk of their debts, even when distant from Kirtland, points out their desire to maintain their integrity.

Before leaving Kirtland, Joseph appointed Oliver Granger to be his business agent and settle remaining debts. By October 1838, progress had been made. The Prophet wrote:

> As I have been accused of "running away, cheating my creditors,["] etc., I will insert one of the many cards and letters I have received from gentlemen who have had the

best opportunity of knowing my business transactions, and whose testimony comes unsolicited:

> *A Card.*
>
> Pain[e]sville, October 19, 1838.
>
> We, the undersigned, being personal acquaintances of Oliver Granger, firmly believe that the course which he has pursued in settling the claims, accounts, etc., against the former citizens of Kirtland township, has done much credit to himself, and all others that committed to him the care of adjusting their business with this community, which also furnishes evidence that there was no intention on their part of defrauding their creditors.
>
> [Signed] Thomas Griffith
>
> John S. Seymour.[38]

In a letter to Granger in 1841, the Prophet indicated concern for the "New York debts" for goods sold in the store and wrote, "I should be much pleased to hear that they were settled." By this time, the mortgage on the temple was paid off, which Joseph Smith acknowledged by adding, "I was very much gratified."[39]

Perhaps the best summary of the banking operation is made by the Prophet himself, just before his resignation from the bank: "It seemed as though all the powers of earth and hell were combining their influence in an especial manner to overthrow the Church at once, and make a final end. Other banking institutions refused the 'Kirtland Safety Society's' notes. The enemy abroad, and apostates in our midst, united in their schemes, flour and provisions were turned towards other markets, and many became disaffected toward me as though I were the sole cause of those very evils I was most strenuously striving against, and which were actually brought upon us by the brethren not giving heed to my counsel."[40]

In an overall perspective, the failure of the Kirtland Safety Society Bank was a refiner's fire for the Church. It was a test. No doubt sensing this dark time over a year earlier, Joseph Smith prophesied that "Satan's kingdom [will] be laid in ruins, with all his black designs; and the Saints will come forth like gold seven times tried in the fire, being made perfect through sufferings and temptations, and that the blessings of heaven and earth will be multiplied upon their heads."[41]

19

APOSTASY, PERSECUTION, AND MOBS

"A dreadful spirit reigns in . . . those who are opposed to this Church. . . . Their leading object seems to be to get all the property of the Church . . . and drive them out of the place." (Hepzibah Richards.)

In 1837-38, the final years of the Church in Kirtland, apostasy and persecution engulfed the Saints. Joseph Smith, in 1836, had prophesied of such severe trials: "Brethren, for some time Satan has not had power to tempt you. Some have thought that there would be no more temptation. But the opposite will come; and unless you draw near to the Lord you will be overcome and apostatize."[1]

At least three things hastened the end of the Church era in Kirtland. One was economic: members were not able to survive rampaging speculation, debt, unemployment, economic problems, and the failure of the bank. The second was an indomitable dark spirit that consumed many of the members and leaders, causing them to leave. The third, organized persecution and violent mob action, came from older residents of the community and from bitter members who apostatized from the Church or were excommunicated.

Economic Factors

An inflationary economy raged in Kirtland from 1830 to 1837 with land prices rising from $6.54 to $44.48 per acre.[2] The *Paines-*

ville Telegraph reported steep inflation and land speculation in 1836:

> For the last eight or ten days there has been rather an unusual degree of activity in buying and selling real estate at this place and Fairport. We are assured by gentlemen who have the means of knowing, that real estate to the amount of ONE HUNDRED AND FIFTY THOUSAND DOLLARS has been sold during the last ten days and at a steady advance in prices from day to day. We would mention one instance among many others, in evidence of the rise. A certain piece of property which sold four or five weeks since for $10,000 was sold last Monday for $20,000. The present proprietor has refused $25,000. A large number of other lots, some of which sold for ten dollars per foot two or three months since are now selling for from $50 to $75 per foot.[3]

In an editorial in the *Messenger and Advocate* in June 1837, Warren Cowdery wrote, "Real estate rose from one to eight hundred per cent[,] and in many cases more." He also referred to "every article of food rising nearly one hundred per cent" in one year.[4] Many of the Saints speculated on rising property values by signing notes, borrowing money, or by loaning money to people who later could not pay. Heber C. Kimball, returning from a mission in October 1836, noted:

> We were very much grieved . . . on our arrival in Kirtland, to see the spirit of speculation that was prevailing in the Church. Trade and traffic seemed to engross the time and attention of the Saints. When we left Kirtland [in May 1836] a city lot was worth about $150; but on our return, to our astonishment, the same lot was said to be worth from $500 to $1000, according to location; and some men, who, when I left, could hardly get food to eat, I found on my return to be men of supposed great wealth; in fact everything in the place seemed to be moving in great prosperity, and all seemed determined to become rich; in my feelings they were artificial or imaginary riches. This appearance of prosperity led many of the Saints to believe

that the time had arrived for the Lord to enrich them with the treasures of the earth, and believing so, it stimulated them to great exertions.[5]

Greed and the desire for riches led to individuals taking unfair advantage of others, resulting in misunderstanding and criticism. An article in the May 1837 issue of the *Messenger and Advocate* described some as "guilty of wild speculation and visionary dreams of wealth and worldly grandeur, as if gold and silver were their gods, and houses, farms and merchandize their only bliss or their passport to it."[6] Members from other areas who were preparing to move to Kirtland were also warned: "Beware of such as attack you as soon as you enter this place, and begin to interrogate you about the amount of money you have, and to importune you for it, with assurances that you shall have it refunded with interest, and that the Lord shall bless you abundantly; yea, and multiply blessings upon you. Of such we say beware. They take advantage of your honest simplicity, obtain your available means, and then desert you."[7]

As the economic problems multiplied, poverty prevailed. In her journal, Caroline Crosby tells of hard days her family had:

> We became very short of provisions, several times ate the last we had and knew not where the next meal was coming from. We then had an opportunity to try the charity of the brethren, who were many of them in the same predicament as ourselves. I recollect that Wm Cahoon called into see us one night, as he was going home with a few quarts of corn meal, and enquired if we had any breadstuff on hand, we told him we had not. He said he would divide what he had with us, and if my husband would go home with him, he would also divide his potatoes and meat which bore the same proportion to his meal. Joseph Young also divided with us several times in the same way, and we with him. We had numerous opportunities of dividing almost our last loaf with the brethren.[8]

While the members clamored for wealth in 1837-38, the Church needed additional financial resources. Loans for temple

211

construction were still outstanding, and money was needed to buy land, print books, support missionaries, assist the needy, including families of men who were away on missions, and finance other operations. Persecution, including property destruction and lawsuits, drained the Saints emotionally and financially. And the bank failure imposed even greater hardships and pressures.

Dark Spirit and Apostasy

A dark spirit seemed to immobilize the Church. Joseph Smith saw this spirit: "As the fruits of this spirit, evil surmisings, fault-finding, disunion, dissension, and apostasy followed in quick succession . . . it seemed as though all the powers of earth and hell were combining their influence in an especial manner to overthrow the Church at once, and make a final end. . . . No quorum in the Church was entirely exempt from the influence of those false spirits who are striving against me for the mastery; even some of the Twelve were so far lost to their high and responsible calling, as to begin to take sides, secretly, with the enemy."[9]

Eliza R. Snow wrote:

A spirit of speculation had crept into the hearts of some of the Twelve, and nearly, if not every quorum was more or less infected. Most of the Saints were poor, and now prosperity was dawning upon them—the Temple was completed, and in it they had been recipients of marvelous blessings, and many who had been humble and faithful to the performance of every duty—ready to go and come at every call of the Priesthood, were getting haughty in their spirits, and lifted up in the pride of their hearts. As the Saints drank in the love and spirit of the world, the Spirit of the Lord withdrew from their hearts, and they were filled with pride and hatred toward those who maintained their integrity. They linked themselves together in an opposing party—pretended that they constituted the Church, and claimed that the Temple belonged to them, and even attempted to hold it.[10]

Another diarist who described conditions in Kirtland was Mary Fielding, who wrote in the summer of 1837:

> I do thank my heavenly Father for the comfort and peace of mind I now enjoy in the midst of all the confusion and perplexity, and rageing of the devil against the work of God in this place. For altho here is a great number of faithful precious souls, yea the Salt of the Earth is here, yet it may be truely called a place where Satan has his seat. He is frequently [stirring] up some of the People to strife & [contention] and dissatisfaction with things they do not understand. . . . I pray God to have mercy upon us all and preserve us from the power of the great enemy who knows he has but a short time to work in. . . . I believe the voice of prayer has sounded in the House of the Lord some days from morning till night and it has been by these means that we have hitherto prevail[e]d and it is by this means only that I for one expect to prevail.[11]

Benjamin Johnson called this time in Kirtland "the first great apostasy" and regarded it as a test he had to pass. His sorrow and disappointment at leaders who failed the test is evident:

> Brethren who had borne the highest priesthood and who had for years labored, traveled, ministered and suffered together, and even placed their lives upon the same altar, now were governed by a feeling of hate and a spirit to accuse each other, and all for the love of *Accursed Mammon*. All their former companionship in the holy anointing in the Temple of the Lord, where filled with the Holy Ghost, the heavens were opened, and in view of the glories before them they had together shouted "Hosanna to God and the Lamb," all was now forgotten by many, who were like Judas, ready to sell or destroy the Prophet Joseph and his followers. And it almost seemed to me that the brightest stars in our firmament had fallen. Many to whom I had in the past most loved to listen, their voices seemed now the most discordant and hateful to me. From the Quorum of the Twelve fell four of the brightest: Wm. E. McLellin, Luke and Lyman Johnson and John Boyington; of the First Pres-

idency, F. G. Williams; the three Witnesses to the Book of Mormon, Oliver Cowdery, David Whitmer and Martin Harris. Of other very prominent elders were Sylvester Smith, Warren Cowdery, Warren Parrish, Joseph Coe and many others who apostatized or became enemies to the Prophet.

I was then nineteen years of age, and as I now look back through more than fifty years of subsequent experience, to that first great Apostasy, I regard it as the greatest sorrow, disappointment and test through which I have ever passed; the first real experience among false brethren, the greatest sorrow and test for the faithful. But with all my faults I did not forget the Lord nor His chosen servants. And in this day of great affliction and separation by apostasy, I felt to call mightily upon His name, that He would never leave me to follow these examples, but that He would keep me humble, even though in poverty and affliction, so only that I fail not.[12]

Approximately one-third of the leaders appear to have succumbed to apostasy, and they drew many others away with them. Some formed churches of their own. One group of about thirty, led by Warren Parrish, called themselves the "Parrish Party." Two men formed "The Independent Church" in Kirtland. George A. Smith described their organization: "Persons who had apostatized from the Latter-day Saints could be admitted into their party upon the terms of entering the room, shaking hands with every member and consecrating their property. This church lasted some two or three months, when a difficulty occurred between the President and the Bishop. The Bishop accused the President of being too familiar with his meat barrel; the President, in turn, accused the Bishop of being too intimate with his sheets. The result was, a split took place between the two chief authorities, and the organization ceased to exist."[13]

George A. Smith also described the direction taken by some other apostates: "One of the members of the first Presidency, some of the seven Presidents of the seventies, and a great many others were so darkened that they went astray in every direction.

They boasted of the talent at their command, and what they would do. Their plan was to take the doctrines of the Church, such as repentance, baptism for the remission of sins, throw aside the Book of Mormon, the Prophet and Priesthood, and go and unite the whole Christian world under these doctrines."[14]

Some who left the Church later sought to be reinstated. Luke Johnson, an apostle who left the Church in Kirtland and later rejoined it in Nauvoo, wrote: "Having partaken of the spirit of speculation, which at that time was possessed by many of the saints and Elders, my mind became darkened, and I was left to pursue my own course. I lost the spirit of God, and neglected my duty."[15] He told the Nauvoo Saints that his heart was with them and that he now wanted to "go with them into the wilderness, and continue with them to the end."[16]

Luke's brother, Lyman, who was the senior apostle, also apostatized in Kirtland. During a visit to Nauvoo, he visited Brigham Young and told him, "If I could believe 'Mormonism' as I did when I traveled with you and preached, if I possessed the world I would give it. I would give anything, I would suffer my right hand to be cut off, if I could believe it again. Then I was full of joy and gladness. My dreams were pleasant. When I awoke in the morning my spirit was cheerful. I was happy by day and by night, full of peace and joy and thanksgiving. But now it is darkness, pain, sorrow, misery in the extreme. I have never since seen a happy moment."[17] His life ended in tragedy, in a drowning.

Brigham Young recalled attending a meeting during this oppressive period when the Prophet was being criticized:

> I rose up, and in a plain and forcible manner told them that Joseph was a Prophet, and I knew it, and that they might rail and slander him as much as they pleased, they could not destroy the appointment of the Prophet of God, they could only destroy their own authority, cut the thread that bound them to the Prophet and to God and sink themselves to hell. Many were highly enraged at my decided opposition to their measures, and Jacob Bump (an old pugilist) was so exasperated that he could not be still. Some

215

of the brethren near him put their hands on him, and requested him to be quiet; but he writhed and twisted his arms and body saying, "How can I keep my hands off that man?" I told him if he thought it would give him any relief he might lay them on. . . .

This was a crisis when earth and hell seemed leagued to overthrow the Prophet and Church of God. The knees of many of the strongest men in the Church faltered. During this seige of darkness I stood close by Joseph, and, with all the wisdom and power God bestowed upon me, put forth my utmost energies to sustain the servant of God and unite the Quorums of the Church.[18]

At least two hundred to three hundred persons apostatized, representing a loss of 10 to 15 percent of the Kirtland membership. About one-third of the Church leaders were either excommunicated, disfellowshipped, or removed from their Church callings. Although almost half of the leaders later repented and returned, it took a heavy toll on the Church's administrative functioning. Heber C. Kimball described this sorrowful time: "A man's life was in danger the moment he spoke in defense of the Prophet of God. During this time I had many days of sorrow and mourning, for my heart sickened to see the awful extent that things were getting to. The only source of consolation I had, was in bending my knees continually before my Father in Heaven, and asking Him to sustain me and preserve me from falling into snares, and from betraying my brethren as others had done; for those who apostatized sought every means and opportunity to draw others after them. They also entered into combinations to obtain wealth by fraud and every means that was evil."[19]

In a January 1838 letter, John Smith, a counselor in the First Presidency, described the time as "a pruning": "I called the High Council together last week . . . and laid before them the case of the Dissenters; 28 persons were, upon mature discussion, cut off from the Church. The leaders are Cyrus Smalling, Joseph Coe, Martin Harris, Luke S. Johnson, John F. Boynton, and W. W. Parrish. We have cut off between forty and fifty of the

Church since you left. Thus you see the Church has taken a high and mighty pruning, and we think she will soon rise in the greatness of her strength."[20]

One leader who temporarily succumbed to the evil influence was Parley P. Pratt. He tells how evil forces overcame him during the summer of 1837:

> After I had returned from Canada, there were jarrings and discords in the Church at Kirtland, and many fell away and became enemies and apostates. . . . At one time, I also was overcome by the same spirit in a great measure, and it seemed as if the very powers of darkness which [were] against the Saints were let loose upon me. But the Lord knew my faith, my zeal, my integrity of purpose, and he gave me the victory.
>
> I went to Brother Joseph in tears, and, with a broken heart and contrite spirit, confessed wherein I had erred in spirit, murmured, or done or said amiss. He frankly forgave me, prayed for me and blessed me. Thus, by experience, I learned more fully to discern and to contrast the two spirits, and to resist the one and cleave to the other. And, being tempted in all points, even as others, I learned how to bear with, and excuse, and succor those who are tempted.[21]

When the evil spirit overtook Parley P. Pratt, he defamed the Church to his friend, John Taylor. This was particularly inconsistent, since he himself had converted John Taylor in Canada. Elder Taylor, who later became President of the Church, responded:

> I am surprised to hear you speak so, Brother Parley. Before you left Canada you bore a strong testimony to Joseph Smith being a Prophet of God, and to the truth of the work he has inaugurated; and you said you knew these things by revelation, and the gift of the Holy Ghost. You gave to me a strict charge to the effect that though you or an angel from heaven was to declare anything else I was not to believe it. Now Brother Parley, it is not man that I

am following, but the Lord. The principles you taught me led me to Him, and I now have the same testimony that you then rejoiced in. If the work was true six months ago, it is true today; if Joseph Smith was then a prophet, he is now a prophet.[22]

Kirtland was so engulfed by the malignancy that the Prophet realized his and other leaders' lives were in danger. His mother reported that he alerted the brethren that the insidious spirit might turn them against him to the point where they would seek to take his life: "But, brethren, beware; for I tell you in the name of the Lord, that there is an evil in this very congregation, which, if not repented of, will result in setting many of you, who are here this day, so much at enmity against me, that you will have a desire to take my life; and you even *would do it,* if God should permit the deed. . . . [T]urn from those principles of death and dishonesty which you are harboring in your bosoms, before it is eternally too late."[23]

Persecution Intensifies in Kirtland

Persecution of the Saints began intensifying in late 1837. Merchants stopped selling grain and other goods to them, mounting an economic boycott that strangled their ability to sustain themselves. Caroline Crosby wrote: "Times became very hard. . . . It seemed that our enemies were determined to drive us away if they could possibly, by starving us. None of the business men would employ a mormon scarcely, on any conditions. And our prophet was continually harassed with vexatious lawsuits. Besides the great [apostasy] in the church, added a [double] portion of distress and suffering to those who wished to abide in the faith, and keep the commandments."[24]

Mob action also escalated in 1837-38. Joseph Smith and Sidney Rigdon were set upon near Kirtland in August 1837 as they returned from their five-week mission to Canada. In a letter to her sister, Mary Fielding described the confrontation:

They were to come home in Dr [Sampson] Avards carrage and expected to arrive about 10 O clock at night but

218

to their great disappointment they were prevented in a most greavous manner. They had got within 4 miles of home after a very fatueging [fatiguing] journey . . . when they were surrounded with a Mob and taken back to Panesvill[e] and secured as was supposed in a Tavern where they intended to hold a mock trial. But to the disappointment of the wretches the Housekeeper was a Member of the Church who assisted our beloved Brethren in making their escape, but as J[oseph] S[mith] says not by a Basket let down through a Window, but by the Kitchen Door. . . .

The first step they took was to find the Woods as quick as possible where they thought they should be safe. But in order [to reach] thereto they had to lay down in a swamp or by an old log just w[h]ere they happened to be so determinately were they pursued by their mad enemy in every direction. Sometimes so closely that Br[other] J[oseph] was obliged to entreat Bro Rigdon, after his exertion in running, while lying by a log to breath[e] more softly if he meant to escape.

When they would run or walk they took each other by the hand and covenanted to live and die together. Owing to the darkness of the night their persuers had to carry lighted torches which was one means of the escape of our beloved suffers as they could see them in every direction while they were clim[b]ing over fences or travling through brush or corn fields untill about 12 O clock. When after traveling as they suppose in this manner 5 or 6 miles they found the road which led homeward and saw no more of their persuers. After traveling on foot along muddy slippery roads till near 3 in the morning they arrived safe at home. . . . I suppose all these things will only add another gem to their Crown.[25]

Some of the most impassioned persecutors were apostate Church members. Oliver Huntington, just fifteen years of age at the time, remembers apostate-inflicted persecution:

It was the life and glory of the apostates to hatch up vexatious lawsuits and strip the brethren of their property and means of removing. It seemed as though all power was given them to torment the saints. The real Mormons were designated by the appelation of Lick skillets, and every Lick skillet had to suffer; the princip[al] ones left were hunted like rab[b]its and foxes who sculk and hide in holes, and so did they. Numbers lay concealed in our house day after day, until their families could be got out of the place, one after another would come and go until we had served a variety with the best we had, and was glad of the privilege of showing favor to the righteous . . . and even the mummies were secreted there to keep them from being destroyed.[26]

Violence perpetrated by apostates even broke out in the temple. Oliver B. Huntington describes such fighting:

Many who turned away and denied the faith . . . became the most bitter enemies of the church, and used to try every means to make a disturbance among the brethren, every day of the week, Sundays not excepted. I remember one Sunday of seeing men jumping out of the windows, I ran to see what the fuss was, and found the apostates had tried to make a real muss, as they had frequently tried before, but on this occasion I saw a dagger, the door keeper held, that was wrenched from one of their hands whilst making his way to the stand. I heard the women scream and saw the men jump out of the windows, them that had chickens hearts, and I shall always remember the sensation that came over me.[27]

The Prophet's mother told of a similar occurrence in a Sunday service in the temple. Her husband, Joseph Smith Sr., in addressing the congregation, became critical of Warren Parrish, who earlier had been accused of issuing bank notes without authorization:

Parrish was highly incensed and made an attempt to drag him [Joseph Smith Sr.] out of the stand. My husband appealed to Oliver Cowdery, who was justice of the peace, to have him brought to order, but Oliver never moved from his seat. William, seeing the abuse which his father was receiving, sprang forward and caught Parrish, and carried him in his arms nearly out of the house. At this John Boynton stepped forward, and drawing a sword from his cane, presented it to William's breast, and said, "if you advance one step further, I will run you through." Before William had time to turn himself, several gathered around him, threatening to handle him severely, if he should lay the weight of his finger upon Parrish again. At this juncture of affairs, I left the house, not only terrified at the scene, but likewise sick at heart, to see that the apostasy of which Joseph had prophesied was so near at hand.[28]

Incredibly, the next day Father Smith and sixteen others were charged by the apostates and arrested for rioting in the temple. Eliza R. Snow, subpoenaed as a witness, wrote: "I found the court scene as amusing as the Temple scene was appalling. The idea of such a man as Father Smith—so patriarchal in appearance—so circumspect in deportment and dignified in his manners, being guilty of riot, was at once ludicrous and farcical to all sane-minded persons. And after the four Gentile lawyers (two for each party) had expended their stock of wit, the court dismissed the case with 'no cause for action,' and Father Smith and his associates came off triumphant."[29]

Lucy Mack Smith described clandestine meetings where many apostates congregated. David Whitmer, the Prophet's former confidant, was involved in these meetings and claimed "power to raise Joseph Smith to the highest heavens, or sink him down to the lowest hell." She recalled: "They made a standing appointment for meetings to be held every Thursday, by the pure church in the house of the Lord. They also circulated a paper in order to ascertain how many would follow them, and it was found that a large number of the Church were disaffected. In this spirit some went to Missouri and contaminated the minds of many of the brethren against Joseph, in order to destroy his influence. This made it more necessary than ever to keep a strict guard at the houses of those who were the chief objects of their vengeance."[30]

Hepzibah Richards wrote to her brother Willard in January 1838: "A large number have dissented from the body of the church and are very violent in their opposition to the Presiden[cy] and all who uphold them. They have organized a church and appointed a meeting in the [Kirtland Temple] next sabbath. Say they will have it, if it is by the shedding of blood. They have the keys already."[31]

The persecution climaxed shortly after midnight on January 16, 1838, when an arsonist set fire to the schoolhouse/printing office. The temple and other buildings, including the Methodist meetinghouse next to the temple, were reportedly scorched. The contents of the printing establishment burned, including many copies of the Book of Mormon. Caroline Crosby gave the following account:

> About the 15th of Jan., I was awakened one night near the middle of the night, by sister Sherwood calling to me and Jane, crying fire. I awoke and as I lay near the window I looked out, and beheld the ground as light as day, while the sky was as black as a thundercloud. A deep solemnity pervaded my mind, and a very strange sensation ran through my whole system. We arose immediately, and opened the door, and beheld the printing office all in flames, and men assembling from every direction in great haste. But they were all too late, they merely threw out a few books, and some of them were scorched. The sparks and shingles were carried to an immense distance. It was the nearest building to the temple but the wind was favorable in protecting it from the flames.[32]

About four months later an attempt was made to burn the temple when a bundle of straw with "a fire brand in it" was thrown through one of the windows.[33]

On one occasion, a constable entered a Mormon home, seized various household items, and then publicly auctioned off the goods. His excuse was that the articles belonged to Joseph Smith and were sold to liquidate debts. When Daniel Wood learned that this constable planned to confiscate his wagon, he took it apart, placed the pieces in the back of his sled, and then covered the parts with hay. The wagon parts, transported by sled out-of-town, were hidden until the wagon could be rebuilt without the constable's knowledge.

Hepzibah Richards wrote a letter about the hostility: "A dreadful spirit reigns in the breasts of those who are opposed to this Church. They are above law and beneath whatever is laudable. Their leading object seems to be to get all the property of the Church for little or nothing, and drive them out of the place. The house of our nearest neighbor has been entered by a mob and ransacked from the top to the bottom under pretense of finding goods which it is thought they had stolen themselves. An attempt has since been made to set the same house on fire while the family were sleeping in bed."[34]

20

THE PROPHET AT THE HELM

"If I obtain the glory which I have in view, I expect to wade through much tribulation." (Joseph Smith.)

The persecution and trials of 1837-38 jolted the Church. Orson F. Whitney, a grandson of Newel K. Whitney and Heber C. Kimball, described the Church at that time as "the good ship Zion, storm-tossed and tempest-driven, her sails rent, her timbers sprung, a portion of her officers and crew in open mutiny, . . . drifting with fearful rapidity toward the rocks and breakers of destruction."[1]

Joseph, facing the storm's fury, guided the Saints and intensified his efforts to unite the faithful. This period constituted one of his severest trials. Pursued by enemies, physically weakened by earlier mob-inflicted injuries, disappointed by friends and trusted companions who tried to overthrow him, disheartened over beloved leaders and Saints who forsook him and the Church, and wearied by lawsuits and the seeming success of his adversaries, he drew even closer to the Lord. As problems mounted, he wrote to the Church in Far West: "Brethren, we have waded through affliction and sorrow thus far for the will of God, that language is inadequate to describe. Pray ye therefore with more earnestness for our redemption."[2]

Despite the severe trials, he proceeded to do the work of God. During this time, he fulfilled a mission to Canada. And when the persecution and trials increased, he went to Far West, Missouri, to organize stakes, purchase land, hold conferences, lay out the town, and prepare to move the Church there. He also struggled to settle his affairs in Kirtland and to repay his debts. An 1838 letter to the Presidency of the Church in Kirtland indicates his intentions: "My business was so deranged that I was not able to leave it in so good a situation as I had anticipated; but if there are any wrongs, they shall all be noticed, so far as the Lord gives me ability and power to do so."[3]

The Prophet maintained his leadership even though some denounced him as fallen and many of his closest friends and associates turned against him. His knowledge of truth received from revelations and visions, combined with his companionship with the Spirit, gave him enough spiritual and temporal stamina to withstand the buffetings of Satan. He knew he couldn't avoid problems; in fact, he told the Saints in a sermon at the end of 1837, "If I obtain the glory which I have in view, I expect to wade through much tribulation."[4] With clarity of purpose and a vision of the future he left Kirtland, his home. But a prophet of God was still at the helm of the Church.

Joseph Smith's Ordeals and Leadership

George A. Smith said that Joseph Smith asked nothing of anyone that he would not be willing to do himself. In writing of Zion's Camp, he told how "most of the men" complained to Joseph of "sore toes, blistered feet . . . poor quality of bread . . . strong honey," and other problems, adding that "even a dog could not bark at some men without their murmuring at Joseph." But, he explained, "the Prophet Joseph took full share to the fatigues of the journey, in addition to the care of providing for the Camp and presiding over it. He walked most of the time and had a full share of blistered, bloody and sore feet, which was the natural result of walking twenty-five to forty miles a day in a hot season of the year. But, during the entire trip he never uttered a murmur or complaint . . . and many of us were careless[,] thoughtless, heedless, foolish or devilish, and yet we did not know it. Joseph had to bear with us and tutor us like children."[5]

Levi Hancock, a loyal member of the presidency of the First Quorum of Seventy, gave further insight into the Prophet's personal trials: "The Prophet Joseph was often in trouble. If his

friends gave him money, he [was] stripped of it all by his enemies. I know for I did all I could to hold up that good man. My
heart would ache for him. He had to stand against thousands
of his pretended friends seeking to overthrow him. It was terrible
the abuse he suffered."[6]

Joseph also had to endure petty criticism from Saints who
had their own ideas as to how a prophet should act or what he
should be. His cousin, George A. Smith, said that one reason
a certain family left the Church was "that they had actually seen
the Prophet come down out of the translating room and play
with his children."[7] And at the dedication of the Kirtland
Temple, he said, "when the dedication prayer was read by
Joseph, it was read from a printed copy. This was a great trial
of faith to many. 'How can it be that the prophet should read
a prayer?' What an awful trial it was, for the Prophet to read a
prayer!"[8]

Those who stood by and defended the Prophet often received abuse themselves. Levi Hancock said that Newel K. Whitney "was cursed by some when he did his best to hold up Joseph.
He would suffer himself to be slandered to save the Prophet
from trouble."[9]

Brigham Young was forced to leave Kirtland on December
22, 1837, because he defended and stood by the Prophet. The
Prophet Joseph Smith said that apostates "had threatened to
destroy [Brigham] because he would proclaim publicly and pri-
vately that he knew by the power of the Holy Ghost that I was
a Prophet of the Most High God, that I had not transgressed
and fallen as the apostates declared."[10]

William E. McLellin, a member of the Quorum of the Twelve
Apostles, became one of the embittered apostates. He had previously been very close to the Prophet, and at a conference in
October 1831 in Orange, Ohio, he had requested that the Prophet
seek a revelation for him so he could know "the will of the Lord"
concerning him. The revelation known as section 66 of the Doctrine and Covenants was given as a result of that request.
McLellin wrote: "General peace and harmony pervaded the conference and much instruction to me. From thence I went home

with Jos[eph] and lived with him about three weeks; and from my acquaintance then and until now I can truely say I believe him to be a man of God. A Prophet, a Seer and Revelator to the church of christ."[11]

After the Church left Kirtland, McLellin happened to meet Heber C. Kimball, with whom he had served in the Quorum of the Twelve and who had been a missionary companion. Elder Kimball's daughter, Helen Mar Whitney, wrote about their conversation at that unexpected meeting. McLellin asked, "Brother Heber, what do you think of Joseph Smith the fallen prophet now? Has he not led you blindfolded long enough; look and see yourself, poor, your family stripped and robbed and your brethren in the same fix, are you satisfied with Joseph?" Heber replied, "Yes, I am more satisfied with him, a hundred fold, than ever I was before, for I see you in the very position that he foretold you would be in; a Judas to betray your brethren, if you did not forsake your adultery, lying and abominations. Where are you and Hinkle and scores of others; have you not betrayed Joseph and his brethren into the hands of the mob, as Judas did Jesus? Yes, verily you have; I tell you Mormonism is true, and Joseph is a true prophet of the living God."[12]

Elder Kimball gained a deep, personal testimony of the Prophet's inspired leadership. Joseph Smith called him to go on a mission to England in June 1837, even though it might not have been a logical thing to do. Though it might seem that Joseph needed his strongest and most stalwart leaders and supporters close to him, he called two of the Twelve, Heber C. Kimball and Orson Hyde, as well as the soon-to-be apostle Willard Richards and other faithful brethren to go to England to establish the Church there. Within a year, when three of the missionaries returned to Kirtland, twenty-six branches were established and thirteen hundred persons baptized. The next year Elder Kimball returned to England on another mission, which produced forty-seven hundred converts.

The influx of converts more than made up for the loss of Kirtland Saints who left the Church. By 1851, there were more than forty-two thousand Church members and 642 congregations in England, and many thousands more had already immigrated to the United States. By 1856, the number of immigrants reached some twenty-four thousand.

Witnesses of Joseph's Divine Calling

Although some persons apostatized in Kirtland, most of the Saints remained stalwart and valiant, and many bore testimony to Joseph Smith's divine calling and his leadership through that difficult period.

Amasa Lyman, who walked seven hundred miles to join with the Saints, said that upon meeting the Prophet for the first time, "serenity and peace of heaven pervaded my soul, and the still small voice of the Spirit whispered its living testimony in the depths of my soul, where it has ever remained, that he was the man of God."[13]

Daniel Tyler recalled one particularly poignant experience:

I attended a meeting "on the flats," where "Joseph" presided. Entering the school-house a little before meeting opened, and gazing upon the man of God, I perceived sadness in his countenance and tears trickling down his cheeks. . . . A few moments later a hymn was sung and he opened the meeting by prayer. Instead, however, of facing the audience, he turned his back and bowed upon his knees, facing the wall. This I suppose, was done to hide his sorrow and tears.

I had heard men and women pray—especially the former—from the most ignorant, both as to letters and intellect, to the most learned and eloquent, but never until then had I heard a man address his Maker as though He was present listening as a kind father would listen to the sorrows of a dutiful child. Joseph was at that time unlearned, but that prayer, which was to a considerable extent in behalf of those who accused him of having gone astray and fallen into sin, that the Lord would forgive them and open their eyes that they might see aright—that prayer, I say, to my humble mind, partook of the learning and eloquence of heaven. There was no ostentation, no raising of the voice as by enthusiasm, but a plain conversational tone, as a man would address a present friend. It appeared to me as though, in case the [veil] were taken away, I could see the Lord standing facing His humblest of all servants I had ever seen. . . . It was the crowning, so to speak, of all the prayers I ever heard.[14]

Daniel McArthur, a workman in Kirtland, said, "To me he [Joseph] seemed to possess more power and force of character than any ordinary man. . . . My testimony is that he was a true Prophet of the living God, and the more I heard his sayings and saw his doings the more I was convinced that he had of a truth seen God the Father and His Son Jesus Christ, as also the holy angels of God. I cannot call to mind that I ever had a doubt enter my heart, since I first heard the gospel preached, which was in the spring of 1832, as to his being a true Prophet. It always seemed to me that if I ever did know anything on this earth I surely knew that he was a Prophet."[15]

When the Prophet lived for a short time on the Morley farm, Lucy Diantha Morley Allen had an opportunity to observe him closely. She declared: "In all that he did he was manly and almost godlike. . . . The only words that express his looks and actions are: 'Surely he was a man of God.' "[16]

Marinda Johnson associated with Joseph and Emma Smith daily when they lived in her parents' home for one year. She said: "During the whole year that Joseph was an inmate of my father's house I never saw aught in his daily life or conversation to make me doubt his divine mission."[17]

Eliza R. Snow, who taught children in Joseph and Emma's home in Kirtland, testified:

I had ample opportunity of judging of his daily walk and conversation, and the more I made his acquaintance, the more cause I found to appreciate him in his divine calling. His lips ever flowed with instruction and kindness; but, although very forgiving, indulgent and affectionate in his nature, when his godlike intuition suggested that the good of his brethren, or the interests of the kingdom of

God demanded it, no fear of censure, no love of appro-
bation, could prevent his severe and cutting rebukes.

His expansive mind grasped the great plan of salvation,
and solved the mystic problem of man's destiny; he was
in possession of keys that unlocked the past and the future,
with its successions of eternities; yet in his devotions he
was as humble as a little child. Three times a day he had
family worship; and these precious seasons of sacred
household service truly seemed a foretaste of celestial hap-
piness.[18]

Eliza's brother, Lorenzo Snow, investigated the Church for
about five years before joining:

I became perfectly acquainted with Joseph Smith the
Prophet, I sat at his table frequently, and had many con-
versations with him. . . . I listened to the teaching of the
Gospel and received these truths with an open heart. I was
determined not to rest there. I was exceedingly anxious to
know without doubt that Joseph Smith was a true
prophet. . . .

I heard the Prophet discourse upon the grandest of subjects. At times he was filled with the Holy Ghost, speaking
as with the voice of an archangel and filled with the power
of God, his whole person shone and his face was lightened
until it appeared as the whiteness of the driven
snow. . . . As soon as I became perfectly convinced and
satisfied in relation to truth of Mormonism[,] everything
that I had thought about in a religious way was changed;
every part of my system became convinced, through the
power of the Holy Ghost, that God is my Father, that Jesus
Christ is my elder Brother, and that Joseph Smith is His
Prophet.[19]

At the height of the Kirtland problems, when many were
apostatizing, Wilford Woodruff bore fervent testimony: "I say
such evidences presented in such a forcible manner ought to
drive into oblivion every particle of unbelief & dubiety from the
mind of the hearers, for such language[,] sentiment[,] principle[,] & spirit cannot flow from darkness. Joseph Smith jr is a

prophet of God r[a]ised up for the deliverance of Israel as true as my heart now burns within me while I am penning thes[e] lines which is as true as truth itself."[20]

Orson Pratt testified of personal knowledge of the Prophet's divine calling:

> I . . . became intimately acquainted with the Prophet Joseph Smith, and continued intimately acquainted with him until the day of his death. I had the great privilege . . . of boarding . . . at his house, so that I not only knew him as a public teacher, but as a private citizen, as a husband and father. I witnessed his earnest and humble devotions both morning and evening in his family. I heard the words of eternal life flowing from his mouth, nourishing, soothing, and comforting his family, neighbours, and friends. I saw his countenance lighted up as the inspiration of the Holy Ghost rested upon him, dictating the great and most precious revelations now printed for our guide. I saw him translating, by inspiration, the Old and New Testaments, and the inspired Book of Abraham from Egyptian papyrus. . . .
>
> I knew that he was a man of God. It was not a matter of opinion with me, for I received a testimony from the heavens concerning that matter.[21]

And finally, "Who can justly say aught against Joseph Smith?" asked Brigham Young. "I was as well acquainted with him, as any man. I do not believe that his father and mother knew him any better than I did. I do not think that a man lives on the earth that knew him any better than I did; and I am bold to say that, Jesus Christ excepted, no better man ever lived or does live upon this earth. I am his witness. . . . I feel like shouting hallelujah, all the time, when I think that I ever knew Joseph Smith, the Prophet whom the Lord raised up and ordained, and to whom He gave keys and power to build up the kingdom of God on earth."[22]

Joseph's Record and Accomplishments

Myriads of journals, letters, and other documents attest to the remarkable leadership of the Prophet Joseph Smith. Among his accomplishments while the Saints were in Kirtland are these:

• He received eighty-four revelations from God that contain clear instruction about major principles of the gospel. Many persons who were present when the revelations were received recorded their testimonies. In one case, at the Johnson home, ten men signed a document bearing testimony to all the world "that these commandments were given by inspiration of God."

• He witnessed, with others, at least eight visions or appearances of the Father and/or the Son. He presided over meetings where many people witnessed divine manifestations that remain unparalleled in our dispensation. He saw in vision, with his counselors, the pattern for the first latter-day temple. He and Oliver Cowdery received priesthood keys of authority from Moses, Elias, and Elijah.

• He organized, through revelation and vision, the Aaronic and Melchizedek priesthoods. He also provided through divine revelation a full organization for the Church, including such restored offices as twelve apostles and quorums of seventies.

• He gave the world additional scriptures, including an inspired translation of the Bible and new records of Moses and Abraham.

• He organized missionary work and set the example himself as a missionary. He also directed that the gospel be taken to many parts of the United States, Canada, and the British Isles.

• He directed the Saints in constructing such buildings as the Kirtland Temple and the schoolhouse/printing office.

• He established an economic order for the Church and its members.

• He established printing operations so that the gospel might be spread through periodicals and books, including the Book of Mormon and the Doctrine and Covenants.

• He suffered severe persecution, hardship, and personal trials. But though his own life was often in jeopardy, he continued to organize the Church, teach and comfort the Saints, and select and train leaders to ensure that the Church would continue.

21

THE CHURCH
LEAVES KIRTLAND

"We turned the key and locked the door
of our homes, leaving our property and
all we possessed in the hands of enemies
and strangers." (William F. Cahoon.)

As violence against the Saints and their leaders escalated, it was finally no longer safe for them to remain in Kirtland. The Prophet, whose life was in gravest danger, was "warned by the Spirit"[1] and decided to move immediately to Missouri. Masses of people followed, leaving behind them their cherished family possessions and comfortable homes. In the first seven months of 1838, more than sixteen hundred Latter-day Saints left the city and headed west, most to travel to Far West, Missouri. By 1839 only about one hundred Church members remained in Kirtland.

Lucy Mack Smith, the Prophet's mother, wrote of her son's final instructions to the brethren in Kirtland: "One evening, before finishing his preparations for the contemplated journey, he sat in council with the brethren at our house. After giving them directions as to what he desired them to do, while he was absent from them, and, as he was about leaving the room, he said, 'Well, brethren, I do not recollect anything more, but one thing, brethren, is certain, I shall see you again, let what will happen, for I have a promise of life five years, and they cannot kill me until that time is expired.' "[1]

The Prophet described the circumstances surrounding his departure:

A new year [1838] dawned upon the Church in Kirtland in all the bitterness of the spirit of apostate mobocracy; which continued to rage and grow hotter and hotter, until Elder Rigdon and myself were obliged to flee from its deadly influence, as did the Apostles and Prophets of old, and as Jesus said, "when they persecute you in one city, flee to another."

On the evening of the 12th of January, about ten o'clock, we left Kirtland, on horseback, to escape mob violence, which was about to burst upon us under the color of legal process to cover the hellish designs of our enemies, and to save themselves from the just judgment of the law.

We continued our travels during the night, and at eight o'clock on the morning of the 13th, arrived among the brethren in Norton Township, Medina county, Ohio, a distance of sixty miles from Kirtland. Here we tarried about thirty-six hours, when our families arrived; and on the 16th we pursued our journey with our families, in covered wagons towards the city of Far West, in Missouri. . . .

The weather was extremely cold, we were obliged to secrete ourselves in our wagons, sometimes, to elude the grasp of our pursuers, who continued their pursuit of us more than two hundred miles from Kirtland, armed with pistols and guns, seeking our lives. They frequently crossed our track, twice they were in the houses where we stopped, once we tarried all night in the same house with them, with only a partition between us and them; and heard their oaths and imprecations, and threats concerning us, if they could catch us; and late in the evening they came into our room and examined us, but decided we were not the men. At other times we passed them in the streets, and gazed upon them, and they on us, but they knew us not.[2]

The Exodus: Persecution Persists

After Joseph left for Missouri, persecution of those close to him in Kirtland increased. A "vexatious" writ was filed by John C. White against Joseph Smith Sr. for "his manner of solemnizing marriages." Luke Johnson, a local constable and a former member of the Twelve, was sympathetic to the Prophet's father. He recalled:

> I begged the priv[i]llege of serving the writ, and arrested the old gentleman [Joseph Smith Sr.], and took him to the magistrate's office. The court not being ready to attend to the case, I put him in a small room adjoining the entrance from the office. I also allowed his son Hyrum to accompany him. I took a nail out from over the window sash, left the room and locked the door, and commenced telling stories in the court room, to raise a laugh, for I was afraid they would hear father Smith getting out of the window; when the court called for the prisoner, I stepped into the room in the dark and slipped the nail into its place in the window, and went back and told the court that the prisoner had made his escape. White and others rushed into the room, and examined the fastenings and found them all secure, which created much surprise how the prisoner had got out.[3]

Eliza R. Snow recalled that "the constable, who manifested the greatest astonishment of all present, finally settled the question by saying, 'It is another Mormon miracle.' "[4]

Most families with sufficient means and equipment escaped the threatening mobs — though not without a great deal of fear and trepidation. Hepzibah Richards wrote in January 1838, "We feel we are in jeopardy every hour."[5] Two months later she wrote, "We suffer from fear, but we hope these days of suffering will not always last."[6]

Luman Shurtliff found Kirtland in early 1838 to be "a hell to all Saints," with fires "laid by the dozens in the basements, windows of the Saints." In their effort to cause the Saints to leave Kirtland, Luman wrote, "the apostates and mobocrats had control of the law in Kirtland, and many of our good Saints were accused of crimes and thefts that they never committed, were tried and convicted and had to pay a big sum of money or get out of town."[7]

Many Latter-day Saints simply abandoned homes and property as they fled Kirtland. William F. Cahoon wrote of his anguish: "I left a good house & rooms in it well finished & furnished of my own," he wrote, "and also a good lot all paid for, which I had labored hard to get. I could not dispose of it, so I turned the key & locked the door and left it & from that day to this I have not received anything for my property. It is now in the hands of strangers, however we left it, and went on our journey to Missouri."[8]

Typical of Saints who faced the uncertainties of the exodus from Kirtland with little or no money or means was Truman O. Angell, the skilled temple carpenter. He and his wife and two small children left in a one-horse wagon. Their first day out of Kirtland, he had to spend his last money to repair the wagon, leaving him with "a rickety wagon, a balky horse, not a penny in my pocket, a family to feed and a thousand miles to go."[9]

Lucy Mack Smith, the Prophet's mother, described her family's experience:

> Sometimes we lay in our tents, through driving storms; at other times we were traveling on foot through marshes and quagmires. Once in particular, we lay all night exposed to the rain, which fell in torrents, so that when I arose in the morning, I found that my clothing was perfectly saturated with the rain. However, I could not mend the matter by a change of dress, for the rain was still falling rapidly, and I wore my clothes in this situation, three days; in consequence of which I took a severe cold, so that when we arrived at the Mississippi river, I was unable to walk or sit up. After crossing this river, we stopped at a hut, a most unlovely place, yet the best shelter we could find. This hut was the birth-place of Catharine's son Alvin. The next day my husband succeeded in getting a comfortable place, about four miles distant, for Catharine and her infant, and they were carried thither on a lumber wagon, the same day.[10]

Kirtland Camp

One effort to see that the Saints traveled to Missouri in safety was the organization of "Kirtland Camp," which was initiated by the seventies. Elias Smith, seventies quorum clerk and historian, described a meeting of the quorum in the temple on March 10, 1838:

> The Spirit of the Lord came down in mighty power, and some of the Elders began to prophesy that if the quorum would go up in a body together, and go according to the commandments and revelations of God, pitching their tents by the way, that they should not want for anything on the journey that would be necessary for them to have; and further that there should be nothing wanting towards removing the whole quorum of Seventies that would go in a body, but that there should be a sufficiency of all things for carrying such an expedition into effect.[11]

James Foster, a president of the quorum, saw in vision a company of about five hundred persons, "moving in order, encamping in order by the way."[12]

Zerah Pulsipher also testified of divine direction to the brethren: "One evening, while we were in the attic story of the Lord's House, and while Joseph Young, I think, was at prayer, I saw a Heavenly messenger, who appeared to be a very tall man dressed in a white robe from head to foot. He cast his eyes on me and on the rest of the Council and said, 'Be one, and you shall have enough,' and soon after the way was opened before us, so that we received money and means for clothing for the poor and to prepare for our removal. James Foster and Jonathan Dunham also saw the angel at the same time I did."[13]

Benjamin Johnson described the company, which had originally been organized to assist needy members of the seventies in their journey to Missouri, as the "Kirtland Poor Camp." "The wealthy had apostatized," he said, "and those who had means enough got an early start; while the poor, by all journeying together could make an outfit and travel with much less expense."[14] Those who could not afford to contribute toward the expenses were told they could pay later. As Zerah Pulsipher said, 'We could not neglect them for all there was against them was that they were poor and could not help themselves," adding, "They wanted to join us and get out of that hell of persecution."[15]

Hepzibah Richards contemplated leaving with Kirtland Camp. In a letter to her sister in Massachusetts, she described the camp's plans:

> Probably an hundred and 25 families or more remain [in Kirtland]. They will go in large wagons covered square on the top with canvas or something that will turn water. Will take their clothing, beds, and cooking utensils and tent by the way. Fifty [yards] of common sheeting will make a tent that will accommodate eighteen persons. Women and children will sleep in the wagons. Some will take along light crick bedsteads, and other measures will be taken to prevent sleeping on the ground as much as possible. They will have runners to go before and lay up provisions, that the inhabitants may not take advantage of their necessities to increase their prices. They will travel five days in a week; stop on Saturdays to bake and wash. Sabbath hold meetings. Will be eight or ten weeks on the road. They design to take along the poor and the lame, deeming it wrong to leave those who have a desire to go but have no means. It will be required of them to refund it as fast as they are able. This will probably be accomplished, but it must be by mighty effort. Duck will be preferred for tent cloth— will turn rain better. The camp will move but slowly. The men will walk much of the way.[16]

Christopher Crary, a non-Mormon resident of Kirtland, described the Saints' pathetic plight as they left Kirtland:

> When their bank failed, all their imaginary wealth vanished; their money was gone; their teams were gone; their provisions were gone; their credit was gone; their stores of goods disappeared. No community could be left in more destitute circumstances, and the only alternative was for them to leave—leave their Temple, their homes, all that they had held dear, and go to, they knew not where. And how to go was a serious question. . . . In 1838 the camp

was ready to start, and left in a body, making a string of teams more than a mile long.[17]

The Kirtland Camp left on July 5, 1838, with 515 members — 249 males and 266 females; 97 horses, 22 oxen, 69 cows, and 1 bull. Heads of families signed a camp constitution in which they agreed to certain regulations that would ensure an orderly journey to Far West. The camp was generally awakened at 4:00 each morning. At 4:20 the three or four families in each of the twenty-seven tents joined together for prayers. By seven or eight o'clock, the Saints were on their way, usually traveling from twelve to twenty miles a day.

Although the journey was hard, the Lord watched over the Saints. As they passed near Bellefontaine, Ohio, a wagon wheel ran over a boy's leg. Elias Smith recorded what happened: "As the Lord would have it, and to the astonishment of all — considering the weight of the load on the wagon — [the boy] received no particular injury, although the wheel ran over [his] leg on a hard road without any obstruction whatever. The wheel made a deep cut in the limb, but after hands were laid on him in the name of the Lord, the boy was able to walk considerable in the course of the afternoon. This was one, but not the first, of the wonderful manifestations of God's power unto us on the journey."[18]

Near Dayton, Ohio, the camp faced severe drought. Zerah Pulsipher wrote: "It was then very dry and the wells so low that it was difficult to get water for our animals in the dry part of the country if we should go on. But we inquired of the Lord for what was best and we were impressed to go on, not knowing what we should do for drink but the day following there fell such a flood of water that the low places in the country were full and we got along very well."[19]

With the help of the Lord and the combined faith and strength of each other, the members of Kirtland Camp traveled 870 miles in about three months, arriving in Far West on October 2, 1838. There they were greeted by the First Presidency and others "with open arms, and escorted . . . into the city." For those who had made the long journey, it was truly a day "long to be remembered."[20]

22

THE CHURCH RETURNS TO KIRTLAND

"The scourge that was placed upon the people . . . is being lifted today. We have a new day here." (Ezra Taft Benson.)

After the Saints had moved to Missouri and then Illinois, the Lord declared that Kirtland would be reestablished and would again be a stronghold of the Church. In 1841, he declared, "I, the Lord, will build up Kirtland." "But," he added, "I, the Lord, have a scourge prepared for the inhabitants thereof." (D&C 124:83.) In his writings and talks, Joseph Smith referred at least nine times to Kirtland's future, particularly in view of this prophecy. The night before his death at the hands of an angry mob in a jail in Carthage, Illinois, in 1844, he reported a "dream or vision" in which he felt he "was back in Kirtland, Ohio . . . and was contemplating how it might be recovered from the curse upon it."[1]

Earlier he had made prophecies to the Saints in Kirtland. For instance, he told Joseph Young that a future "stake at Kirtland . . . will be one of the princip[al] ones of Zion." Then, apparently referring to the faithful Saints who comprised the early Kirtland stake, he said that their posterity would be those who would be involved in reestablishing the stake there. Joseph Young reported that he also heard his brother, Brigham Young, make similar statements.[2]

In a letter to members in Kirtland in October 1841, Hyrum Smith, as "Patriarch for the whole Church," also said that while the Saints must leave their land and property in Kirtland, "yet your children may possess them, but not until many years shall pass away. . . . Thus saith the Lord, . . . and then I will send forth and build up Kirtland, and it shall be polished and refined according to my word."[3]

Two things are clear from Hyrum's letter and from other statements, revelations, and prophecies: a "curse" or "scourge" was to come upon Kirtland, and Kirtland would eventually be built up again.

What was that curse or scourge? There are three possibilities.

1. The scourge came when the body of the Saints left Kirtland, with the gospel and its blessings withdrawn from the community. In past gospel dispensations, the Lord placed scourges upon a land by withdrawing the prophets. It seems reasonable to conclude that one aspect of the scourge was that the Prophet Joseph Smith had left from Kirtland. Some of those who remained in Kirtland eventually joined other churches or religious movements.

2. A second possibility might be Kirtland's continual decline in population. At the time the Saints were there in the 1830s, it was one of the largest towns in northern Ohio, with an estimated population of 3,230. Kirtland and a neighboring town, Cleveland, had about equal populations. But by 1890 Kirtland's population dwindled to 909 while Cleveland's mushroomed to 261,000.

3. Not only did the population of Kirtland dwindle, but commerce and industry also declined after the Saints left, while other areas in northeastern Ohio, such as Cleveland, Youngstown, and Akron, became major industrial centers.

New Growth for the Church in Ohio

The Church began to rebuild in northeastern Ohio in the early 1950s, when property was purchased in Cleveland for a chapel, the first LDS meetinghouse to be built in that area since the 1830s. The *Cleveland Press* editorialized: "If Joseph Smith, the dedicated and courageous founder of the Mormon Church, were living today, he would take special pride in the news that a new Mormon Chapel shortly will be built on Lake Avenue

KIRTLAND PROPHECIES

Date	Event	To Be "Built-up" or "Established"	To Be a Principal Stake	Posterity to Be Involved	Lifting of Scourge
1834	Blessing of Sidney Rigdon[1]	X			
1834	Blessing of Zebedee Coltrin[2]	X			
1836-41	Joseph Smith Statement[3]	X	X	X	
1836-41	Brigham Young Statement[4]	X	X	X	
1837	Joseph Smith Speech[5]	X			
1840	Joseph Smith Letter[6]	X			
1840	Joseph Smith Speech[7]	X			
1840	Joseph Smith Letter[8]	X			
1841	Revelation[9]	X			X
1841	Hyrum Smith Letter[10]	X		X	X
1844	Joseph Smith "Dream or Vision"[11]				X

1. *History of the Church* 2:51.
2. *History of the Church* 2:51.
3. Joseph Young Sr. to Lewis Harvey, November 16, 1880.
4. Ibid.
5. *History of the Church* 2:479.
6. Joseph Smith to Brother Granger, July 1840, in Dean C. Jessee, *The Personal Writings of Joseph Smith*, 476.
7. *History of the Church* 4:204.
8. *History of the Church* 4:226.
9. D&C 124:83.
10. *History of the Church* 4:443-44.
11. *History of the Church* 6:609. (Joseph Smith still considered the lifting of the scourge to be a future event.)

near Edgewater Park. The building would, for him, undoubtedly be the confirmation of his own faith, once shared by too few in northern Ohio, that the Church had the spiritual strength and economic substance to live and grow."[4]

President David O. McKay dedicated the building on May 2, 1954. At that time the Church's membership in the Cleveland area was about one thousand. President McKay subsequently directed that the Church purchase the historic John Johnson home in Hiram. This first purchase of historic property in the Kirtland area was completed March 23, 1956.

Another landmark occasion brought President Spencer W. Kimball to northeastern Ohio on January 28, 1976, for a meeting to commemorate the 143rd anniversary of the revelation known as the Word of Wisdom, which was received in Kirtland in 1833. About nineteen thousand people attended the missionary-oriented session in the Cleveland Coliseum, and it has been estimated that nearly one thousand baptisms resulted from the meeting. President Kimball made initiatives after this visit that resulted in acquisition of the Whitney store and other properties in Kirtland.

The first ward in Kirtland since the 1830s was created on June 5, 1977. Jack Davis, who was called as the bishop, is a latter-day witness that the Lord is building up Kirtland. Reflecting on his move to the area, he told members of his ward, "I was in another area and working in a job unrelated to the job I have here in Kirtland. For the first time in the history of our company, an individual was assigned to a job in which he was not experienced and given new responsibilities. People wondered why it was done—I wondered why it was done. Little did I know. But in the 38th section of the Doctrine and Covenants, we are given a clue as to why I—and many of you—came here: 'Wherefore, for this cause I gave unto you the commandment that ye should go to the Ohio.' There is no doubt in my mind that the Saints who have now gathered in the Ohio were directed to be here by the Lord for the building up of this area."[5]

The year 1979 was a significant one for the Saints in northern Ohio. On August 7, the stakes there, with a membership of some ten thousand, were organized into the Cleveland Region. And on October 14, while serving as president of the Quorum of the Twelve Apostles, Ezra Taft Benson broke ground for a meetinghouse in Kirtland, the first building of the Church to be built there since the temple was completed in 1836.

The Scourge Is Lifted

While in Kirtland, President Benson declared, "The scourge that was placed upon the people in that prophecy [D&C 124:83] is being lifted today." He then added, "Our prophecy said that yet your children may possess the Kirtland lands, but not until many years shall pass away. Those many years have, I feel, passed away, and now is the time. Now is the time to arise and shine and look forward to great progress in this part of the Lord's vineyard."[6]

Those who heard President Benson will never forget this day. Stake President Gordon Watts, a descendent of early Kirtland pioneer Israel Barlow, described his feelings as the scourge was lifted, saying, "It was as if a light broke through the heavens. Kirtland would never be the same." Joseph H. Young, mission president and a descendant of Brigham Young, wrote in his journal that night that "a great spirit was felt by all." He compared the singing of the closing hymn, "The Spirit of God Like a Fire Is Burning," to how it must have been at the Kirtland Temple dedication when the same hymn was sung. "We were all so moved that the building rocked with the sound of our singing," he wrote.

Three years later, on October 17, 1981, President Benson returned to dedicate the new meetinghouse. "I feel that I have been walking on sacred ground," he commented, "and my soul is subdued and my feelings rather tender. . . . As long as The Church of Jesus Christ of Latter-day Saints endures, and that will be forever, Kirtland, Ohio, will have great significance."[7]

Many persons at the dedication testified that they felt the presence of the early Kirtland Saints. Zane F. Lee, architect of the meetinghouse, is a descendant of Levi Hancock, who was present at the dedication of the Kirtland Temple. He reported

247

that "when the choir and congregation sang the hymn 'The Spirit of God Like a Fire Is Burning,' I felt the same spirit of exultation that has been described in the dedication of the Kirtland Temple. . . . I felt at that moment that angels were singing with us and many beyond the veil rejoiced in the renewal of this work so long delayed."[8]

Another significant milestone in Kirtland was the organization of a stake there on October 16, 1983. President Benson, who presided on that occasion, reiterated that the Church in Kirtland would continue to grow and and that the prophecies of rebuilding were coming to pass. "We have barely scratched the surface of missionary work in the Kirtland area," he said.[9]

Zane F. Lee, who was called to serve as stake president, wrote: "During the conference in which the Kirtland Stake was organized, I felt very close to Joseph Smith, who was president of the Kirtland Stake some 150 years before. I felt that he was present and approved of the proceedings. The feelings I had were such that I considered him as a very dear friend. I had never felt that way about Joseph before. I felt that he wanted me to continue or renew the work of saving souls in the area of the Kirtland Stake that he had started in the 1830s. My heart was filled to overflowing."[10]

A Mission Is Created

The first mission in northern Ohio, the Cleveland Ohio Mission, was established by the Church on July 1, 1977, with Donald S. Brewer as the president. He had originally received a call to serve a Spanish-speaking mission in South America, but the call was subsequently changed to Ohio.

President Brewer recalled a dream that he had before he went to Ohio. "I saw myself standing in front of the Kirtland Temple speaking with a stranger," he said. "I looked up at the temple and marveled at its beautiful simplicity. Details of stone, glass, size, and surrounding shrubbery were indelibly stamped on my memory. It was not until the next morning that I became aware that I had been dreaming. It had been so real that I actually felt I could describe every detail of the temple and the surrounding area."

When he arrived in Kirtland, President Brewer went immediately to the temple, which he had not previously seen. He recorded his impression: "Now here I was in Ohio, standing in front of the Kirtland Temple on the exact spot I had been standing on in my dream some two months earlier. Was it the same as I had seen in my dream? Indeed it was—every detail was there, even to the proper direction—facing east. The vacant lot through the shrubbery and the two-story block building down the street were exactly as I had seen them in my dream, and yet this was the first time that I had ever been to Kirtland!"[11]

The first missionaries assigned to Kirtland since the 1840s arrived on January 5, 1978. They lived in the later-to-be-restored Newel K. Whitney store, which had been purchased over twenty years earlier by the late Wilford C. Wood, whose family was holding it until the Church could use it.

There had been some concern about the Church's assigning missionaries to Kirtland, since the community had an ordinance forbidding door-to-door soliciting. There was also concern that the missionary efforts would be misunderstood by officials of the Reorganized Church of Jesus Christ of Latter Day Saints (RLDS), which had been organized after Joseph Smith was martyred and the main body of the Saints left Nauvoo, Illinois, for the Rocky Mountains. The RLDS church now owned the Kirtland Temple. To resolve the first problem, President Brewer decided to invite the citizens of Kirtland to the Whitney store building to a series of lectures on the Church, which would allow the missionaries to make appointments with those who were interested in hearing more about the Church. To resolve the second problem, he met with the local presiding official of the RLDS congregation and explained what the LDS church's plans were. The only thing the RLDS representative asked was that the missionaries make it clear that they represented "the church out in Utah."[12]

Soon after the missionaries arrived in Kirtland, the ban on proselyting in the community was removed.

On July 1, 1984, the stakes in Akron and Kirtland were assigned to the newly created Akron Ohio Mission, which would also contain the major Church history sites in Ohio. Stanley Smoot, president of the mission, relates: "A few months after our arrival, a mission president's seminar was held in Kirtland. . . . We visited the genealogical library and heard of the great posterity program then being initiated and launched in the Kirtland Stake and in that region. We were thrilled beyond our ability to express when both I and Mary Ellen found that we had roots in Kirtland. Abraham Owen Smoot was my great-grandfather. He joined the Church in 1835. . . . Mary Ellen's great-grandfather, Daniel Wood, was also a resident of Kirtland. . . . In June of 1838, because of the persecution of the Saints, he was obliged to sell all his holdings at a discount and leave with the Saints. . . . His descendant, Wilford Wood, purchased the Whitney store [for the Church]. . . . The experiences that we enjoyed in Kirtland and Ohio are second to none in our life."[13]

The Newel K. Whitney store was restored, and under President Gordon B. Hinckley's direction, President Benson dedicated it on August 25, 1984. In his prayer, he called the store "a hallowed place of glorious revelation." He later said, "I'm satisfied that the growth and progress in Kirtland is most satisfying to the Lord."[14]

The Church in Hiram and Chardon

Hiram, Ohio, site of one of the largest branches of the Church in 1832, has participated in the prophesied rebuilding of the Church. A branch was organized there on April 15, 1984, and began meeting in the John Johnson home. Less than two years later, on March 22, 1986, President Benson, who had recently been sustained as President of the Church, broke ground for a meetinghouse on the historic John Johnson farm. The building was dedicated and the Hiram Ward organized in a historic meeting on March 29, 1987. Ordained as bishop was Joseph Nelson, a descendant of Omer Call, who lived in the area in the 1830s. "It has been made clear to me by Heavenly Father that Hiram is still a chosen area," Bishop Nelson said, "and there is a great work that must go forward. Satan is still working hard as he did in the 1830s to keep very special and growth experiences from taking place. But I know that his influence will be overcome and a continuation of miracles in Hiram will be a reality."[15]

Chardon, the county seat where Joseph Smith visited frequently, is central to the Chardon Ward, created from a division of the Kirtland Ward on April 29, 1984. Richard L. McClellan, first bishop of the Chardon Ward, is a descendant of John P. Greene, president of the 1830s Parkman Branch, which covered much of the same area as the new ward. Bishop McClellan talked about his Kirtland ancestors: "Susan Kent was one of only two members of her family to leave Kirtland with the Church. Her father, Daniel Kent, lived and died on the land where my children's soccer league now plays. He is buried not far from our home. Russell King Homer visited the Prophet in Kirtland, assisted the Church, and was told his posterity would be blessed. Other ancestors, John P. Greene and his son Evan, both labored on the Kirtland Temple. John P. Greene was a major investor in the Kirtland Safety Society Bank. I can imagine their heartbreak at losing everything and fleeing west. I can also imagine the comfort they felt with the prophecy that Kirtland would someday be a land of inheritance for their descendants. One hundred and fifty years later, my family is here, beneficiaries of these prophecies. The members of the Church in northeastern Ohio enjoy a profound awareness of the unique role of the Kirtland period in the history of the Church. A special sense of dedication lingers still."[16]

Searching for Lost Descendants

In his diary, under the date of November 19, 1832, Joseph Smith wrote a blessing for Sidney Rigdon. Referring to Sidney's posterity, he indicated that "one shall hunt after them" the way one would hunt after an animal that "hath strayed in the wilderness, & straitway findeth him and bringeth him into the fold." He then promised that "thus shall the Lord watch over his generation that they may be saved."[17] In October 1835, the Prophet and other leaders united in prayer for several blessings:

to be delivered from their afflictions; for solution to the Missouri problems; for protection against the mob; and for their posterity to be preserved and not fall.[18]

Kirtland is the only site of early Mormon history where large numbers of members and relatives were left behind when the Church moved out. Those leaving expressed great concern for their loved ones, many of whom left the Church and remained in Kirtland. The prophecies of Joseph and Hyrum Smith connecting the rebuilding of Kirtland with descendants of those early families are now being fulfilled. When the Kirtland Stake was organized again in 1983, a substantial portion of the members were descendants of the earlier Kirtland Saints.

President Ezra Taft Benson has been an instrument in fulfilling these prophecies. From 1979 to 1986 he made five trips to the Kirtland area and met each time with nonmember descendants. During these trips he hosted receptions, visited the dairy farm of a descendant of John Johnson, and met in reunions with Whitney and Johnson families. In 1986, he met with many persons who were baptized after his trip in 1979, including families surnamed Young, Woodruff, Kimball, Rigdon, Whitney, Rich, Dudley, Ormsby, and Wood. His efforts spurred a search for other descendants of early Kirtland residents. "There is a new generation, and we love them," he said. "They are our Father's children."[19] As a result of these efforts, members of the Kirtland Stake began a special effort to find descendants of early members who still remained in the area. Family organizations in the West were also asked to reunite families by identifying and locating long-lost cousins.

One of the first families to reestablish ties between the eastern and western family branches was the posterity of John and Elsa Johnson. A descendant, Grant Johnson of Ogden, Utah, was called with his wife on a mission to the Kirtland area. Convinced that all of John and Elsa's children were known to the western family organization, Grant was not prepared for the surprise he received upon being assigned to labor in Hiram. There he met distant cousins who showed him an old family Bible that identified five additional children not previously known. A highlight of his mission came when a busload of the western Johnsons journeyed to Ohio and were introduced to many previously unknown eastern cousins.

The Whitney family had a similar experience. Fred Whitney Rockwood, president of the Whitney family organization, reported, "As a result of the challenge of President Benson, we organized the Samuel and Suzanna Whitney family organization to include these nonmembers parts of our family in Kirtland who didn't come west with the Church. We have identified about 1,500 descendant records we didn't have. . . . We have seen relationships develop between different branches of the family that heretofore haven't know each other. We have pictures and history never known before."[20]

Stanley Smoot related the following story:

> At a Kirtland Stake conference . . . Karl Anderson, regional representative, asked the Saints to call their kin names in the phone book to see if they were related. . . . Sister Smoot started calling all of the Smoots in the phone book, and one day in Canton, Ohio, she ran across a couple who said their roots extended to the Smoots of Maryland. We visited with them in their home and were shown a book written by Vera Abston of Texas. It included eight generations of Smoots. . . . We located the branch from North Carolina, and through this experience and subsequent miracle events, . . . the Smoot family was able to begin the temple work for this Smoot family. On June 9, 1988, 485 were baptized, . . . with the potential of that many more soon to follow.[21]

Mormons in Modern Kirtland

The Church of Jesus Christ of Latter-day Saints returned to Kirtland and is part of the community again. A spirit of warmth, love, and acceptance exists between the Church and the community. No longer a small frontier community, however, Kirtland now has six thousand residents, and over five million people live in a radius of seventy-five miles.

When President Gordon B. Hinckley of the First Presidency

presided at the dedication of the restored Newel K. Whitney store in August 1984, the event received local and state attention from the city of Kirtland, the county of Geauga, and the state of Ohio. Edna Davis, who represented Geauga County, referred to the early Kirtland settlers and said, "We would like to show The Church of Jesus Christ of Latter-day Saints that we're a lot more friendly folk right now than we were in the 1830s."[22] A proclamation from the state of Ohio paid tribute to "the industrious and courageous pioneers of the Western Reserve who gave Kirtland a prominent place in Ohio history."[23]

Mayor Mario V. Marcopoli of Kirtland proclaimed the week surrounding the dedication as "Heritage Days" to focus attention on the early Kirtland settlers.

A tragic event, reminiscent of the night when flames consumed the schoolhouse/printing office, occurred on the morning of May 4, 1986, when an arsonist set fire to the newly built Kirtland meetinghouse. In contrast to the earlier event, however, which resulted from malice toward the Church, the modern-day burning was attributed to someone who selected random targets, and was not directed at the Church. After the fire, hundreds of townspeople visited the charred remains and offered sympathy and support. Fire fighters were especially touched when a small girl placed a bunch of flowers in front of the smoldering building. Other churches in the community immediately offered assistance, and many persons offered to help rebuild the structure and to contribute to the reconstruction. "This is not the Mormon Church that burned," one resident commented. "It is *our* church."[24]

In a unique way, the Church had finally become an accepted part of the community. The "rebuilding of Kirtland," progressing in both spiritual and physical dimensions, is testimony to the words of President Benson: "We have a new day here and a great opportunity and a great day ahead of us." Joseph Smith's Kirtland, once relegated to the role of forgotten history, is literally fulfilling the words of the Lord, that it shall be built up and "polished and refined according to my word."

NOTES

Chapter 1. Joseph Smith Goes to Kirtland

1. Vera Morley Anderson, "History and Travels of the Life of Isaac Morley Sr.," in Richard Henrie Morley, "The Life and Contributions of Isaac Morley" (Master's thesis, Brigham Young University, 1965), 3.

2. *History of Geauga and Lake Counties, Ohio* (Philadelphia, 1878), 246.

3. Parley P. Pratt, *Autobiography of Parley P. Pratt* (Salt Lake City: Deseret Book, 1950), 27.

4. Ibid., 37.

5. "History of Joseph Smith," *Times and Seasons* 4 (August 15, 1832): 289.

6. John W. Rigdon, "Lecture on the Early History of the Mormon Church," MS., Archives, The Church of Jesus Christ of Latter-day Saints (hereafter cited as LDS Archives).

7. A. W. Cowles, *Moore's Rural New Yorker* 23 (January 23, 1843): 61.

8. "History of Joseph Smith," *Times and Seasons* 4 (September 1, 1843): 304.

9. Ibid.

10. Ibid., 289-90.

11. *Saints' Herald* 29:192.

12. Ibid.

13. John Murdock, "A Brief Synopsis of the Life of John Murdock, Taken from an Abridged Record of His Journal," MS. in possession of author, 9-11.

14. "Philo Dibble's Narrative," in *Early Scenes in Church History* (Salt Lake City, 1882), 75.

15. *Painesville Telegraph,* November 16, 1830.

16. Extracts from Lydia Partridge's Writings, Family History of Edward Partridge Jr., in Richard L. Anderson, "The Impact of the First Preaching in Ohio," *Brigham Young University Studies* 11 (Summer 1971): 489.

17. "Philo Dibble's Narrative," 77.

18. Edward W. Tullidge, *The Women of Mormondom* (New York, 1877), 41-43.

19. "A Leaf from an Autobiography," *Woman's Exponent* 7 (August 15, 1878): 51.

20. Orson F. Whitney, *Conference Report, The Church of Jesus Christ of Latter-day Saints,* April 1912, 50 (hereafter cited as *Conference Report*).

21. "A Leaf from an Autobiography," *op. cit.*

22. Joseph Smith Jr., *History of The Church of Jesus Christ of Latter-day*

Saints, 2nd ed. rev., 7 vols. (Salt Lake City: Deseret News, 1960), 1:145-46 (hereafter cited as *History of the Church*).

Chapter 2. Faithful Saints Gather to Kirtland

1. Oliver B. Huntington, Diary, 1842-1847, pt. 1, 6-27, photocopy, Manuscript Collection, Harold B. Lee Library, Brigham Young University, Provo, Utah.

2. *Journal of Discourses*, 26 vols. (Liverpool: George Q. Cannon, 1855-1886), 11:295.

3. *History of the Church* 1:332.

4. Tullidge, *The Women of Mormondom*, 412.

5. "Caroline Barnes Crosby (1807-1884)" in Kenneth W. Godfrey, Audrey M. Godfrey, and Jill Mulvay Derr, *Women's Voices: An Untold History of the Latter-day Saints* (Salt Lake City: Deseret Book, 1982), 52.

6. Ibid., 52-53.

7. *History of Geauga and Lake Counties*, 248.

8. W. W. Phelps to Sally Phelps, January 17, 1836, Microfilm Letters, Family History Department, The Church of Jesus Christ of Latter-day Saints (hereafter cited as Family History Department).

9. *History of the Church* 2:468-69.

10. Millet Family History, "A Brief History of Artemus Millet," MS., 70-71, LDS Archives.

11. John Tanner, "Sketch of an Elder's Life," in *Scraps of Biography* (Salt Lake City, 1883), 12.

12. Ibid., 14-15.

13. Ibid., 16.

14. Leonard J. Arrington, "The John Tanner Family," *Ensign* 9 (March 1979): 48-49.

15. Huntington, Diary, 26.

16. Ibid., 27.

17. Ibid., 28.

18. Ibid., 19.

Chapter 3. Hardship and Conflict in Kirtland

1. Mary Fielding Smith to "My Dear Sister," July 8, 1837, in Godfrey, Godfrey, and Derr, *Women's Voices*, 61.

2. Tanner, "Sketch of an Elder's Life," 15.

3. *Journal of Discourses* 7:101.

4. The various journal entries are under dates indicated, in volume 2, *History of the Church*.

5. *History of the Church* 3:11.

6. Ibid., 1:265.

7. "Memoirs of George A. Smith," 10, typescript, Harold B. Lee Library, Brigham Young University, Provo, Utah.

8. Joseph Smith to Edward Partridge and Others, March 30, 1834, in Dean C. Jessee, comp. and ed., *The Personal Writings of Joseph Smith* (Salt Lake City: Deseret Book, 1984), 316.

9. Benjamin F. Johnson, *My Life's Review* (Independence, Missouri: Zion's Printing and Publishing Co., 1947), 24.

10. Ira Ames, Journal, 1835, entry in Max H. Parkin, *Conflict at Kirtland* (Provo, Utah: Department of Seminaries and Institutes of Religion, 1967), 206-7.

11. Oliver Cowdery to William W. Phelps and John Whitmer, January 21, 1834, Oliver Cowdery Letterbooks, Huntington Library, San Marino, California.

12. "Memoirs of George A. Smith," 28-29.

13. "Jonathan Crosby Autobiography," 15, in Parkin, *Conflict at Kirtland,* 161.

14. W. W. Phelps to his wife Sally, May 26, 1835, in Parkin, *Conflict at Kirtland,* 161.

15. Huntington, Diary, 27-28.

16. *History of the Church* 2:515.

17. *Journal of Discourses* 13:106.

18. Ibid., 8:277-78.

19. Jacob K. Butterfield to Persia Butterfield, November 4, 1836, in Parkin, *Conflict at Kirtland,* 164.

20. Dean C. Jessee, "Kirtland Diary of Wilford Woodruff," *Brigham Young University Studies* 12 (Summer 1972): 371.

21. *Latter-day Saints Messenger and Advocate* 3 (January 1837): 444.

22. Ibid., 3 (June 1837): 520.

23. Ibid., 521.

Chapter 4. Staggering Trials for Joseph and Emma

1. There has been some confusion regarding the location of Joseph Smith's home in Kirtland. The home adjacent to and immediately north of the cemetery on Chillicothe Road has for years been identified as his father's home. Property records indicate that Joseph Smith Sr. purchased the property in 1837 and paid taxes on it in 1838 and 1839. (We are indebted to Dr. Keith W. Perkins for his careful research of property and tax records in Kirtland.) This home, however, is apparently where Joseph Smith Jr.

and his wife, Emma, lived. Sources indicate their home was on the French farm, which places it north of the temple and on the west side of the main street that ran in front of the temple (Chester or Chillicothe Road), on the opposite side of the street from McFarland's blacksmith shop. An early photograph in the Historical Department of the Church also identifies this home as the Prophet's. It is therefore placed in this location on the Kirtland map on the back endsheet of this book. See Warren S. Snow, Autobiography, 1-2; "History of Brigham Young," *Millennial Star* 27 (1865): 5; *Infancy of the Church* (Salt Lake City, 1889), 43; Franklin D. Richards, Journal, June 8, 1844; LeRoi C. Snow, "How Lorenzo Snow Found God," *Improvement Era*, February 1937, 83; "The Memoirs of Joseph Smith III (1832-1914)," *The Saints' Herald*, November 6, 1934, 2.

2. *Patriarchal Blessing Book*, vol. 1, LDS Archives.

3. Murdock, "A Brief Synopsis of the Life of John Murdock," B-5.

4. *History of the Church* 1:261-64.

5. Warren Newsletter in Parkin, *Conflict at Kirtland*, 204.

6. *History of the Church* 1:265.

7. "Truth Will Prevail," *Times and Seasons* 5 (September 2, 1844): 624.

8. Joseph Smith Jr. letter, in Jessee, *The Personal Writings of Joseph Smith*, 238-39. Spelling and punctuation have been corrected and modernized for ease in reading.

9. Ibid., 252-53.

10. Marvin S. Hill, C. Keith Rooker, and Larry T. Wimmer, *The Kirtland Economy Revisited* (Provo: Brigham Young University Press, 1977), 30-33.

11. *History of the Church* 2:502.

12. Parkin, *Conflict at Kirtland*, 212.

13. *Millennial Star* 26 (August 20, 1864): 535.

14. E. D. Howe Autobiography 45, in Parkin, *Conflict at Kirtland*, 211.

15. *Painesville Telegraph*, in Parkin, *Conflict at Kirtland*, 215.

16. Lucy Mack Smith, *History of Joseph Smith by His Mother*, Preston Nibley, ed. (Salt Lake City: Bookcraft, 1958), 190-91.

Chapter 5. The Prophet Joseph at Home

1. Journal entries appear under date, as cited in volume 2 of *History of the Church*.

2. Ibid., 493.

3. Ibid., 325.

4. Ibid., 332.

5. "History of Luke Johnson," *Millennial Star* 27 (December 31, 1864): 5.

6. *History of the Church* 2:304.

7. Ibid., 327.

8. Ibid.

9. Ibid., 325.

10. Joseph Smith to the editor, *Messenger and Advocate* 2 (December 5, 1835): 240.

11. *History of the Church* 2:314-15.

12. *Juvenile Instructor* 27 (January 1, 1892): 24.

13. Lorenzo Snow, "Reminiscences of the Prophet Joseph Smith," *Deseret Evening News* 50 (December 12, 1899): 17.

14. LeRoi C. Snow, "How Lorenzo Snow Found God," 83.

15. Ibid.

16. Christopher G. Crary, *Pioneer and Personal Reminiscences* (Marshalltown, Iowa, 1893), 21.

17. *Journal of Discourses* 1:215.

18. Ibid., 3:121.

Chapter 6. Family Heritage and Support

1. *History of the Church* 4:191.

2. LeRoi C. Snow, "How Lorenzo Snow Found God," 84.

3. Eliza R. Snow, *Biography and Family Record of Lorenzo Snow* (Salt Lake City, 1884), 10.

4. "Minutes of The Church of Jesus Christ of Latter-day Saints, 1830-1844," in *Far West Record*, Donald Q. Cannon and Lyndon W. Cook, eds. (Salt Lake City: Deseret Book, 1983), 22.

5. Lucy Mack Smith, *History of Joseph Smith*, 198.

6. Ibid., 204-5.

7. Ibid., 211.

8. Ibid., 215-17.

9. Lucy Mack Smith, MS., 151-52, LDS Archives.

10. Ibid., 152.

11. Lucy Mack Smith, *History of Joseph Smith*, 231-32.

12. Ibid., 152.

13. *History of the Church* 4:191.

14. Ibid., 2:338.

15. Daniel Tylor, "Incidents of Experience," in *Scraps of Biography*, 26.

16. Lorenzo Dow Young, "Lorenzo Dow Young's Narrative," in *Fragments of Experience* (Salt Lake City, 1882), 43-45.

17. Hyrum Smith, Journal, in Pearson H. Corbett, *Hyrum Smith, Patriarch* (Salt Lake City: Deseret Book, 1976), 103.

18. *History of the Church* 2:519.

19. Lucy Mack Smith, *History of Joseph Smith*, 246.

20. Corbett, *Hyrum Smith, Patriarch*, 164.

21. *History of the Church* 4:443-44.

22. Ibid., 2:443.

Chapter 7: The Missionary Prophet Leads by Example

1. Mary A. Noble, Journal, in the journal of Joseph Bates Noble, Manuscript Collection, Harold B. Lee Library, Brigham Young University, 19.
2. *History of the Church* 2:170.
3. Ibid., 1:271.
4. Jessee, *The Personal Writings of Joseph Smith,* 239. Punctuation has been added for ease in reading.
5. *Lydia Knight's History* (Salt Lake City, 1883), 17-19.
6. Mary A. Noble, Journal, 18-19.
7. Jessee, *The Personal Writings of Joseph Smith,* 322. Spelling and punctuation have been modernized for ease in reading.
8. Edward Stevenson, *Reminiscences of Joseph the Prophet and the Coming Forth of the Book of Mormon* (Salt Lake City, 1893), 4-5.
9. *History of the Church* 2:168-69.
10. Tullidge, *Women of Mormondom,* 235.
11. *Juvenile Instructor* 27 (March 15, 1892): 173.
12. *Millennial Star* 25:439, in *History of the Church* 1:297.
13. B. H. Roberts, *The Life of John Taylor* (Salt Lake City: Bookcraft, 1963), 37-38.
14. Ibid., 40.
15. *Conference Report,* April 6, 1898, 57.
16. Matthias F. Cowley, *Wilford Woodruff: History of His Life and Labors* (Salt Lake City: Bookcraft, 1964), 39.
17. LeRoi C. Snow, "How Lorenzo Snow Found God," 83.
18. Ibid., 107.
19. *Conference Report,* April 6, 1898, 57.
20. Ibid.

Chapter 8. Missionaries Go Forth from Kirtland

1. *History of the Church* 2:378.
2. *Instructor* 2 (October 1946): 462.
3. "Memoirs of George A. Smith," 29.
4. Cannon and Cook, *Far West Record,* 23.
5. Davis Bitton, "Kirtland as a Center of Missionary Activity 1830-1838," *Brigham Young University Studies* 11 (Summer 1971): 500.
6. Wilford Woodruff to John Whitmer, January 2, 1836, *Messenger and Advocate,* January 1836, 255.
7. Bitton, "Kirtland as a Center of Missionary Activity," 505.
8. Pratt, *Autobiography,* 128-29.

9. Bitton, *op. cit.*, 506-7.

10. *Instructor,* October 1946, 462.

11. Pratt, *Autobiography,* 48-51.

12. Orson Hyde, "History of Orson Hyde," *Millennial Star* 26 (November 19, 1864): 776.

13. *Journal of Discourses* 13:89, 7:229.

14. Cowley, *Wilford Woodruff,* 83-85.

15. Tullidge, *Women of Mormondom,* 113.

16. Pratt, *Autobiography,* 127-28.

17. *History of the Church* 2:219.

18. *The Orson Pratt Journals,* Elden J. Watson, comp. (Salt Lake City, n.p., 1975), 60.

19. "History of Brigham Young," *Millennial Star* 26 (September 3, 1864): 569.

20. Ibid., pp. 568-69.

21. Orson F. Whitney, *Life of Heber C. Kimball* (Salt Lake City: Bookcraft, 1945), 80.

22. Tullidge, *Women of Mormondom,* 112.

23. Ibid., 114-15.

24. Ibid., 115.

25. Joseph Smith, Diary, in Jessee, *The Personal Writings of Joseph Smith,* 146.

26. Whitney, *Life of Heber C. Kimball,* 94.

27. Ibid., 131-32.

28. Tullidge, *Women of Mormondom,* 246-47.

29. Pratt, *Autobiography,* 130.

30. Ibid., 166-67.

31. "Diary of Mary Elizabeth Rollins Lightner," *Young Women's Journal* 16 (December 1905): 556-57.

32. *History of the Church* 2:469.

33. *The Return* 1 (May 1889): 74.

34. Eliza R. Snow, *Biography of Eliza R. Snow,* 8-9.

Chapter 9. New Scriptures Come Forth

1. *History of the Church* 1:152n.

2. Ibid., 1:245.

3. "Philo Dibble," *Juvenile Instructor* 27 (May 15, 1892): 303-4.

4. *Journal of Discourses* 16:42.

5. Ibid., 12:158.

6. Minutes of the St. George (Utah) School of the Prophets, December 23, 1883, quoted in Paul H. Peterson, "An Historical Analysis of the Word of Wisdom" (Master's thesis, Brigham Young University, 1972), 20.

7. Cannon and Cook, eds., *Far West Record,* 27.

8. Ibid., 28.

9. *History of the Church* 1:226.

10. Kirtland Council Minute Book, 1832-37, typescript, 3-4, LDS Archives.

11. Ibid., 104-5.

12. Pratt, *Autobiography,* 62.

13. *Millennial Star* 32 (August 11, 1874): 498.

14. "Philo Dibble," 303.

15. Philo Dibble, "Early Scenes in Church History," in *Four Faith Promoting Classics* (Salt Lake City: Bookcraft, 1968), 81.

16. *Journal of Discourses* 9:89.

17. *Autobiography of Edward Stevenson 1820-1897,* Joseph Grant Stevenson, ed. (Provo, Utah: Stevenson's Genealogical Center, 1986), 7.

18. Robert J. Matthews, "New Translation of the Bible," *Brigham Young University Studies* 11 (Summer 1971): 420.

19. *History of the Church* 1:215.

20. Cannon and Cook, *Far West Record,* 23.

21. Ibid., 23-24.

22. *History of the Church* 1:369.

23. Ibid., 2:349.

24. *Journal of Discourses* 20:65.

25. *History of the Church* 2:235.

26. Oliver Cowdery to Mr. Wm. Frye, Esq., December 22, 1835, in Stanley R. Gunn, *Oliver Cowdery, Second Elder and Scribe* (Salt Lake City: Bookcraft, 1962), 235-36.

27. Ibid., 237.

28. *History of the Church* 2:236.

29. *Journal of Discourses* 7:176.

30. *History of the Church* 2:238.

31. Ibid., 2:334.

32. Jessee, "Kirtland Diary of Wilford Woodruff," 371.

Chapter 10. Appearances of the Father and the Son

1. School of the Prophets, October 3, 1883, LDS Archives.

2. "The Life of Levi Hancock," 33.

3. F. Mark McKiernan and Roger D. Launius, eds., *An Early Latter Day Saint History: "The Book of John Whitmer"* (Independence, Missouri: Herald House, 1980), 66-67.

4. Address of Zebedee Coltrin at a meeting of high priests in Spanish

Fork, Utah, in Hyrum L. Andrus and Helen Mae Andrus, *They Knew the Prophet* (Salt Lake City: Bookcraft, 1974), 27.

5. The Prophet's writings establish March 18, 1833, as a day when many of the brethren in the School of the Prophets saw the Savior and were promised that "the pure in heart should see a heavenly vision." (See note 6.) He also indicated that each had "a record of what he saw." Both the Zebedee Coltrin and the John Murdock accounts occurred in approximately this time frame, and both men are known to have attended the School of the Prophets in its first session; therefore, since no other accounts exist of visions on this date, it is assumed the vision took place on this date.

6. *History of the Church* 1:334-35.

7. Murdock, "A Brief Synopsis of the Life of John Murdock," 14.

8. School of the Prophets, October 3, 1883.

9. *History of the Church* 2:379-81. This vision was added to the Doctrine and Covenants in 1981 as section 137.

10. *History of the Church* 2:435. This vision is section 110 of the Doctrine and Covenants.

11. *Journal of Discourses* 14:273.

12. Ibid., 25:158.

13. *History of the Church* 2:310.

14. Ibid., 2:381-82.

15. Ibid., 2:387.

16. Harrison Burgess, "Sketch of a Well-Spent Life," in *Labors in the Vineyard* (Salt Lake City, 1884), 67. See also *History of the Church* 2:387.

17. *History of the Church* 2:432.

18. *Millennial Star* 26 (January 23, 1964): 51.

19. Lightner, address at Brigham Young University.

Chapter 11. Schooling a People

1. "The Life of Levi Hancock," 51.

2. *Journal of Discourses* 12:158.

3. *History of the Church* 12:176.

4. Lucy Mack Smith, *History of Joseph Smith*, 224.

5. School of the Prophets, October 3, 1883.

6. Lyndon W. Cook, *Revelations of the Prophet* (Provo, Utah: Seventy's Mission Book Store, 1981), 189.

8. Ibid., 2:236-37.

9. James H. Eells to Brother Levitt, April 1, 1836, in William Mulder and A. Russell Mortensen, eds., "By No Means Men of Weak Minds," *Among the Mormons* (New York: Alfred Knopf, 1958), 88.

10. "Elder William Farrington Close," *Juvenile Instructor* 28 (August 15, 1892): 492-93.

11. Jared Carter, Autobiography (1830-33), as cited in Bitton, *Mormon Diaries and Autobiographies* (Provo, Utah: Brigham Young University Press, 1977), 62.

12. *History of the Church* 1:175.

13. Ibid., 1:342.

14. Oliver Cowdery Letterbook, 22, Huntington Library.

15. *Evening and Morning Star* 2 (December 1833): 120.

16. Milton V. Backman, Jr., *The Heavens Resound* (Salt Lake City: Deseret Book, 1983), 121.

17. *History of the Church* 2:273.

18. Ibid., 2:250.

19. Ibid., 2:528.

Chapter 12. "A Storehouse Unto This Church"

1. Orson F. Whitney in *Conference Report*, June 1, 1919, 47.

2. Cannon and Cook, *Far West Record*, 23.

3. Lyman Wight Journal, in Richard Lloyd Anderson, "First Preaching in Ohio," *Brigham Young University Studies* 2 (Summer 1971): 484.

4. McKiernan and Launius, *An Early Latter Day Saint History: "The Book of John Whitmer,"* 37.

5. "The Life of Levi Hancock," 28.

6. *History of the Church* 1:146-47.

7. Joseph Knight Jr., "Incidence of History 1827-1833," in Cook, *Revelations of the Prophet*, 85.

8. *History of the Church* 2:433.

9. Ibid., 1:336.

Chapter 13. Zion's Camp: A Forging Process

1. *History of the Church* 2:39.

2. Pratt, *Autobiography of Parley P. Pratt*, 107-9.

3. *Millennial Star* 27 (July 22, 1865): 455.

4. *History of the Church* 1:454.

5. Lucy Mack Smith, *History of Joseph Smith*, 225.

6. *History of the Church* 2:39.

7. Backman, *The Heavens Resound*, 185-86.

8. *History of the Church* 2:63-64.

9. *Painesville Telegraph*, May 9, 1834, in Cook, *Revelations of the Prophet Joseph Smith*, 325.

10. *History of the Church* 2:64-65.
11. Backman, *The Heavens Resound,* 185-86.
12. *History of the Church* 2:103.
13. Ibid., 2:104.
14. *Chardon Spectator and Geauga Gazette* (Chardon, Ohio), July 12, 1834.
15. George A. Smith, Journal, in *Instructor* 81 (July 1946): 323.
16. *History of the Church* 2:73.
17. Ibid., 2:182.
18. *Journal of Discourses* 2:10.
19. Ibid., 13:158.

Chapter 14. The Restoration of Offices and Organization

1. *History of the Church* 2:182, n. 1.
2. "The Life of Levi Hancock," 33.
3. Cannon and Cook, *Far West Record,* 20-23.
4. Ibid.
5. It should be noted that the organization of the First Presidency occurred in several steps. These steps are outlined by Lyndon W. Cook in *Revelations to the Prophet Joseph Smith,* 170-71, 192. They are also traced in the headings to sections 81 and 90 of the Doctrine and Covenants. The organization on March 18, 1833, had particular significance and appears to be the final step. The language used in the revelations and by Joseph Smith specifically denotes the counselors as being made equal to the Prophet in "holding the keys of this last kingdom." Joseph set both of his counselors apart and ordained them to be equal in both the holding of the keys and the presidency of the high priesthood. (See Kirtland Council Minute Book, 17.) This would certainly imply that neither had been ordained with this significance before the March 1833 date. The Lord must have also considered this as a very significant event. Following the ordinations, members of the School of the Prophets, who had just witnessed the organization of the First Presidency, were visited by Deity and angels and witnessed many other things. (See *History of the Church* 1:334-35.)
6. *History of the Church* 1:334.
7. Special entry, Manuscript History of the Church, December 18, 1833.
8. *History of the Church* 4:190.
9. LeRoi C. Snow, "How Lorenzo Snow Found God," 84.
10. *History of the Church* 2:31.
11. Ibid., 2:181.
12. Ibid., 2:182.
13. Ibid.

14. Ibid., 2:185-86.
15. *Journal of Discourses* 12:86.
16. *History of the Church* 2:201.
17. Ibid., 2:181.
18. Ibid., 2:201.
19. Godfrey, Godfrey, and Derr, *Women's Voices*, 48.
20. "A Leaf from an Autobiography," *Women's Exponent*, October 1, 1878.
21. Lorenzo Snow, "Reminiscences of the Prophet Joseph Smith," *Deseret News* 50 (December 23, 1899): 17.

Chapter 15. Building a House of the Lord

1. The inscription on the front of the temple read "House of the Lord, built by the Church of the Latter-day Saints in 1834."
2. *Eliza R. Snow, an Immortal: Selected Writings of Eliza R. Snow* (Salt Lake City: Nicholas G. Morgan, Sr., Foundation, 1957), 54.
3. This $40,000 figure is used by many early sources, including John Corrill, *A Brief History of the Church of Christ of Latter Day* (St. Louis, 1839), 21; Christopher Crary; James Eells; Frederick Mather; and *History of Lake and Geauga Counties.*
4. *Eliza R. Snow, an Immortal*, 59.
5. *Journal of Discourses* 2:31.
6. Mrs. Peter S. Hitchcock, *Lake County Historical Society Quarterly* 7:4.
7. *History of the Church* 1:349.
8. Truman O. Angell, Journal, MS., Special Collections, Lee Library, Brigham Young University, 4.
9. Truman O. Angell to John Taylor, March 11, 1885, LDS Archives.
10. Angell, Journal, LDS Archives, 5.
11. *Journal of Discourses* 2:31.
12. Lucy Mack Smith, *History of Joseph Smith*, 230.
13. Ibid., 230-31.
14. *History of the Church* 1:400.
15. Lucy Mack Smith, *History of Joseph Smith*, 231.
16. *History of the Church* 1:336.
17. Johnson, *My Life's Review*, 16.
18. *Journal of Discourses* 10:165.
19. *Times and Seasons* 6 (April 15, 1845): 867-68.
20. *History of the Church* 2:328.
21. Jessee, *The Personal Writings of Joseph Smith*, 103.
22. Ibid., 104.
23. *Juvenile Instructor*, January 15, 1880, 283.
24. Ibid.

25. Lorenzo Young, "Young's Narrative," in *Fragments of Experience* (Salt Lake City, 1882), 43.

26. *Times and Seasons* 6 (April 15, 1845): 867.

27. *History of the Church* 2:399.

28. Tullidge, *Women of Mormondom,* 76.

29. Biography of Artemus Millet, *Millet Family Book,* 93-95.

30. Johnson, *My Life's Review,* 15-16.

31. Andrew Larson, *Erastus Snow,* 466.

32. *Times and Seasons* 6 (January 15, 1845): 771.

33. *History of the Church* 1:450.

34. Crary, *Pioneer and Personal Reminiscences,* 33.

35. For an approximation of the debt, see *Messenger and Advocate* 3 (April 1837): 488; John Corrill, *A Brief History of the Church of Christ of Latter Day Saints,* 21.

36. *Times and Seasons* 6 (April 15, 1845): 867.

37. Parkin, *Conflict at Kirtland,* 206.

38. *History of the Church* 2:386-87.

39. *Times and Seasons* 6 (July 15, 1845), 972.

40. Joel Hills Johnson, Journal, in Parkin, *Conflict at Kirtland,* 208.

41. *History of the Church* 1:450.

42. Johnson, *My Life's Review,* 24.

Chapter 16. "A Pentecost and a Time of Rejoicing"

1. *History of the Church* 2:309.

2. Sidney Rigdon, Newel K. Whitney, and Oliver Cowdery to John A. Boynton, Kirtland, Ohio, May 6, 1834, Huntington Library.

3. *History of the Church* 2:432-33.

4. Tyler, "Incidents of Experience," 32.

5. *Journal of Discourses* 18:132.

6. William W. Phelps, "The Spirit of God Like a Fire Is Burning," *Messenger and Advocate* 2 (March 1836): 280-81.

7. Eliza R. Snow, *Biography of Lorenzo Snow,* 11.

8. *History of the Church* 2:432-33.

9. Ibid., 2:381.

10. Ibid., 6:184.

11. Minutes of the Salt Lake City School of the Prophets, October 10-11, 1883, as cited in Hyrum L. and Helen Mae Andrus, *They Knew the Prophet* (Salt Lake City: Bookcraft, 1974), 29.

12. *Journal of Discourses* 18:132.

13. *History of the Church* 2:386-87.

14. Burgess, "Sketch of a Well-Spent Life," 67.

15. Tullidge, *Women of Mormondom*, 207-8.

16. Ibid., 101.

17. Ibid., 207.

Chapter 17. The Temple Is Dedicated

1. *History of the Church* 2:414.

2. *Eliza R. Snow, an Immortal*, 59.

3. *History of the Church* 2:426; also *Messenger and Advocate* 2 (March 1836): 280-81.

4. Benjamin Brown, "Testimonies for the Truth," *Gems for the Young Folks* (Salt Lake City: 1881), 65.

5. Tullidge, *Women of Mormondom*, 95.

6. Truman O. Angell, Journal, as cited in Lyndon Cook, *Brigham Young University Studies* 15, no. 4 (Summer 1975): 550.

7. Heber C. Kimball, *Journal of Discourses* 9:376.

8. Tullidge, *Women of Mormondom*, 95.

9. *Saints' Herald*, March 24, 1915, 289.

10. *Journal of Discourses* 11:10.

11. *History of the Church* 2:428.

12. Leonard J. Arrington, "Oliver Cowdery's Kirtland Ohio 'Sketch Book,' " *Brigham Young University Studies* 12 (Summer 1972): 426.

13. *History of the Church* 2:435-36; also D&C 110:1-10.

14. *History of the Church* 2:309-10.

15. Lauritz G. Petersen, "The Kirtland Temple," *Brigham Young University Studies* 12 (Summer 1972): 402.

16. *Journal of Discourses* 2:31.

17. *History of the Church* 2:197.

18. Ibid., 2:309.

19. Whitney, *Life of Heber C. Kimball*, 92.

20. Wilford Woodruff, *Leaves from My Journal* (Salt Lake City, 1881), 28.

21. Tyler, "Incidents of Experience," 32.

22. Newel Knight, Journal, in *Scraps of Biography*, 94.

23. "Memoirs of George A. Smith," 36.

24. The Millet Family Record, 2.

25. "History of Brigham Young," *Millennial Star* 26 (September 3, 1864): 569.

26. *History of the Church* 2:432.

27. Ibid., 2:368.

28. Ibid., 2:368-69.

29. Caroline Barnes Crosby, in Godfrey, Godfrey, and Derr, *Women's Voices*, 49.

30. Jessee, "Kirtland Diary of Wilford Woodruff," 375-76.

31. *History of the Church* 2:474.

32. Caroline Barnes Crosby, in *Women's Voices,* 48.

33. *History of the Church* 2:356.

34. Crary, *Personal Reminiscences,* 29.

35. Huntington, Diary, photocopy, 27, Harold B. Lee Library, Brigham Young University.

Chapter 18. The Kirtland Safety Society Bank

1. *Messenger and Advocate* 3 (April 1837): 488; also *History of the Church* 2:480.

2. Hill, Rooker, and Wimmer, *Kirtland Economy,* 25-29.

3. *History of the Church* 2:478-79.

4. Ibid., 2:515-17.

5. D. Paul Sampson and Larry T. Wimmer, "The Kirtland Safety Society: The Stock Ledger Book and the Bank Failure," *Brigham Young University Studies* 12 (Summer 1972): 427.

6. Hill, Rooker, and Wimmer, *Kirtland Economy,* 61.

7. *History of the Church* 2:467.

8. Ibid., 2:470-71.

9. Ibid., 2:468.

10. Ibid.

11. Dale W. Adams, "Chartering the Kirtland Bank," *Brigham Young University Studies* 23 (Fall 1983): 471.

12. Hill, Rooker, and Wimmer, *Kirtland Economy,* 67.

13. *Painesville Republican* (February 16, 1837), as cited in Hill, Rooker, and Wimmer, *Kirtland Economy,* 50.

14. Hill, Rooker, and Wimmer, *Kirtland Economy,* 55.

15. *Messenger and Advocate* 3 (July 1837): 536.

16. Jessee, "Kirtland Diary of Wilford Woodruff," 381.

17. *Geauga and Lake Counties, Ohio,* 248.

18. *Messenger and Advocate* 3 (July 1837): 539.

19. Ibid., 536-37.

20. Hill, Rooker, and Wimmer, *Kirtland Economy,* 61.

21. Jessee, "Kirtland Diary of Wilford Woodruff," 383-84.

22. *Messenger and Advocate* 3 (January 1837): 443.

23. Adams, "Chartering the Kirtland Bank," 477.

24. Hill, Rooker, and Wimmer, *Kirtland Economy,* 52.

25. Adams, "Chartering the Kirtland Bank," 480.

26. Samuel Eliot Morison, *The Oxford History of the American People* (New York: Oxford University Press, 1965), 455.

27. Jonathan Crosby, Autobiography, 15-16, in Parkin, *Conflict at Kirtland,* 242-43.

28. *History of the Church* 2:497.

29. Sampson and Wimmer, "Kirtland Safety Society," 428.

30. Hill, Rooker, and Wimmer, *Kirtland Economy,* 66.

31. *Messenger and Advocate* 3 (July 1837): 539-40.

32. *History of the Church* 2:507-8.

33. *Journal of Discourses* 11:11.

34. Lucy Mack Smith, *History of Joseph Smith,* 240-41.

35. Hill, Rooker, and Wimmer, *Kirtland Economy,* 65.

36. Crary, *Personal Reminiscences,* 59.

37. Huntington, Journal, 27.

38. "History of Luke Johnson by Himself," *Millennial Star* 26 (December 31, 1864): 5.

39. Hepzibah Richards to Willard Richards, January 18, 1838, in Godfrey, Godfrey, and Derr, *Women's Voices,* 75.

40. *History of the Church* 3:164-65.

41. Joseph Smith to Oliver Granger, January 26, 1841, in Jessee, *The Personal Writings of Joseph Smith,* 490.

42. *History of the Church* 2:487-88.

43. Ibid., 2:353.

Chapter 19. Apostasy, Persecution, and Mobs

1. Tyler, "Incidences of Experiences," 33.

2. Hill, Rooker, and Wimmer, *Kirtland Economy,* 21.

3. "Real Estate Speculation," *Painesville Telegraph,* January 29, 1836, in Parkin, *Conflict at Kirtland,* 230-31.

4. *Messenger and Advocate* 3 (June 1837) 521.

5. Whitney, *Life of Heber C. Kimball,* 99.

6. *Messenger and Advocate* 3 (May 1837): 509.

7. Ibid., 506.

8. Caroline Barnes Crosby, in Godfrey, Godfrey, and Derr, *Women's Voices,* 55.

9. *History of the Church* 2:487-88.

10. Ibid., 2:487-88n.

11. Mary Fielding Smith to her sister Mercy, September 1, 1837, in Godfrey, Godfrey, and Derr, *Women's Voices,* 63-64.

12. Johnson, *My Life's Review,* 28-29.

13. *Journal of Discourses* 11:6-7.

14. Ibid., 11:11.

15. Luke Johnson, part 2 of "History," *Millennial Star* 27 (1865): 6.

16. Manuscript History of Brigham Young, 1846-47, 72, in Keith Perkins, "A House Divided," *Ensign*, February 1979, 58.

17. *Journal of Discourses* 19:41.

18. Manuscript History of Brigham Young, 1801-44 (Salt Lake City: Elden Jay Watson, 1968), 16-17.

19. Whitney, *Life of Heber C. Kimball*, 101.

20. John Smith to George A. Smith, January 1, 1838, in Parkin, *Conflict at Kirtland*, 252.

21. Pratt, *Autobiography*, 168.

22. Roberts, *Life of John Taylor*, 40.

23. Lucy Mack Smith, *History of Joseph Smith*, 240.

24. Caroline Barnes Crosby, in Godfrey, Godfrey, and Derr, *Women's Voices*, 64-65.

25. Mary Fielding, in Godfrey, Godfrey, and Derr, *Women's Voices*, 64-65.

26. Huntington, Diary, 29.

27. Ibid., 28-29.

28. Lucy Mack Smith, *History of Joseph Smith*, 241.

29. Eliza R. Snow, *Biography of Lorenzo Snow*, 21-22.

30. Lucy Mack Smith, *History of Joseph Smith*, 243.

31. Hepzibah Richards to Willard Richards, January 18, 1838, in Godfrey, Godfrey, and Derr, *Women's Voices*, 71.

32. Caroline Barnes Crosby, Autobiography, 1838, in Parkin, *Conflict at Kirtland*, 265.

33. Joseph Smith's Kirtland Revelations Book, 122.

34. Hepzibah Richards to Dear Friends, March 23, 1838, in Godfrey, Godfrey, and Derr, *Women's Voices*, 76.

Chapter 20. The Prophet at the Helm

1. Whitney, *Life of Heber C. Kimball*, 103.

2. Joseph Smith to John Corrill and Church in Zion, September 4, 1837, in *History of the Church* 2:508.

3. Ibid., 3:11.

4. *Juvenile Instructor* 27 (March 15, 1892): 173.

5. "Memoirs of George A. Smith," 25.

6. "The Life of Levi Hancock," 51.

7. "Memoirs of George A. Smith," 10.

8. *Journal of Discourses* 11:9.

9. "The Life of Levi Hancock," 51.

10. *History of the Church* 2:529.

11. William E. McLellin to Samuel McLellin, August 4, 1832, in *The Revelations of the Prophet Joseph Smith*, 106.

12. Helen Mar Whitney, "Early Reminiscences," *Mormon Heritage* 1 (November 1985): 13.

13. *History of the Church* 1:333.

14. *Juvenile Instructor* 27 (February 15, 1892): 127-28.

15. Ibid., 128-29.

16. *Young Women's Journal* 17 (December 1906) 538.

17. Tullidge, *Women of Mormondom,* 404.

18. Ibid., 65-66.

19. *The Improvement Era* 40 (February 1937): 83-84, 105.

20. Jessee, "Kirtland Diary of Wilford Woodruff," 390-91.

21. *Journal of Discourses* 7:176-77.

22. Ibid., 9:332; 32:51.

Chapter 21. The Church Leaves Kirtland

1. Lucy Mack Smith, *History of Joseph Smith,* 247-48.

2. *History of the Church* 3:1-3.

3. Luke Johnson, part 2 of "History," *Millennial Star* 27 (1865): 6.

4. Eliza R. Snow, *Biography of Lorenzo Snow,* 23.

5. Godfrey, Godfrey, and Derr, *Women's Voices,* 71.

6. Ibid., 76.

7. Luman Andros Shurtliff, Journal, typescript, 30, Harold B. Lee Library, Brigham Young University.

8. William F. Cahoon, Autobiography, 45, MS., LDS Archives.

9. Angell, Journal, 5.

10. Lucy Mack Smith, *History of Joseph Smith,* 251-52.

11. *History of the Church* 3:88.

12. Ibid.

13. Parkin, *Conflict at Kirtland,* 269.

14. Johnson, *My Life's Review,* 32.

15. Parkin, *Conflict at Kirtland,* 269.

16. Hepzibah Richards to Rhoda Richards, March 23, 1838, in Godfrey, Godfrey, and Derr, *Women's Voices,* 78.

17. Crary, *Personal Reminiscences,* 35.

18. *History of the Church* 3:113.

19. Parkin, *Conflict at Kirtland,* 276.

20. *History of the Church* 3:147.

Chapter 22. The Church Returns to Kirtland

1. *History of the Church* 6:609.

2. Joseph Young Sr. to Lewis Harvey, November 16, 1880.

3. *History of the Church* 4:443-44.

4. Artel Ricks, "Hyrum's Prophecy," *Improvement Era*, May 1956, 344; *Cleveland Press*, June 8, 1953.

5. Jack Davis, address at Cleveland Ohio stake conference and Kirtland Ward meetinghouse dedication, October 17, 1982.

6. Ezra Taft Benson, address at groundbreaking for the Kirtland Ward meetinghouse, October 14, 1979, Ms., LDS Archives.

7. Ezra Taft Benson, address at dedication of the Kirtland Ward meetinghouse, October 17, 1982, Ms., LDS Archives.

8. Zane F. Lee to Karl R. Anderson, June 16, 1988.

9. Ezra Taft Benson, October 17, 1982, transcript of videotape, Kirtland Stake library.

10. Lee to Anderson, June 16, 1988.

11. Donald S. Brewer, journal, 1978, photocopy in author's possession.

12. Donald S. Brewer to Elder David B. Haight of the Council of the Twelve, December 17, 1977, photocopy in author's possession.

13. Stanley Smoot, interview with author, June 18, 1988.

14. Ezra Taft Benson, address at dedication of the Newel K. Whitney Store, August 25, 1984, videotape, Kirtland Stake library.

15. Joseph Nelson, interview with author, June 16, 1988.

16. Richard L. McClellan to Karl R. Anderson, June 27, 1988.

17. Jessee, *The Personal Writings of Joseph Smith,* 22.

18. *History of the Church* 2:291.

19. Ezra Taft Benson, October 17, 1982.

20. Fred Whitney Rockwood, interview with author, June 16, 1988.

21. Stanley Smoot, interview with author, June 28, 1988. As of February 1989, temple ordinances had been performed for 866 individuals.

22. Edna Davis, remarks at dedication of the Whitney store, August 25, 1984, videotape in Kirtland Stake library.

23. Gordon B. Hinckley, address at dedication of the Whitney store, videotape in Kirtland Stake library.

24. Conversation with author at the scene of the fire.

INDEX

Abraham, book of, 105
Abston, Vera, 253
Adams, Dale W., 201
Agriculture in Kirtland, 21
Akron, Ohio, 250
Allen, Charles, 137
Allen, Lucy Diantha Morley, 230
Ames, Ira, 25
Angell, Polly, 163
Angell, Truman O., 157, 238
Angels: companionship of, in
  Zion's Camp, 135, 142-43;
  protection provided by, 165,
  175; visions of, in Kirtland
  Temple, 170, 175-77, 182-83
Animals, Joseph Smith's kindness
  toward, 46-47
Anti-banking company, 196-97
Apostasy: Joseph Smith
  prophesies of, 209; spirit of,
  engulfs Kirtland, 212-18; of
  Church leaders, 213-17
Apostles. *See* Twelve Apostles
Arrington, Leonard, 18
Articles of agreement for Kirtland
  Safety Society, 195
Ashery, 132-33
Astronomy, 104-5
Authority, keys of, restored in
  Kirtland Temple, 172-73

Backman, Milton V., Jr., 140
Banks, failure of, 193, 201-2. *See
  also* Kirtland Safety Society
Baptism of Ohio converts, 6-8,
  90-91
Barnes, Lorenzo, 77
Barnum, Samuel, 44
Basset, Heman, 130

Benson, Ezra Taft: on "new day"
  in Kirtland, 243, 254; breaks
  ground for Kirtland
  meetinghouse, 247; dedicates
  meetinghouse, 247; organizes
  stake in Kirtland, 248; dedicates
  Newel K. Whitney store, 250;
  breaks ground for
  meetinghouse on Johnson
  farm, 250; instrumental role of,
  in fulfilling Kirtland
  prophecies, 252
Bent, Samuel, 55
Bible, Joseph Smith's translation
  of, 93, 100-102
Bishops, calling of, 127-28
Board kiln, 160
Bodyguards of Church leaders,
  24-25
Book of Mormon, 89-90, 124-25
Boycott, economic, of Saints, 25-26
Boynton, John, 14, 91, 150, 169,
  216, 221
Brewer, Donald S., 248-49
Brick kiln, 133, 159
Brown, Benjamin, 182
Brown, Sherman, 76
Bulldog, Parley Pratt escapes
  from, 79-80
Bump, Jacob, 18-19, 205-6, 215-16
Burgess, Harrison, 175-76
Businesses: established in
  Kirtland, 28; run as part of
  United Order, 133
Butterfield, Jacob, 28-29

Cahoon, Reynolds, 159
Cahoon, William, 120-21, 201, 211,
  235, 237-38

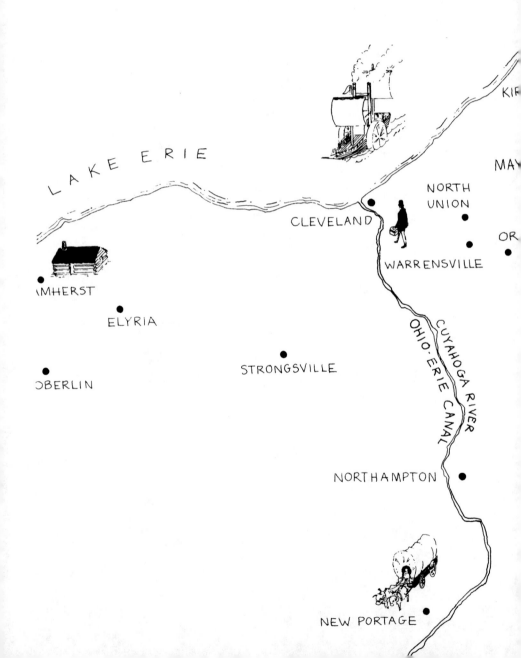

Important Locations in
Northeastern
Ohio
in the 1830s

LAKE ERIE

KIR

MA\

CLEVELAND

NORTH
UNION

OR

WARRENSVILLE

\MHERST

ELYRIA

CUYAHOGA RIVER

OHIO-ERIE CANAL

STRONGSVILLE

)BERLIN

NORTHAMPTON

NEW PORTAGE

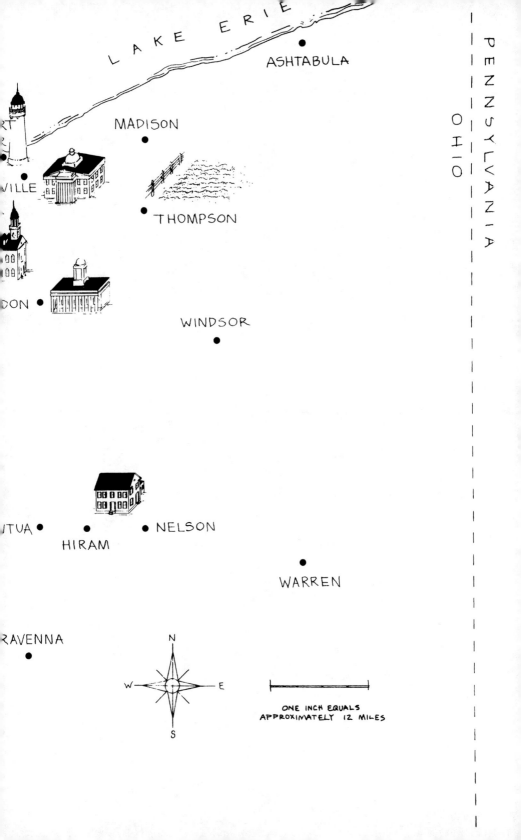

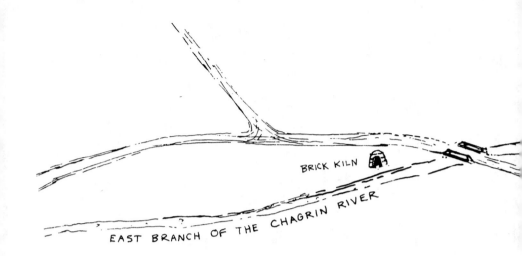

BRICK KILN

EAST BRANCH OF THE CHAGRIN RIVER

JOSEPH SMITH JR. H

CEMETERY

TEMPLE

JOS
V

SCHOOLHOUSE +
PRINTING OFFICE

SIDNEY

BANK

HYRUM S

STONE QUARRY

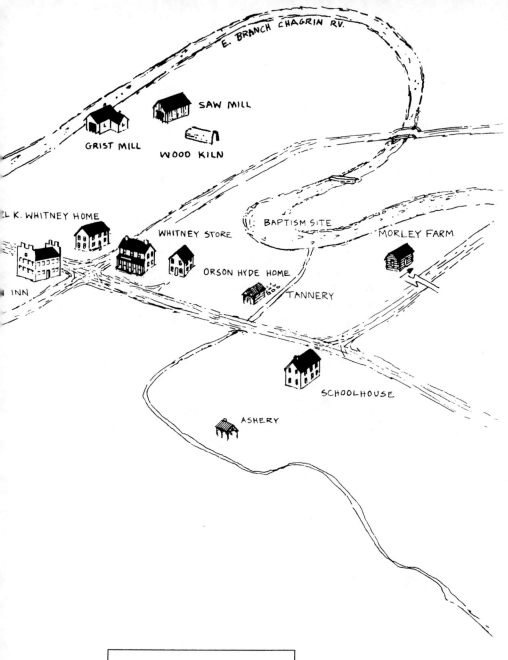

E. BRANCH CHAGRIN RV.

SAW MILL

GRIST MILL

WOOD KILN

L K. WHITNEY HOME

WHITNEY STORE

BAPTISM SITE

MORLEY FARM

ORSON HYDE HOME

INN

TANNERY

SCHOOLHOUSE

ASHERY

Important Sites in
Kirtland
in the 1830s

About the Author

Karl Ricks Anderson has lived in Ohio, near the Kirtland area, for nearly thirty years. He has served as president of the Ohio Cleveland Stake and as a regional representative. He has also been a seminary teacher, family relations teacher, counselor in a bishopric, elders quorum president, stake high councilor, and an institute instructor for the Church Educational System.

A native of Ogden, Utah, he received his B.S. and MBA degrees from the University of Utah. In his career, he was an executive in a computer software consulting firm. He and his wife, the former Joyce Hirschi, have seven children.